Barbara Hanna Wasik
Donna M. Bryant

Second Edition

Procedures for Helping Families

For information:

Sage Publications, Inc.
2455 Teller Road
Thousand Oaks, California 91320
E-mail: order@sagepub.com

Sage Publications Ltd.
6 Bonhill Street
London EC2A 4PU
United Kingdom

Sage Publications India Pvt. Ltd.
M-32 Market
Greater Kailash I
New Delhi 110 048 India

Printed in the United States of America

Library of Congress Cataloging-in-Publication Data

Wasik, Barbara Hanna.
Home visiting: Procedures for helping families / by Barbara Hanna Wasik and Donna M. Bryant.—2nd ed.
p. cm.
Includes bibliographical references and index.
ISBN 0-7619-2054-4 (pb)
ISBN 0-7619-2053-6 (cloth)
1. Home-based family services.—United States.
I. Bryant, Donna M.,
1951- II. Title.
HV697 .W37 2000
362.82'83.—dc21 00-010329

01 02 03 04 05 06 10 9 8 7 6 5 4 3 2 1

Acquiring Editor: Nancy Hale
Production Editor: Diane Foster
Editorial Assistant: Cindy Bear
Typesetter/Designer: Barbara Burkholder
Cover Designer: Samar Hashemi

Contents

Foreword

Today we are likely to use the phrase "early intervention" without stopping to question what the phrase really means. During the 1960s, early intervention became a part of our educational, social, and health service programs. Since then new ideas have emerged about what it means to "intervene" in the lives of children and what constitutes "early." Human development—and with it the opportunity for intervention—continues throughout every stage of the life span, but these life long opportunities do not diminish the importance of intervention prior to the time a child reaches school age. Indeed, critical efforts to optimize child health and development are now routinely made during infancy, during the prenatal period, and, in some cases, even before conception.

Early intervention, as it is broadly conceived today, can take any number of approaches to problem solving or prevention in any area important to the lives of children and families. *Early intervention* generally refers to actions taken before a child reaches school age, even as far back as the prenatal or preconceptual period. Systematic and intentional interventions in a family's or child's environment—with the ultimate goal (or goals) of enhancing education readiness, improving child health, or supporting parents—are commonly accepted today by theorists and practitioners of developmental and clinical psychology, psychiatry, pediatrics, social work, and other fields.

Home visitation is a logical manifestation of the need to intervene expeditiously, thoughtfully, and effectively when children and their parents are at risk for social, educational, and medical problems. The field of home visitation is built on an ecological approach and on the following assumptions: (a) that the early childhood period and the experiences that occur during that time have important implications for later child and adult development; (b) that genetic, biological, and environmental problems can be overcome or attenuated through efforts initiated early in the life of the family; (c) that the solutions to the challenges facing families today must be as diverse and individualized as the problems—and the families—themselves; and (d) that such interventions must be based on empirical studies of child development and family dynamics. Home visitation has become a powerful tool for intervening effectively—and respectfully—in the lives of young children and their families, perhaps the ultimate concrete application of these principles. Embracing such an approach in principle, however, does not automatically bring with it an understanding of the fundamental tenets of home visitation. Anyone engaged in working with children and families in their homes will find material here to aid them as they provide support, evaluation, and preventative or remedial services to their clients.

Home visitation programs may seem like a new phenomenon, springing up as a part of 20th century reforms, but as Barbara Wasik and Donna Bryant ably illustrate, children's own homes have for centuries been one of the most optimal sites for intervention. More recent programs, however, at their best have evolved to reflect a somewhat more enlightened ethos than was reflected in many of the home visiting programs of the early and mid-20th century. The authors of this volume implicitly base their work on, and celebrate the importance of a critical set of variables.

First, they acknowledge that home visiting programs are most effective when they seek not to supplant parental values and authority, but to respect and build on the primacy of mothers and fathers and to help parents and all other members of the family to build upon their own strengths as they create loving, supportive, healthy environments for their children. Second, Wasik and Bryant embrace a two-generation approach, giving theorists and practitioners the tools to build a foundation for improved child development by giving parents the tools to improve their lives and their parenting skills.

Third, as experienced home visitors, trainers, and program developers themselves, the authors are fully cognizant of the professional, academic, and policy issues related to home visiting. Their realistic acknowledgment of the need to support the entire field by proving that working with children and parents in this context has demonstrable positive effects, not only in the lives of the parent and child they may see in the morning of a given day, but in a more general way in the communities and service systems in which the programs are embedded, will have broad implications for the field. Taking this broad view is essential in a field in which the bottom line is typically buttressed by outcomes having less to do with individual health and happiness than with cost effectiveness and attenuating a client group's long-term need for services.

As a lifelong advocate for children and families, I applaud Wasik and Bryant for their efforts in writing this book. The outcomes for home visitors—and the families about which they care and for whom they work so hard—will be positive and long-lasting.

—Edward Zigler, PhD
Sterling Professor of Psychology
Yale University
New Haven, Connecticut

Preface

We published the first edition of this book in 1990. At that time, we saw a need to share with home visitors information on the history and philosophy of home visiting and to provide them with specific information on many of the skills essential for home visiting. We hoped that the readers of the book would be home visitors from a variety of programs with many different backgrounds, including health, social service, psychology, and education. We wanted the book to be useful for community or lay home visitors, also. In addition, we wrote for trainers and supervisors of home visitors and for local, state, and federal administrators responsible for establishing, managing, or funding home visiting programs. These individuals remain our audience for this second edition.

We wrote the first book based on the need we perceived from our combined experiences in home visiting. We have been involved in home visiting since the 1970s as home visitors, trainers, developers, and evaluators of programs. Much of our work was in two early intervention programs that included home visiting: Project CARE and the Infant Health and Development Program. As we hired, trained, and supervised the home visitors in these programs, we found very little information written specifically for home visitors. We planned the 1990 book to address this need.

Home visiting programs that were in their infancy in the 1980s have experienced considerable growth, and a number of home visiting programs have expanded nationwide. Prevention and intervention programs delivered via home visiting can now be found across all health, education, and social services. As a result of this considerable expansion, the need for updated information on home visiting has continued. Consequently, we prepared this edition. We have expanded the section on the historical events in the history of home visiting partly because we personally find this topic so interesting and partly to give home visitors a sense of the long tradition of home visiting. We have also added more information about current theories about family development and interaction and adult problem solving and related those to the day-to-day practice of home visiting.

Not only has growth occurred in the number of home visiting programs but the empirical database supporting home visiting has grown considerably in the past decade. We describe several of the better known home visiting efforts and report on more recent research findings. We enjoy bringing readers up-to-date on the research base of home visiting and helping the field think about how to build on this knowledge base.

During the past decade, we have continued to meet with home visitors, trainers, supervisors, and program directors across the country. As a result, we have expanded and refined some of our training procedures. These changes are reflected in the chapters on personnel issues, helping skills, and managing home visits. We have also expanded information on visiting families in stressful situations to reflect the expansion of knowledge in this area. We have updated information on assessment and evaluation procedures, and we have concluded by reviewing some of the advances of the past decade and noting directions for the next decade.

Our work with home visitors has been supported over the years with funding from the Robert Wood Johnson Foundation; the Packard Foundation; the State of North Carolina; the Administration for Children, Youth, and Families; and the Office of Educational Research and Improvement. We are grateful to these agencies for making it possible for us to do the work we enjoy.

Many people provided assistance in the preparation of the first edition of this book, and we still owe a debt of gratitude to them. At this time, we want to acknowledge those who have contributed to the development of this second edition. Two graduate students in school psychology at the University of North Carolina, Molly Murphy and Jennifer Smith, provided invaluable assistance in helping to update information, tracing references, making suggestions, and editing. Beth Tanner of the Frank Porter Graham Child Development Center and Kathleen Bueche of the School of Education provided eagle-eyed editorial assistance. To Marie Butts, who was the glue that held together the preparation of the first volume, we say thank you for taking on this task again.

We especially want to recognize Claudia Lyons, one of our original coauthors. Claudia's career has taken her on new paths, and she was not able to participate in the preparation of this second volume. Nevertheless, her influence can still be seen throughout the book. She was our colleague in the Infant Health and Development Program, spending weeks in the field on training, supporting, and learning from the IHDP home visitors. She provided wise insight and considerable effort in the preparation of the first volume. We still owe a special thanks to this very valued colleague and friend. Her sensitivity to the needs of home visitors and her skills in training are legacies that remain in this book.

Each of our husbands, John Wasik and Don Stanford, provided support to us throughout the writing of this book. To each we say thank you; we deeply appreciate your patience and encouragement.

1

A Historical Overview

Friendly visitor, district visitor, homemaker, visiting teacher, visiting nurse, family social worker, home visitor, family physician—all have provided care and support to families through visits in the home. Professional and lay workers, paid and volunteer, they have brought to families child care information, emotional support, health care, knowledge of community resources, help in learning to cope with everyday problems and, at times, homemaker services. Although such services currently address a variety of family needs, traditionally most home visit programs were prompted by conditions of poverty, illness, or the need for infant and child care.

In this book, *home visiting* is defined as the process by which a professional or paraprofessional provides help to a family in their own home. This help focuses on social, emotional, cognitive, educational, and/or health needs and often takes place over an extended period of time. Among professional groups in our society, nurses, social workers, and teachers are major providers of home services, although other professionals (including physicians, psychologists, psychiatrists, counselors, physical therapists, and speech therapists) also provide services in the home. Members of religious organizations have a long history of caring for individuals in their own homes. Many paraprofessionals or lay workers provide home-based family support. These individuals often share common characteristics or experiences with the families they visit. Parents, for example, may be recruited to visit other parents. We will use the term *home visitor* for any of these professional or paraprofessional helpers.

Home visiting may be initiated for a variety of reasons. It may be offered as a universal service to families; for example, a local health center may provide home visiting by nurses to all first-time parents of newborns within its geographic area. Such services could include support and encouragement to the new parents as well as information on nutrition and infant care. Home visiting may be offered as a prevention or intervention procedure prompted by the special needs of children. As a prevention effort, home visiting services may be offered to families whose children are at risk for school failure. As an intervention effort, educational agencies may provide home visiting by teachers to parents of each developmentally delayed child within a school district. In both types of services—intervention and prevention—home visitors could help parents learn ways of enhancing their child's social and cognitive development. In other instances, families may request services such as help with caring for a physically disabled or chronically ill family member. The judicial system may also require some families to participate in home visits, as in child neglect or abuse cases or child custody disputes.

Structural changes in the family, including a high divorce rate and large numbers of teenage parents and single-parent families, have resulted in an increased number of women and children living in poverty (Zigler & Black, 1989). The problems associated with poverty (e.g., high rates of infant mortality and premature births, child abuse and neglect, drug abuse, high school dropouts) have received increased attention in recent years (Bronfenbrenner, 1987; Moynihan, 1986). Many families face other difficult situations, such as job stress and insecurity, disruptive family relations, few social supports, and chronic illness (Rutter, Champion, Quinton, Maughan, & Pickles, 1995). Numerous social, educational, and health agencies are emphasizing home visiting as an extremely valuable procedure for helping families address these pervasive personal and social concerns.

Home visiting offers many advantages for working with families. It often helps overcome barriers to available services, such as illness, physical disability, lack of transportation or child care, low motivation, or alienation from the educational, social, or medical establishment. As a result, needed services reach many individuals and families who otherwise might not receive help. Home visiting can reduce the need for hospitalization by providing the support necessary for individuals to stay with their families. Home visiting is also influenced by the increased interest in self-care, the lower costs of home care when compared with institutionalization, and the increased willingness of insurance providers to cover the costs of home care (Berg & Helgeson, 1984). Home visiting provides a unique opportunity to obtain relevant information about a family's environment, resources, and needs, and it enhances a service provider's ability to individualize services. Also, by reaching out to people in their own homes, one conveys a message of respect and appreciation of the family needs. Visiting in the home allows the family to be in more familiar surroundings.

Additional advantages of home visiting for families with children stem from several assumptions related to parenting and parent-child interactions. The first assumption is that parents are usually the most consistent and caring people in the lives of their young children. For a majority of parents, bonding and caring for their children begins in infancy and continues throughout childhood, adolescence, and beyond.

A second assumption is that parents can learn positive, effective ways of responding to their children if they are provided with support, knowledge, and skills. Some parents have less access to parenting role models and knowledge about children than do other parents. Helping these parents to acquire knowledge and skills can be done in the home and can have a very positive influence on their children's development.

A third assumption is that for parents to respond most effectively and positively to their children, their own needs must be met. Parents who are out of work, worried about housing or food, or are experiencing emotional problems from events such as divorce or other family stress often find it difficult to care for their children. Through home visiting, one can provide support to parents, help them become more effective in addressing their day-by-day concerns, and help them with parenting competencies.

In this chapter, we will trace the history of home visiting, from its early beginnings to the present, in order to place in perspective current home visiting practice and to learn from and build on the work of the early leaders in this field. The few existing historical accounts of home visiting generally focus on events within specific professions such as social work, nursing, education, or medicine. Levine and Levine (1970) present a historical account of visiting teachers and social workers, Holbrook (1983) describes the social worker's role in home visiting, Buhler-Wilkerson (1985) describes the history of public health nursing, and Donahue (1985) presents a comprehensive view of the historical antecedents of today's nursing profession, including early efforts in home visiting, institutional care, and community care. In this chapter, we will highlight historical developments across different professions and with diverse populations to provide the reader with an understanding of the rich heritage shared by those who engage in home-based services.

History of Home Visiting

It is difficult to date the beginning of formal home visiting because caring for those in need has traditionally been a responsibility assumed by relatives, friends, and neighbors, with societal efforts developing gradually when informal support was not adequate. Although home visiting is often noted as developing during the past two centuries, organized visits to the sick in their own homes were occurring as early as 200 and 300 A.D. During this time, early Christian religious groups, as part of their charitable works of mercy, reached out to the sick by going to their homes (Donahue, 1985). Within this religious tradition, changes occurred over the centuries as care sometimes became more prevalent in institutions and sometimes in homes, often determined by sanitary conditions in institutions (Donahue, 1985; O'Sullivan, 1982). These religious groups have continued to be a strong presence in visiting the sick at home.

Formal home care was also prevalent in Elizabethan England when services were provided to paupers in their homes (Fink, Wilson, & Conover, 1963). These services were known as "outdoor relief" because they were provided outside rather than inside institutions. This practice of providing care at home was adopted in colonial America as the dominant method of public care for poor children and their families. By the 19th century, a shift in philosophy occurred and institutional care came to be considered superior to home care for poor children. When families could not provide for them, neglected them, or left them orphaned, children were taken from their homes and placed in almshouses (Fink et al., 1963). This practice was also true in England, where widows were not provided support in their homes; rather, their children were sent to almshouses where hundreds of children often resided. The state of New York built almshouses in every county to house and educate poor children. By the mid-19th century, almshouses had been established in all major seaboard cities (Moroney, 1987). Such efforts were not without strong critics who described the negative effects of these arrangements in breaking up families rather than keeping them together (Bremner, 1971). As a result, during the 19th century, some states continued home care, and the state of New York began to shift its emphasis to home care.

While these changes were occurring, the foundation was being laid for the provision of home care by trained home visitors. Florence Nightingale, through her efforts on the part of the sick poor, was a pioneer in this field. Her first public comments on home visiting appeared in a letter to William Rothbone in November 1861 (Monteiro, 1985). Rothbone, a member of the District Provident Society in Liverpool, had employed a nurse to care for the sick in his geographic district (Richmond, 1917). When Rothbone tried to expand these services to other districts, he could not find trained nurses, so he turned to Nightingale for support. She recommended that nurses be specifically trained for his project and proposed a plan for the training and employment of women in hospital, district, and private nursing. Following her advice, Rothbone opened a training school in Liverpool the following year.

Nightingale's concern with the sick, especially those who were poor, continued throughout her life. She linked the importance of home care with nursing care. In 1867 she wrote, "never think that you have done anything effectual in nursing in London till you nurse, not only the sick poor in workhouses, but those at home" (cited in Monteiro, 1985, p. 181). Although one of the major themes of her writings was the need for adequate training of nurses, she also called for rural health missioners, or nonnurse health visitors, to provide hygiene instruction for mothers living in rural towns and villages (Nightingale, 1894). Her final reports on district nursing and home care overlapped with an era of major social and cultural changes in America, from the 1890s to the time of the First World War.

Nightingale's efforts in England were predated by a religious order in France, the Congregation of Bon Secours. In 1824, in a departure from what had then become the norm of providing institutional care, the women of this order began to care for the sick in their own homes. This religious order expanded to Ireland in 1861 and to England in 1870. In 1881, they went to Baltimore, Maryland, where they began to address, through home visiting, the prevalence of disease, poverty, and unsanitary living conditions, conditions also being experienced by families in other large American cities at this time (O'Sullivan, 1982).

The Expansion of Home Visiting in America

Since the late 19th century, a number of circumstances contributed to organized formal efforts in the United States to help those in need. An increasing number of poor people living in urban settings, especially those who were sick, could not afford institutional care and needed support in the home. To assist those who were visiting the poor, in 1883, the Charity Organization Society of New York City published a handbook for visitors. The organization's purpose was to coordinate philanthropic resources. This work emulated the charity organization movement begun in London in 1869 that used volunteers to "visit, counsel, and instruct the poor" (Bremner, 1971, p. 52).

At the turn of the 20th century, when immigration was combined with continuing urbanization, further increases occurred in the number of urban poor, and a corresponding increase occurred in the social conditions associated with poverty (Levine & Levine, 1970). These demographic changes influenced the development of the visiting nurse, visiting teacher, public health nurse, and social worker. Many new child and family services were developed to address the conditions associated with urbanization and immigration, especially poverty, contagious diseases, unhealthy living conditions, high infant mortality, school dropouts, and delinquency. During this time, the helping professions were all strongly influenced by the philosophical view that environmental conditions were major contributors to personal problems and illness. Consequently, intensive efforts were directed at changing poor social conditions, particularly those contributing to illness, accidents, infant mortality, and school problems.

The role of the visiting nurse continued to expand, and two additional roles for service were developed: visiting teachers and social workers. These professions have strong roots in the settlement house movement in New York, Boston, Philadelphia, and Chicago. Settlement houses were established in communities with high levels of poverty. The settlement house workers, typically well-educated, upper-class women, served to improve social conditions and provide support for individual families (Addams, 1935).

In the early 1900s, visiting school teachers began working in the major urban cities of the United States. The visiting teacher was developed as a liaison between the school and the home because workers in the settlement houses saw the need to improve educational conditions for children by working with the children's teacher. These visiting teachers, forerunners of the school social worker, worked with families when children showed academic difficulties or were truant or incorrigible, or when there were adverse home conditions (Levine & Levine, 1970). When the visiting teacher began her work, she used an ecological approach, becoming familiar with the neighborhood, the attitudes of the people toward education, the settings in which people worked and lived, recreational opportunities, school programs, and services of public and private agencies. By being in the community, the visiting teacher came to know the family and child and could use her relationships with the schools to help the family and school work together. Classroom teachers also benefited from the input of the visiting teachers because they often received information about the child's family that made it easier to understand the child and provide attention to any special needs. As a result of these positive home-school experiences, "a resident in each of the settlement houses took on the special assignment of calling on the families of children who presented special problems of an educational, social or medical nature" (Levine & Levine, 1970, p. 128).

The sociocultural events that influenced the development of home services by teachers also strongly influenced the initiation of the field of social work. In the preface to her classic book, *Friendly Visiting Among the Poor,* Richmond (1899) acknowledged the influence of the associated charities that had organized Boston's friendly visitors almost two decades earlier. Addams's (1935) work at Hull House in Chicago was also a significant event in the development of social services. Although social work history and tradition have been intricately woven with home visiting, Holbrook (1983) observed that home visiting has not been addressed by most social work historians.

Providing mental health services in the home setting is usually associated with the beginning of social work. Early social workers focused on helping individuals and reforming society's institutions. Holbrook (1983) noted that social work developed during the Progressive Era of the early 1900s as a reaction to the survival-of-the-fittest advocates and the Social Darwinism philosophy of the late 19th century. Rather than promoting those philosophies, social workers tried to protect individuals from social and natural deprivation (Hollis & Wood, 1981). During this time, the child-saving movement was born to save the children of the working and dependent classes from the social conditions of poverty, urban industrialization, and slum life.

Historically, social workers served as a bridge between medicine, law, and the home (Holbrook, 1983). They were described as concerned with

> the positive measures of hygiene, such as the better housing of the patient, better nutrition, better provision for sunlight and fresh air, and above all, instructions to the patient as to the nature of his disease and the methods to be pursued in combating it. (Cabot, 1919, p. xv)

Because of their familiarity with families and their homes, social workers often assisted members of the legal profession by obtaining family information important in legal decision making.

Visiting nurses also added preventive care to their efforts. By 1910, most large urban visiting nurse associations "had initiated preventive programs for school children, infants, mothers, and patients with tuberculosis" (Buhler-Wilkerson, 1985, p. 1157). Many existing agencies, however, regarded public health and prevention as their domain and objected to the visiting nurses' involvement in these areas. Buhler-Wilkerson (1985) reported that the nursing leadership was "outraged by such assertions. Visiting nurses, they insisted, had always been teachers of prevention and hygiene and had, in fact, 'blazed the trail' for all of the health departments' new preventive programs" (p. 1159). Although debates about the roles of visiting nurses and public health nurses in treatment and prevention have continued into the present, in practice, both groups of nurses have been actively involved in home care throughout this century. Today's community health nurses provide services to the entire community (Leahy, Cobb, & Jones, 1982).

During the same time period in which child and family services underwent a rapid development in America, the progressive education movement also expanded. Philosophers, educators, and psychologists such as John Dewey (1915), William James (1899), and Lightner Witmer (1897, 1915, cited in Levine & Levine, 1970) argued strongly for their views of education, education's role in society, and the relationship of psychology to education. Within this atmosphere, Witmer developed the first psychological clinic in 1896 and focused on educational processes, community services, and prevention. He engaged teachers, parents, nurses, and housemothers in the therapeutic process with children based on his belief in the importance of adults in children's natural environments (Levine & Levine, 1970).

By the 1920s, the social reform movement, prevalent from the turn of the century, began to lose momentum. In the social work field, professional training became heavily influenced by psychiatric and psychoanalytic thinking. Freudian psychology came to be accepted by social work as the most useful basis for understanding personality (Hollis & Wood, 1981). This major shift paralleled developments in psychology in which the dominant mode of therapy from the 1920s to the 1950s was based on psychoanalytic theory, which emphasized individual traits in personality in contrast to environmental or situational effects on personality. Social casework became formalized, and social work began to focus less on environmental or social conditions and more on the psychological problems of individuals, resulting in a trend toward clinic-based services.

Even as the reform or preventive aspect of home visiting was changing in the United States, homemaker services were initiated by several casework agencies in Baltimore, Chicago, and Philadelphia in the 1920s (Fink et al., 1963). Although these services were initially provided to families with young children, they were expanded over time to include care for the chronically ill, handicapped, and elderly. These home visitors were motivated by the practical concerns of making it possible for individuals to remain in their own homes rather than by the social reform concerns that motivated earlier workers.

Home care or house calls have historically been a part of American medicine (Cauthen, 1981). Their role in home visiting has been important not only in the provision of direct services but also in facilitating the acceptance of services delivered to families in their homes. Yet during the first half of the 20th century, home care by physicians dropped significantly. House calls decreased from 40% of all patient-physician encounters in 1930 to 10% in 1950 (Meyer & Gibbons, 1997).

In summary, although there were early precursors to these services, home visiting did not become an organized, prevailing component of public agencies until the beginning of the 20th century. Then, over a relatively brief period of time, home visiting developed as a service delivery process in all three major areas of human services: health, education, and social services. In the following section, significant events of the 20th century that influenced home visiting are described.

Early Public Support for Home Visiting

The beginning of the 20th century saw a major public commitment to assist dependent and needy children in their homes rather than in institutions. In 1909, President Theodore Roosevelt convened the first White House conference on children. Noting that "home life is the finest and highest product of civilization," Roosevelt called for keeping children with their parents, "such aid being given as may be necessary to maintain suitable homes for the rearing of children" (Bremner, 1971, pp. 375-376).

The adoption of widows' pension laws in 1911 was one of three major advances in services for children resulting from this conference. These laws were based on a belief that it was appropriate to use public money to help mothers care for their children in their own homes (Fink et al., 1963). The White House conference also led to the establishment of the U.S. Children's Bureau and the organization of the Child Welfare League of America. These efforts all sanctioned the use of public funds for daily support of families in their homes, thus encouraging and supporting the practice of home visiting.

Home visiting was also influenced by the Great Depression and its aftermath, when many communities did not have the financial resources to meet their needs or did not have a conceptual framework to address the complexities of the problems in their own communities (Roberts & Heinrich, 1985). As a result, federal relief was initiated, with a major effort developed under the Civil Works Administration, in which more than 10,000 nurses were employed to work in local health agencies, with home visiting as an important part of their work.

The nation's involvement in the Second World War also significantly influenced home nursing. Because medical and nursing staffs in hospitals were greatly depleted by the war effort, many patients who would normally have been cared for in hospitals were treated at home.

> Families, already stressed, were expected to care for critically ill members, help with home births, or care for mothers and infants discharged early from the hospital. These family caretakers needed much instruction, support, and assistance with direct nursing care and looked to the public health nurse for this help. The American Red Cross organized courses in home nursing and training programs for nurse's aides. By the end of 1942, over 500,000 women had completed the American Red Cross home nursing course, and nearly 17,000 nurse's aides had been certified. (Roberts & Heinrich, 1985, p. 1165)

Financial assistance for the care of children in their own homes was strengthened by the federal government's passage of the Social Security Act of 1935. This act not only provided for social insurance and public assistance but also provided for maternal and child health services, services for crippled children, and child welfare services. The wording of the Social Security Act has changed over time, typically increasing its appropriateness for children. The Public Welfare Amendment of 1962 specifically described, as a child welfare service, the option of strengthening children's own families when possible, an option that home visiting is particularly well suited to help accomplish.

Home Visiting From the 1950s to the Present

At mid-century in the United States, the home became recognized as a desirable setting for the care of children with disabilities. Until the mid-1950s, parents of children with disabilities were generally advised to place the children in state or private institutions. Not until after this time did professionals begin to view positively the role of parents in the rearing of children with disabilities and to provide support to the parents to allow them to do so. Also, the deinstitutionalization movement of the 1960s led to an increase in attention on community- and home-based care for other populations.

Several factors influenced the shift in focus away from institutional care toward home care and support of the family. One factor was the change in the perceptions of professionals toward parents. As professionals recognized the bidirectionality of cause-and-effect relationships between parent and child (Bell, 1971), it became acceptable to incorporate parents as active partners in intervention procedures rather than blame them for their child's maladaptive behavior. This positive view of parents helped to bring about an increase in home care for children because society no longer strongly believed that the child had to be removed from negative parental influences.

The study of cost-effectiveness also became prevalent in the 1960s, influencing community- and home-based interventions. Federal and state agencies began to reevaluate the potential benefits of home and local community programs versus large institutional programs, in part because of the lower cost of home programs. As an example of this interest, a number of efforts were developed during the 1970s that were aimed at keeping delinquent youths in their own community, typically in a group home. In many of these group homes, located near the youths' families, the treatment program was modeled on family life, and a major objective was to help the youths learn behaviors necessary to live with their own families (Phillips, Wolf, Fixsen, & Bailey, 1970).

In the 1970s, increased concerns about maternal and child health sparked an increased interest in home visiting. One of the first people to speak out for young mothers and their infants was a pediatrician, Henry Kempe, who was motivated by the failure of society to take responsibility for providing the services during infancy necessary to prevent child abuse. Kempe (1976) noted that although there had been calls for early screening of infants for specific diseases, the emotional growth and development of the child was often neglected. He called for giving "adequate attention to the whole child, his family, their total health status, including those emotional as well as physical factors that might affect the child's welfare" (Kempe, 1976, p. 946). Kempe strongly recommended the universal provision of home health visitors for families of newborns, stressing that every child is entitled to effective, comprehensive health care. When parents do not or cannot provide for this care, society must.

Psychiatrists have also had a role in home visiting, most often associated with community mental health movements. Deinstitutionalization in the 1960s and 1970s brought about an increased interest in the psychiatric home visit (Sullivan & Cohen, 1990). During the 1960s, several writers addressed the role of psychiatrists in home visits, often with a focus on providing visits for the poor (Behrens, 1967; Brown, 1962). Psychiatrists recognized early on the advantages of providing help to families by meeting with them in their own homes, but home visits by psychiatrists have not been prevalent. Recently, several writers have called for an increased role for psychiatrists in home visiting. Thompson and Fox (1994, p. 304) ask, "How long can we psychiatrists pay lip service to the idea of providing psychiatric and medical care in the community without ourselves going to patients' homes?"

As noted earlier, the number of house calls by physicians declined significantly in the first half of the 20th century. By 1980, house calls accounted for only 0.6% of patient-physician encounters (Meyer & Gibbons, 1997). This decrease has been influenced by advancing technology (requiring access to specific equipment and resources in order to deliver the best medical care) and by a belief that home visits by physicians are not cost-effective. In contrast to these earlier influences, there is now an increasing need for physician house calls due to the increased use of medical equipment in homes and the number of homebound, frail, and elderly patients (Adelman, Fredman, & Knight, 1994). Consequently, renewed attention is being focused on house calls by physicians, especially for the elderly and those so ill that travel is difficult. For example, home-based care for persons with AIDS has developed during the past 20 years as both a medical and mental health service delivery system (Frey, Oman, & Wagner, 1997). Schools of medicine have begun to incorporate home visits as part of medical training (Cauthen, 1981; Steinkuller, 1992; Wells, Benson, Hoff, & Stuber, 1987) as writers call for increased training of residents in home care and increased recognition of its benefits.

Although the number of physician house calls is low, the number of health-related home visits in the United States has continued to grow. The annual Medicare budget in 1996 for homecare was $19 billion. More than 160 million home visits per year by visiting nurses, physical therapists, occupational therapists, and home health aides are being paid for by Medicare (Campion, 1997).

Examples of Home Visiting Programs in the United States

One of the largest home visiting programs in America is the Head Start Home-Based Program, initiated as a demonstration program in 1972 and continuing through today (Love, Nauta, Coelen, Hewett, & Ruopp, 1976). Communities may select the Head Start home visiting option as an alternative to center-based programs, and many center-based programs include home visiting. At least 90% of the families in Head Start are low-income, with children between the ages of 3 to 6 years. A Head Start home visitor's role is to assist, encourage, and support parents in their parenting and family responsibilities (U.S. Department of Health and Human Services [U.S. DHHS], 1993). The home visitor makes regular contact with parents, provides information and support to parents, and encourages and facilitates interaction between parents and children.

Early Head Start (EHS) was initiated in 1995, representing a new phase of Head Start that was designed to serve low-income pregnant women and families with infants and toddlers up to the age of 3. In 1999, approximately 500 EHS grantees served approximately 40,000 children from birth to age 3. EHS programs must focus on child, family, and staff development and community building and can do so in a number of ways. Some programs are exclusively center-based, with parent involvement at the centers, other programs are exclusively home-based, with all contacts taking place in homes and communities, and still other programs offer both modalities of service. A study of 3,400 families in 17 of the first EHS programs was begun in 1996, and the longitudinal results of the program's effects on children and families became available in 2000.

In the 1970s, some states and private foundations began to develop new home visiting initiatives. In Hawaii, the Kamehameha Schools provided home visiting services for native Hawaiian children, beginning with the mother during the prenatal period and continuing until the children were 3 years old (Roberts, 1988). The Kansas Healthy Start Program and the Colorado Parent-Infant Project were both developed to provide for maternal and child health through home visits. These latter two programs were influenced by

Kempe's (1976) proposal calling for health visitors for all children. Minnesota included home visiting as part of a program for children from birth to the age of 6 that emphasizes the parent as the child's major teacher (Weiss, 1989). In the state of Washington in the late 1990s, approximately 75% of families accepted home visiting services offered after the birth of a child (K. Barnard, personal communication, 1999).

The state of Missouri facilitated the development of the Parents as Teachers home visiting program in the 1980s. Visitors help parents strengthen their parenting skills, enhance their knowledge of child development, and prepare their young children for school (Winter & Rouse, 1991). It is a widely implemented, universal access program that now serves more than 500,000 families in 49 states as well as several foreign countries. Designed to serve all families regardless of income level, this program reaches out to all families with a newborn to provide information and advice on child care and parenting.

Healthy Families America is a home-based program designed to prevent child abuse and neglect. It is modeled on the Healthy Start Program begun in Hawaii in the 1980s (Sia & Breakey, 1985). The Hawaii program was built on the beliefs and procedures of Kempe (1976) for providing services to high-risk families.

In the early 1980s, the Ford Foundation funded a number of home visiting programs to serve the needs of low-income families. These programs, called Child Survival/Fair Start Programs, served a variety of cultural and ethnic groups across the country to improve pregnancy outcomes, infant health, and family conditions that are associated with child development. The populations who were served included migrant Mexican American farm workers, young Black mothers in the South, Appalachian families, and Haitian immigrants (Halpern & Larner, 1988; Larner & Halpern, 1987).

Home visits by school systems have also been receiving increased interest. Current interest in home visiting is partly based on concerns similar to those that existed at the beginning of the 20th century, namely providing services to children of immigrant families or families for whom English is a second language. Home visiting provides an opportunity to engage the parent in a joint home-school intervention program for children with academic or behavioral difficulties. Examples of successful home-school collaborations have been reported by Kelley (1990) and Kahle and Kelley (1994).

Home Visiting in Europe in the 20th Century

Both historically and currently, European models of home visiting have influenced practice in the United States. In particular, the widespread acceptance of home visiting for prenatal and postnatal care throughout Europe has been viewed in this country as a model for practice (Miller, 1987).

Possibly the most comprehensive home visiting program of any country was initiated in Denmark based on legislation passed in 1937. This family and child care system has been an exemplary model of successful service delivery and for this reason we will describe this country's services in more detail. In Denmark, every pregnant woman is visited at least once, usually by a midwife or a home visiting nurse. Within the first week of returning home after delivery, the mother and child are visited. Denmark's highly developed system dates back to the late 1800s, when worldwide concern was expressed about the practice of placing children of unwed mothers and abandoned or orphaned children with private families, in which the children were often mistreated (Wagner & Wagner, 1976). A strong impetus for Denmark's program was a 6-year pilot study conducted in the 1930s that demonstrated substantial effects of home visiting on the reduction of infant mortality and morbidity during the first year of life.

The Danish response to the concern with placing children in institutions and the results of the pilot study was to set up a nationwide network of local lay citizens to serve as advocates for children in individual communities. These local citizen groups, the Child and Youth Committees (CYC), became a standing committee of every district or township, including elected officials and lay volunteers. The roles of the CYC have been protection, promotion, and prevention.

The CYCs have been staffed by social workers, family helpers, or both. The use of family helpers as ancillary workers became necessary because of an insufficient number of social workers to provide the necessary services. In some localities, the social worker supervised the work of 10 to 20 family helpers. Depending on the family's needs, a family helper was assigned to visit on a daily, weekly, or monthly basis. Priority was placed on trying to resolve problems within the context of the family. Problems that were addressed ranged from parental depression to teenage pregnancy (Wagner & Wagner, 1976).

In 1963, the Public Health Nursing Services Act recommended health home visitors, but the practice did not become universally available until 1971, when these services were mandated (unless families declined) (Kamerman & Kahn, 1993). In 1980, 259 of the 277 townships in Denmark had a visiting nurse program, thus assuring that 88% of all Danish infants were being seen regularly by a registered nurse who specialized in infant health. Midwives and physicians are legally required to report all births to a home visitor. Fewer than 2% of Danish families refuse this service (Dawson, 1980; Wagner & Wagner, 1976). In some areas, high-risk infants are followed until they enter school. The Danish family helper has no exact equivalent in the United States, but the increasing concerns about maternal and child health are leading the United States in the direction of home visiting for young mothers (Weiss, 1989).

Norway also has an organized home helper program. Because of a shortage of domestic help and hospital beds prior to the 1940s, women's organizations in Norway began to address the questions of how to bring help into homes of women who, through illness, childbirth, or other emergency, could not carry out household responsibilities (Langholm, 1961). A full expansion of these efforts occurred in 1947, when the Norwegian Parliament voted the first state allowance for home helpers. A State Home Help Council was appointed in 1949, and the activities of home helpers were officially described by the Ministry of Social Affairs. In 1956, the Ministry of Family and Consumer Affairs was assigned responsibility for coordinating the work of home helpers and home nurses. Specific training for home helpers and home nurses was required unless the helpers were authorized trained nurses or met other specific requirements.

The now classic work by Bowlby (1952) on the importance of the relationship between maternal care and child health, published by the World Health Organization, significantly influenced the nature of family services. In England, in particular, Bowlby's (1952) work served as a strong stimulus for the country to promote services that would prevent the breakup of the family. Prior to the 1950s, children in situations of crisis, abandonment, incapacity, or illness were placed in the care of others (e.g., foster homes, institutions). Skilled help was not available to assist the child's natural family in dealing with the situation. The Children's Act of 1948 emphasized the natural strength of the family. As a result, casework no longer focused primarily on removing children from families living in conditions of poverty or overcrowding. Rather, social policies were developed to address these environmental conditions, and the caseworker focused on interpersonal needs rather than social conditions (Heywood, 1959).

In England in 1978, the Warnock Committee Report on children with special education needs strongly advocated for a specific person to be identified as a point of contact for each parent. Support for home visiting of families who had a severely disabled child also came from the Resource Worker Project in London, a 2-year project designed to evaluate the effectiveness of resource workers. In this project, very specific roles were played by workers who provided support and services to families with a severely disabled child. A basic component of the project was a commitment to maintain regular contact with families to assist them with concerns about their disabled children. In addition to providing family support, regular contacts with the families made it possible for the resource workers to monitor the children's development and changes in the families' circumstances on an ongoing basis without having to depend on a parent to write or telephone for services (Glendinning, 1986).

The breadth of involvement with the family was judged to be one of the most successful features of the Resource Worker Project. Glendinning (1986) noted that "the resource workers' involvement encompassed a very broad range of medical, social, educational, practical, financial, recreational, and emotional issues" (pp. 201-202). Although the workers thought of themselves and were seen by the families as social workers, they became "involved in the whole spectrum of problems experienced by families looking after a disabled child" (p. 202). The breadth of help was seen as central to the role of the resource worker.

Currently, in the United Kingdom (England, Scotland, and Wales), a wide range of services are available related to childbearing and home care (Miller, 1987). In England and Wales, prenatal home visiting services are generally initiated as a check on those who do not attend prenatal clinics. In Scotland, by contrast, a community midwife attends and counsels every pregnant woman at home. She makes monthly visits to women who plan to deliver their infants at home until the 32nd week of pregnancy, and then she visits weekly until delivery. Miller (1987) reports a relatively structured postpartum program in all parts of the United Kingdom. For instance, a midwife makes a home visit each day for a minimum of 10 days after delivery, and once the midwife's responsibilities end, a health visitor continues the home visits.

In Switzerland, prenatal home visits are made only for medically defined risks or if requested by the pregnant woman for an acceptable reason. After delivery, home visits are routinely made to all families by a nurse with training in maternity and infant care. At least one visit is made within the first 14 days after discharge from the hospital, and another visit is made 4 months later.

In Belgium, home visiting is a featured part of maternity care, with a nurse visiting the home twice in the prenatal period. At least one home visit occurs during the first 2 months postpartum, with earlier and more frequent visits for high-risk families. In Ireland, free home visiting is available to the entire population, with special emphasis on perinatal care, child health, and elderly care. As evidence of the acceptance of home visiting, usage of these services from 1975 to 1983 increased 50% (Miller, 1987).

The Netherlands has an impressive system of postpartum care. Whether delivery is in the home or a hospital, the lying-in period is 10 days. During this time, mothers and their infants are visited at home by a caregiver for up to 8 hours a day for the first 10 days postpartum, with an average of 64 hours of visits for each family. The home visitor helps care for the infant and mother, advises on infant care, and assists with housekeeping.

Home visits in Europe are not only provided by nurses, social workers, and family helpers but also by teachers. In writing about home visiting by teachers in England, Hannon and Jackson (1987) noted that the idea of home visiting could be traced back to preschool intervention work in the United States that began in the 1960s. The results of the early intervention programs, especially Gray and Klaus's (1970) Early Training Program and the Ypsilanti Perry Preschool Project (Weikart, Bond, & McNeil, 1978), as well as the writing of Bronfenbrenner (1974), were instrumental in prompting home visiting as an educational intervention. As a result, educational home visiting was initiated in England in a number of settings with preschool children (e.g., Raven, 1980; Smith, 1975) and later for children with disabilities (Cameron, 1984). Psychiatric home visits were prevalent in England and Canada in the 1950s and 1960s, predating interest in the United States (Carse, Panton, & Watt, 1958).

Dowie (1983), in a study of home visits by psychiatrists in the United Kingdom, found that in 1982, British psychiatrists made more than 90,000 home visits, with each psychiatrist making an average of 90 visits (cited in Kates, Webb, & LePage, 1991). These visits accounted for 14% of all outpatient consultations.

In summary, home visiting in Europe is a widely accepted practice for helping families. The promotion of family life is viewed as the responsibility of the government. Home visits are provided during times of universal need, as in the birth of a child, or for families experiencing stresses beyond their management abilities. Home visits by physicians are a more common practice in Europe than in the United States.

Other International Efforts

Offering help to families in their homes is prevalent throughout the world. The Portage model of early intervention, developed in Michigan to focus on helping parents in their role as the child's teacher (Shearer & Shearer, 1972), is now found in the United Kingdom, Japan, India, the Philippines, Norway, Latvia, and Cyprus. Training and technical assistance is also taking place in Middle Eastern countries and in the Nordic region of Europe (Shearer, 1998). The *Portage Guide to Early Education* (Bluma, Shearer, Frohman, & Hilliard, 1976), a comprehensive description of this program has been translated into 37 languages and introduced in more than 78 countries.

International interest in home visiting is clearly illustrated by the large number of research studies evaluating home visiting in many diverse places. In Israel, Muslim mothers are asked to provide support for other women in their own communities. The Home Instruction Program for Preschool Youngsters was initiated in Israel and has been implemented in many other locations, including the United States. In other areas of the Middle East, visitors bring help to mothers and infants and to the sick and poor. In Turkey, researchers are implementing early intervention programs through home visiting with parents and children (Kagitcibasi, 1996). In Canada, visiting by many professionals is a widespread practice, ranging from visits for families of preterm infants (Barrera, Doucet, & Ketching, 1990) to visits by psychiatrists. In Latin America, there are also home visiting programs (e.g., Super, Herrera, & Mora, 1990; Villar et al., 1992).

Research on the Effects of Home Visiting

Several areas of home visiting have received considerable research attention, including home visiting for children being raised in poverty and children at biological risk (including low birthweight infants, preterm infants, and infants with disabilities). Home visiting programs for maternal and child health, care during pregnancy, and postnatal care have received considerable attention. Other research programs have focused on home visiting for the prevention of out-of-home placements for adolescents and for delinquent adolescents more broadly. The treatment and prevention of child abuse and neglect has been another significant area of interest with home visiting. In addition, many programs have focused on universal services, offering home visiting to all parents of newborns under the assumption that support for parenting is an important social responsibility.

Home Visiting for Low-Income Families

Many home visiting efforts developed from concerns about poverty in the 1960s, the same concerns that prompted the initiation of Project Head Start. Reviews of this work are included in reports by Gray and Wandersman (1980), Bryant and Maxwell (1997), and Farran (2000). The research focused on children from poverty backgrounds included an early study by Schaefer and Aaronson (1977), in which home tutors focused on verbal stimulation with children. The data suggested a brief, positive change in cognitive scores for children in the intervention program but no long-term benefits.

Later, research in the 1970s and 1980s often compared infants and young children in home visiting intervention programs with infants and young children in control groups. Such studies were conducted by Gordon and Guinagh (1978), who addressed the question of program intensity, studying the effects of home visiting programs of 1, 2, or 3 years duration for children from low-income families. Field, Widmayer, Stringer, and Ignatoff (1980) reported significant cognitive gains at 4 and 8 months for preterm infants in a home visiting program compared with children whose families were not in the program. In a second study that compared a home visit plus parent training program and a nursery plus parent training program, children in both treatment programs obtained higher scores on measures of mental and motor development than control children who received no intervention (Field, Widmayer, Greenberg, & Stoller, 1982).

Gray and Ruttle (1980) conducted a family-focused home intervention program for children from low-income families. Although the intervention program was individualized for each family, language, teaching style, competence, and behavior management were emphasized with all families. The results showed that during preschool, children in the intervention program scored higher on cognitive development measures than control children. The Mother-Child Home Program was developed by Levenstein (1988) to reduce the risk of school failure for children from low-income families and to increase the mothers' parenting skills and self-esteem. Home visitors take toys into the home and demonstrate their use, emphasizing language and interaction. Replication of this home program in Bermuda found no significant treatment effects (Scarr & McCartney, 1988).

The authors of this book, with colleagues Craig Ramey and Joseph Sparling, developed and conducted Project CARE (Carolina Approach to Responsive Education), a research program designed to evaluate the effects of a developmental day care program and family home visiting program for low-income children. At ages 3 and 5, children whose families received family education in the home and who participated in an educational day care program scored significantly higher on cognitive measures than children whose families received only family education through home visiting or children in the control group (Ramey, Bryant, Sparling, & Wasik, 1985; Wasik, Ramey, Bryant, & Sparling, 1990).

Low Birthweight Infants

Home visiting has been evaluated as an intervention strategy for low birthweight infants. In one study, low birthweight infants who participated in an intervention program in which home visits were made for 2 years performed significantly better on mental and physical development measures than did control children (Resnick, Eyler, Nelson, Eitzman, & Buccizrelli, 1987). Another study of low birthweight infants combined in-hospital visits with the mother and at-home visits for 3 months (Rauh, Achenbach, Nurcombe, Howell, & Teti, 1988). Mothers in the intervention group made a better initial adjustment to their low birthweight infant, and at 3 and 4 years of age, children who received the intervention scored significantly higher on mental development measures than children who did not receive the intervention. These effects from an intervention delivered early in a child's life support the importance of involving the parents at a crucial time.

The Infant Health and Development Program, modeled on both the Abecedarian Project (Ramey & Campbell, 1987) and Project CARE (described above), included a major home visiting component. The program goal was to study the effects of home intervention and day care on the cognitive, social, and physical development of low birthweight infants from birth to age 3 (Infant Health and Development Program, 1990; Ramey et al., 1992). Results of children at age 3 showed that those in the intervention group performed higher on cognitive tests than children in the nonintervention group (Gross, Spiker, & Haynes, 1997). Kana et al. (1995), in a randomized experimental study, found significant effects on children's positive social interactions as a result of an intervention promoting parent adaptation to the preterm infants combined with a program to promote infant behavioral responsiveness.

Maternal and Child Health

Home visiting for maternal and child health has been a major focus for public health nursing (Byrd, 1997), and a number of reviews of home visiting exist (Baldwin & Chen, 1989; Combs-Orme, Reis, & Ward, 1985; Deal, 1994; Olds & Kitzman, 1993). Byrd (1997) provided a historical account that began with one of the first evaluation studies of nurse home visiting by Shyne, LeMat, and Kogan (1963) and continued with studies through the early 1990s. One example of a public health nursing intervention was the Mobile Unit for Child Health, which focused on both medical and cognitive needs through prenatal counseling for teenage, unmarried, low-income mothers as well as infant stimulation for their children. Significant cognitive gains were seen at ages 2 and 3 for children in the intervention groups (Gutelius, Kirsch, MacDonald, Brooks, & McErlean, 1977). Ross (1984) found that infants who had been visited in the home during the first year of life by a nurse and occupational therapist scored significantly higher at the age of 1 year on a measure of general development when compared with a matched control group. In a matched sample study to reduce maternal depression for mothers of infants, mothers who were in a home visit intervention improved more in reported depression and daily hassles than mothers not in the intervention (Gelfand, Teti, Seiner, & Jameson, 1996).

Olds and Kitzman (1990, 1993) and Olds et al. (1999) have conducted a total of three research programs evaluating the effects of a nurse home visiting program for pregnant women and mothers of infants. These research programs have all used randomized experimental designs. Results from these studies, described in Chapter 3, have provided support for some child and family outcomes but not for other outcomes.

Child Abuse and Neglect

Home visiting has been described as the treatment of choice for child abuse and neglect, and as a result there has been considerable interest in providing home-based services for both prevention and intervention (Wasik & Roberts, 1994a). Objectives of these programs include helping parents learn positive child-rearing techniques and effective coping skills, reducing stress, and increasing home safety. Among the well-known programs addressing abuse and neglect are the Hawaii Healthy Families (Duggan et al., 1999) and Healthy Families America (Daro & Harding, 1999) programs. In addition, significant work in this area has been conducted by Lutzker, Wesch, and Rice (1984).

Out-of-Home Placement

Since the 1970s, the prevention of out-of-home placement for children and youths has been a major focus of home visiting services. These services are commonly referred to as *family preservation services*. Although there were predecessors to providing family preservation services before 1970, the theoretical perspectives that guide the field (i.e., social learning theory, family systems theory, crisis intervention theory, ecological perspectives on child development) were not articulated until later (Wells, 1995). (See Chapter 2 for a discussion of theories guiding home visiting practices.) Among the most well-known family preservation services are those of the Homebuilders Model, initiated in 1974 (Kinney & Dittmar, 1995; Kinney, Haapala, & Booth, 1991). These services are currently available in most of the United States as well as in a number of countries abroad (Kinney & Dittmar, 1995). In-home, family-focused interventions have also been implemented to reunify families separated by a child placed in out-of-home care. In one research study, findings suggested that family-strengthening services may promote reunification and permanence (Walton, Fraser, Lewis, Pecora, & Walton, 1993).

The David and Lucile Packard Foundation has published two reports devoted to home visiting as part of its *The Future of Children* journal. In the 1993 journal issue on home visiting, several topics were addressed, including conceptual frameworks, research, and implementation. In 1999, the home visiting issue of *The Future of Children* focused on the outcomes of some of the best documented home visiting programs. Because of the interest in this publication, the National Research Council sponsored a conference for program directors and researchers to discuss issues of effectiveness. The report concluded that the results were strong enough to guide policy makers and practitioners but that a number of weaknesses in the evaluations preclude generalization (Gomby, 1999).

Legislation Influencing Home Care

Home visiting has been affected by federal legislation such as Public Law (P.L.) 96-272. Known as the Adoption Assistance and Child Welfare Act of 1980, this legislation encouraged professionals to keep children in their natural homes while maintaining the child's safety (Wells, 1995). The purpose was to shift federal funding from out-of-home placement in foster care to prevention and family reunification. A number of home-based family intervention programs have resulted from this legislation, many with a family therapy focus (Christensen, 1995). Among these interventions are programs such as Homebuilders, which provides intensive family preservation services. In 1993, the Family Preservation and Family Support Initiative was passed, making additional funds available for family-oriented services.

In 1986, Congress passed P.L. 99-457, Amendments to the Education of the Handicapped Act, the most far-reaching family legislation of the decade. Part H, Early Intervention Programs for Handicapped Infants and Toddlers, mandated services to all 3- to 5-year-old children with handicapping conditions. It also established a state grant program that focused on the needs of infants and toddlers with disabilities, from birth to age 2, and their families. States were required to develop policies to put the major components of Part H into effect by 1991.

One of the most important components of P.L. 99-457 is the Individualized Family Service Plan, which requires coordinated and individualized services within the context of the family for any child with special needs. This requirement is significant in its focus on the needs of families as well as children. Following the passage of P.L. 99-457, the Surgeon General of the United States reiterated the commitment to family-centered, community-based coordinated care (Koop, 1987). Home visiting is seen as an important process for providing these needed family services.

The federal Even Start Family Literacy programs, serving both adults with low literacy or low education levels and their children, are required to provide home visiting services. The Even Start program was initially authorized by 1988 amendments to the Elementary and Secondary Education Act of 1965, and was then amended by the National Literacy Act of 1991 and reauthorized in 1994 (P.L. 102-73). Also, the recent initiation of Early Head Start, serving children from birth to age 3, has spawned the development of many new home visiting programs throughout the United States.

Summary

In this chapter, we have considered the development of home visiting over time as well as the cultural and social events that have influenced the practice of home visiting. From the early history of home visiting to its current role in society, many people have discovered and rediscovered the value of home visiting. It has persisted as a family service across time and across countries, serving both special populations and the general population. The continued expansion of home visiting as a means of addressing current social and family needs requires a continued effort to assure the highest quality in providing services. The healthy skepticism engendered by recent evaluations should encourage continued study of the ways to strengthen home visiting and better focus our efforts.

2

Theories and Principles of Home Visiting

Many questions have been asked about why and how to provide care and support to those in need. In this chapter, we will address theories and principles that have given direction to the practice of home visiting. First are theories about children's development, family dynamics, and interpersonal relationships. These theories include ecological theory, family systems theory, cognitive-behavioral theories, and social problem-solving theories. We then present Richmond's (1899) principles of relief for guiding the practice of "friendly visitors" to illustrate the relationship between many current principles of care and those she wrote about more than 100 years ago. Third, shifts in principles of care guiding services in health, education, social services, and mental health across the 20th century are described. We conclude with a set of principles for home visitors derived from our own work in home visiting, informed by the theories and work of others.

Theories Influencing Home Visiting

Ecological Theory of Human Development

The ecological theory of human development as proposed by Bronfenbrenner (1979, 1989) has been especially influential in family-focused programs (Minuchin, Colapinto, & Minuchin, 1998;

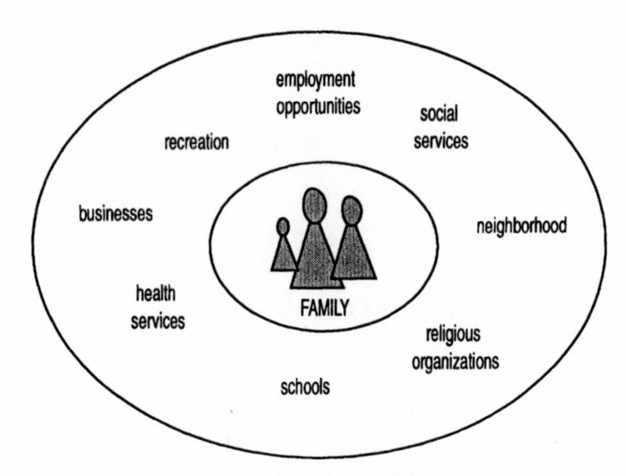

Figure 2.1 Brofenbrenner's Ecological Model

Stephens, 1979). In his theory, each person is seen as nested within a set of increasingly complex environments, beginning with the family (see Figure 2.1). The family is nested in a community that includes a neighborhood, schools, religious institutions, businesses, employment opportunities, and social and health services. State and federal policies are at a more distant level, but they nevertheless influence the family. Among the policies influencing families are those related to child care, education, social services, Medicare, Medicaid, and economics. Bronfenbrenner's (1979, 1989) stress on considering social and community variables when planning for families is similar to what home visitors in the early 1900s already recognized as important: Change in social conditions can lead to change in the lives of families. The availability of jobs, child care, transportation, and health and education services all directly influence family life.

Ecological theory serves as an organizing framework for home visiting by helping programs recognize influences and resources beyond the immediate family. As an illustration, social support plays a significant role in the well-being of individual family members and the family as a whole (Moroney, 1987; Rutter, 1987). When social support is strong, as in a positive marital relationship or close, caring relatives and friends, benefits accrue to both children and parents. When social support is lacking or inadequate, emotional distress, depression, and physical illness are more likely.

Many research studies validate the importance of social support. Families who report four or more close friendships seem to cope better with rearing their child with special needs than families who report few close friends (Rees, 1983). Women with a network of friends were found to complete a behavioral training program more often than socially isolated women (Wahler, 1980). Women with low levels of social support are much more likely to develop complications during pregnancy than women with high levels of support (Nuckolls, Cassel, & Kaplan, 1972).

Bronfenbrenner (1995) extended his theory to include principles related to life course development. One principle states, "The lives of all family members are interdependent. Hence, how each family member reacts to a particular historical event or role transition affects the developmental course of other family members, both within and across generations" (Bronfenbrenner, 1995, p. 642). This expansion of ecological theory leads us into family systems theory, the next theory with relevance for home visiting.

Family Systems Theory

All helpers need a framework for thinking about families. They also need an appreciation of the complexity of providing services to a family. Many individual problems are related to family patterns and it is often necessary to involve other family members, both to understand one person's problem and to help in its resolution. Knowledge gained from family systems theory and family therapy procedures can help programs conceptualize individual and family-focused services. Providing services to an individual is often easier and more manageable than providing services to a family. Even when addressing the needs of an individual, knowledge of family dynamics helps one identify relationship patterns that may be interfering with an individual's coping skills, ability to benefit from program services, and general well-being. On many occasions, home visitors need to be able to interact with all family members first, because they are often present during visits and, second because change is often more likely when all the important individuals living in the house are involved. When providing intervention services for children, involving the family is essential. Consequently, it is important to understand family dynamics and to be skilled in working with families. Although we identify some skills in this book, working with families requires intensive training and supervision.

As early as the 1950s and 1960s, therapists who pioneered in helping individuals in the context of the family recognized the importance of relationships between family members (Bateson, Jackson, Haley, & Weakland, 1956; Bowen, 1966; Haley, 1976; Jackson, 1957; Minuchin, 1974; Satir, 1983). Their observations and studies of families led these therapists to describe the family as a unit with interlocking relationships; a system in which each individual influences and is influenced by other family members (Kerr & Bowen, 1988; Satir, Banmen, Gerber, & Gomori, 1991).

In describing the basic principles of systems theory as applied to family therapy, Minuchin (1985) noted the importance of two major principles. The first is that "any system is an organized whole, and elements within the system are necessarily interdependent" (p. 289). Here we will refer to the family as a system and groupings within a family as subsystems. For example, parents are a subsystem within a family, so too are siblings. Interactions within and between these subsystems are directly related to the family's overall functioning. Interactions that are positive, constructive, and supportive are consistent with well-functioning families. Negative, critical, and nonsupportive interactions contribute to family dysfunction.

A second principle Minuchin (1985) identified is that patterns in a system occur in a circular manner, not in a linear manner. Cause and effect in relationships cannot be explained simply as one event causing another. In human relationships, multiple events often interact in complex ways to influence actions. *Circularity* calls into question earlier views that recognized the parent's influence on the child but did not recognize the child's influence on the parent. Recognition of circularity (or *bidirectionality*, as described by Bell, 1971) includes the child's influence on the parent. The principle of circularity applies to all relationships in a family as each member influences and is influenced by other members.

Another tenet of family systems theory addresses the role of boundaries between generational subsystems such as parents and children (Minuchin, 1974). These boundaries need to be both flexible and clear. Many responsibilities are specific to one subsystem as, for example, the need for one parent to support the other. When one parent fails to support the other parent or to fulfill his or her own parental responsibilities, or when one parent and child align against the other parent, the well-being of the family may be threatened.

Families are also influenced by a myriad of rules, routines, and traditions. These expectations can help families function effectively. They might include having a common mealtime, attending a weekly religious event, or celebrating special occasions. They may range from watching a weekly television program together to going to the same place every year for a vacation. Rules can be spoken or unspoken. They can also be restrictive and limiting and contribute to family dysfunction (Satir et al., 1991). One family may have the expectation that one does not express positive emotions (e.g., affection, joy) or negative emotions (e.g., anger, regret). Another family may insist that everyone must always be present at a weekly family event and show little tolerance for individual preferences. Understanding a family's rules and expectations and how these influence individual functioning helps a home visitor work more effectively and responsively with that family.

Knowledge of family systems theory can prompt programs to recognize important family relationships beyond that of mother-child. Involving fathers, grandparents, boyfriends, and older and younger siblings can often be essential to success by helping families jointly identify desired outcomes, discuss ways of reaching these outcomes, and make commitments to work together. Research studies continue to support a relationship between the quality of the interactions between family members and the well-being of each person in the family (Cox & Paley, 1997). Of special importance is the marital relationship itself and its role in child and adolescent functioning.

When one home visiting program for mothers and their infants analyzed both their program data and home visitor narrative reports, researchers noted that the objective of working with several family members had not been easy to accomplish.

> While the grandmothers and other adults often were very supportive of their daughters, the young women living in these households were less able to implement the changes in the home environment suggested by program visitors than were mothers living

> alone . . . The key variable is . . . likely to be the complexity of the household organizations. These households were complex networks of extended families. The households we categorized as mother-grandmother often included the separated or divorced siblings of the mothers and their children, and sometimes married adult siblings living with their spouse as well as their own children. . . . The household rules and routines that permit these complex arrangements to work are not easily changed to accommodate the needs of one person's infant, especially when that person is the newest parent in the household. (Cole, Kitzman, Olds, & Sidora, 1998, p. 46)

As can be seen from this example, establishing a working relationship with key members of a family can be very complex and can have unpredictable outcomes. Home visitors need to understand the complexity of these relationships and work to develop effective ways of involving all family members.

Cognitive/Behavioral Theories

Many home visiting programs are specifically designed to help families engage in problem management and problem resolution. Addressing problems in daily living may require new behaviors and new ways of thinking about one's situation. Helpers need to have knowledge about the principles of behavior change and the role of cognitive processes in influencing behaviors and feelings. Cognitive/behavioral principles are compatible with a broader systems approach, recognizing that both immediate and more distant events influence our behavior.

Basic principles of behavior change emphasize (a) the importance of either the setting or environment on behavior and (b) the importance of consequences on behavior. Even programs that describe their goal as emphasizing changes in parent attitudes generally judge success by whether the parent's actions change. Consequently, having knowledge of how new behaviors are learned or how existing behaviors are changed needs to be an essential component of training. Individuals may be more or less likely to engage in some behaviors as a result of what their friends are doing, the setting they are in, or the stresses they are experiencing. Setting variables include our everyday surroundings, neighborhood safety, the physical comforts of our home, and play materials for children. In a safe neighborhood, parents will more likely let children play outside than they will in an unsafe neighborhood. If home visitors are knowledgeable about how the environment influences behavior, they will be less likely to try to "fix" people and more likely to help them make constructive changes in their environments (Gambrill, 1997), such as finding housing in a safer neighborhood.

Because of the effects of consequences on our actions, visitors need to be knowledgeable about the different effects of positive and negative consequences. Mothers who are supported and encouraged to engage in more positive parenting behaviors by their spouse or other adults in the house will be more likely to do so than mothers whose child-rearing behaviors do not have status or support in their homes. Children who are encouraged and supported for appropriate social behaviors will be more likely to engage in these behaviors. Home visitors are also sources of encouragement for parents, supporting them and giving them positive feedback as they try out new ways of responding.

Principles of behavior change also include modeling and prompting. These strategies can be use by home visitors to help families try out new skills or practice existing skills in new situations. Parents, in turn, can use modeling and prompting to encourage new skills and actions of their children.

Cognitive skills, such as the ability to set goals and priorities, identify solutions, and make decisions, are often listed among the top priorities of many programs. A visitor may focus on helping parents think through current dilemmas and consider solutions. He or she can help parents see how some of their beliefs might interfere with their ability to take action.

We say things to ourselves such as "I know I can do this. I can be successful." We also say things such as "There is no need to try. I always fail at whatever I try." Parent beliefs and attitudes that are incompatible with good, positive parenting practices are also concerns of those who provide family services. These beliefs can include unreasonable expectations about the abilities of a 3- or 4-year-old child, leading a parent to believe that the child is rebellious or stubborn. Helping parents identify these beliefs is often an important component of home visiting programs.

Theories of Interpersonal Problem Solving

Another significant theoretical area of home visiting is that of interpersonal or social problem solving. All of us must deal with the day-to-day hassles of daily life as well as challenges and opportunities. How we do so is strongly influenced by our social problem-solving skills. *Social problem solving* refers to the cognitive-behavioral-affective processes by individuals or groups to "identify, discover, or invent effective means of coping" with everyday problems in living (D'Zurilla, 1988, p. 86). Helping individuals address problematic situations is fundamental to almost all therapeutic procedures (see, e.g., Egan, 1998; Haley, 1987).

Jahoda (1958) was one of the first researchers to identify the importance of the relationship between problem-solving skills and mental health. In the 1960s and 1970s, several other individuals began to write about the close relationship between problem solving and mental health, including D'Zurilla and Goldfried (1971). They emphasized the importance of teaching individuals a strategy for dealing with real-life social and personal problems (D'Zurilla & Goldfried, 1971; D'Zurilla & Nezu, 1982; Goldfried & Davison, 1976).

Of increasing concern to professionals is the relationship between problem solving and the adjustment of the family. Concern in this area has led some writers to suggest that the absence of conflict resolution skills can lead to the dissolution of the family (Patterson, Weiss, & Hops, 1976). Others have written that failure to use effective problem-solving skills in child rearing can lead to serious emotional and behavioral problems in children (Kelley, Embry, & Baer, 1979). Many researchers have noted the relationship between poor problem-solving skills and depression (Nezu, 1987). Several psychologists have used problem-solving procedures in intervention programs for families (see, e.g., Blechman, 1974; Foster & Robin, 1998; Robin, 1979, 1981), for teachers and parents of young children (Shure & Spivack, 1972, 1978), and for parents of children with disabilities (Intagliata & Doyle, 1984).

In 1978, as part of Project CARE, we developed a model of an early intervention program for children and their families from low-income backgrounds. With this model, we wanted to help parents build on their coping and problem-solving skills to manage current concerns in their lives. We also believed that these strategies could help parents address future needs in their lives (Ramey, et. al., 1985; Wasik, Bryant, & Lyons, 1990). Many professional fields, such as nursing (Miles, 1986), social work (Kadushin, 1976), counseling (Egan, 1998), and psychology (Wasik & Fishbein, 1982), have taught problem-solving skills to those in training. We believe that parents also deserve opportunities to learn these skills.

The problem-solving approach we developed incorporates ecological and family systems theory as well as behavioral and cognitive principles. The objective is to help families learn effective ways of coping with day-to-day concerns, reaching goals, and addressing disappointments and concerns (Wasik, Bryant, Lyons, Sparling, & Ramey, 1997). The model includes seven steps or processes important to social and interpersonal situations. These processes include identifying problematic situations, selecting goals, generating possible solutions, considering consequences, making decisions, implementing decisions, and evaluating outcomes. We elaborate on this model in Chapter 5.

In summary, our brief overview of the four theories that underlie many home visiting programs shows that each deals with the complexity of family interactions. Because of this complexity, training and supervision are essential to prepare helpers to develop working relationships in which they can facilitate constructive change and growth in families. It is equally important for home visitors to recognize the limitation of their own training and skills and know when to ask for help and when to refer families to other professionals. Intensive work with families requires intensive training and supervision.

Mary Richmond's Principles of Relief

After we were thoroughly immersed in designing, administering, and evaluating home visiting programs, we came upon a much earlier set of home visiting guidelines and principles that are now more than 100 years old. These are the six relief principles identified by Richmond in her 1899 book, *Friendly Visiting Among the Poor* (see Table 2.1). We were impressed by the appropriateness of these principles to home visiting a century later, an appropriateness that most likely stems from the universality of human needs; the commonality

TABLE 2.1 Richmond's 1899 Principles of Relief

- Relief should be given individually and privately in the home, and the head of the family should be conferred with on all questions of relief.
- We should seek the most natural and least official sources of relief, bearing in mind the ties of kinship, friendship, and neighborliness, and we should avoid the multiplication of sources.
- Relief should look not only to the alleviation of present suffering but also to promoting the future welfare of the recipient.
- Instead of trying to give a little to many, we should help adequately those that we help at all.
- We should help the poor to understand the right relations of things by stating clearly our reasons for giving or withholding relief and by requiring their hearty cooperation in all efforts for their improvement.
- We must find that form of relief that will best fit a particular need.

SOURCE: Richmond, M.E. (1917). *Social diagnosis*. New York: Russell Sage.

of concerns among helping professionals as they contemplate appropriate, effective, and responsive services; and the similarity of procedures suggested for effectively serving families.

Richmond's principles reveal an impressive set of professional guidelines. Her first principle called attention to the importance of home services, described how services should be delivered in the home, and stated that the "head of the family should be conferred with on all questions of relief" (p. 149). This statement is a forerunner of today's emphasis on recognizing and responding to the roles and values of all immediate household members when helping one or more members of a family.

Richmond's second principle emphasized the importance of finding the least official source of relief (a principle not unlike the current principles underlying the Individuals With Disabilities Education Act [IDEA]), with services provided in an environment that is as unrestrictive as possible (Johnson, McGonigel, & Kaufmann,

1989). Her third principle identified the need to look beyond present suffering to address future needs of families, a principle advocated by others (e.g., Dunst & Trivette, 1987) and exemplified in programs that promote a family's ability to cope effectively with its own problems.

Her fourth principle related to public policy and how resources should be allocated. She called for "helping adequately" those who are helped rather than providing too little for too many. This issue is one that state and federal agencies and national organizations continue to address as they consider proposals for universal home visiting versus more intensive services for those most likely to encounter problems or who are already experiencing hardships (Gomby, Culross, & Behrman, 1999).

Richmond's fifth point, that we should help the poor to understand the right relation of things by stating clearly our reasons for giving or withholding relief and by requiring their hearty cooperation in all efforts for their improvement, addressed the need for clear communication and called for active client participation "in all efforts for their improvement" (Richmond, 1899, p. 160). On the latter point, Richmond predated similar current suggestions for the "maximum feasible participation" guideline of Head Start and the emphasis on parent or client involvement in identifying needs and services. This principle, however, also suggests the authority of the home visitor in making decisions about whether support will be provided.

Finally, Richmond recommended that visitors find the form of relief that would best fit the family's particular need. This guideline is also consistent with today's emphasis on providing individualized services to families by developing individualized family service plans (IFSPs). In summary, Richmond's principles, by embodying the enduring qualities in a helper-client relationship, continue to provide direction for today's visitors.

As noted in Chapter 1, although beliefs consistent with those of Richmond's prevailed from the 1890s to the 1920s, a shift occurred during the 1920s toward services for individuals, not for families, and services provided within clinic or other institutional settings. Beginning in the 1950s, we began to see a return to family and home-based services, a shift that gained considerable momentum in the 1980s. Other principles guiding home visiting have changed over time, and these are considered in the next section.

Shifts in Principles of Care

Principles of care are defined as guidelines for providing high-quality care that are inclusive of current beliefs about the role of the family in children's physical, mental, and social well-being. They have derived primarily from an interest in serving children in the family setting. These principles of care can be adhered to in a single program or across programs, and they can pertain to an educational intervention as well as a health intervention (Wasik, Roberts, & Lam, 1994).

Of the many principles and concepts promoted recently to guide the care of children in our country, three have been widely articulated by writers across the areas of health care (Hutchins & McPherson, 1991; Koop, 1987), mental health (Friedman, 1986; Knitzer, 1982), and education (Johnson et al., 1989; McGonigel, Kaufman, & Johnson, 1991; Weiss, 1989). These concepts are family-centered, community-based, and coordinated systems of care. Hutchins and McPherson (1991) observed that the

> evolution in medical technology for children with special health care needs has been accompanied by an evolution in concepts of care. Broadened diagnostic categories, comprehensive concern for the whole child, and coordinated services that are family-centered and community-based have become part of the national agenda. (p. 141)

The term *family-focused* (or *family-centered*) refers to services that are responsive to the needs of the total family. These services include the following: recognition of the family as the constant in most children's lives; facilitating parent-professional partnerships; sharing unbiased information with parents; recognition of family strengths, diversity, values, and customs; and promoting flexible and responsive services (Hutchins & McPherson, 1991).

Community-based services are generally defined by a sharing of commitments among a group of people for mutual assistance and work toward common goals (Hobbs, Perrin, & Ireys, 1985). Communities are not simply defined by geographic boundaries but by individuals who share common institutions or psychological bonds. Community characteristics as part of community-based family support have been defined as providing social support, promoting informal support ties, and advocacy on the part of the population served (Weiss & Halpern, 1990).

The purpose of coordinating services is to enable a child and his or her family to receive the services to which they are entitled. Although *service coordination* and *service integration* are often used interchangeably, they may represent two different concepts (Roberts, Akers, & Behl, 1996). Service integration is most frequently viewed as a systemwide effort more directly involving cross-agency coordination. Whereas service coordination is generally viewed as occurring at the client level.

Another principle of care is cultural competence, arising from concerns about the responsiveness of services to values and beliefs of diverse families. Beginning as a sensitivity to the needs of families, this concept has evolved to include definable competencies in working with families from diverse backgrounds (Roberts & Evans, 1994; Slaughter-Defoe, 1993; Zayas, Evans, Mejia, & Rodriguez, 1997).

The theories described earlier—ecological theory, family systems theory, cognitive/behavioral theory, interpersonal problem solving—in combination with the principles of care presented here have influenced a shift in the philosophy of human services in general and child services in particular. To consider their effect on practice, we will look at the following three critical questions that must be addressed by any home visiting program and by any agency that funds such programs: Who is the client? How is the client served? What is the role of the helper?

In Table 2.2, we have identified points of discussion and debate under each of these three questions. For the most part, we have seen a shift over time for each question from those philosophical positions listed on the left side of Table 2.2 toward those positions on the right side. Some of these shifts may be more evident in the writings of our times than they are in actual practice, but many of these philosophical positions have also been incorporated into public policy.

Who Is the Client?

In Chapter 1, we described how, at the beginning of the 20th century, visiting nurses, teachers, and social workers all emphasized the importance of focusing on family needs (Whall, 1986). In the 1920s, a shift toward a focus on individuals and their personalities promoted

TABLE 2.2 Philosophical Positions on Family Support

Who is the client?	
Child	Family
Individual	Family system
Encapsulated	Ecological
Handicapped	Universal
How is the client served?	
Restrictive	Broad
Predetermined	Negotiated
Standard	Individualized
Exceptional	Normalized
Deficit	Strength
Treatment	Prevention
What is the role of the helper?	
Expert	Collaborator
Problem solver	Facilitator

a change from a family-and-home focus to individual clinic-based services.

Historically, the question of who the client is had a more simplistic answer. The client was the adult or child in need of help, an individual typically described as having a disability or being at risk for a social, emotional, or physical difficulty. As noted in Chapter 1, a child was typically removed from the family under stressful home conditions or when the child needed treatment. In the 1960s, when the focus shifted to home care for exceptional children, the child was still the primary focus of attention.

Many programs have now returned to an appreciation that the family unit, rather than an individual, may best be considered the client. Beginning in the 1970s, we saw changes in conceptualizing and identifying the client, especially a change from the child to the family and from an individual family member to the family as a system. Changes have also occurred from an encapsulated view of the family to an ecological view and from a focus on people with disabilities to a focus on services for all families in times of stress or when major changes occur, such as the birth of the first child.

The seeds for this shift to a family focus originated in part in the policies of Head Start that called for the family's participation in the services that were offered (Zigler & Freedman, 1987). Practical concerns also influenced this shift. When home-based services were provided for a child with disabilities, the visitor often found parental concerns as critical as child needs. This shift from the child to the family has helped to reaffirm the family's preeminent role and responsibility in child rearing. It is also consistent with strong societal beliefs in the role of the family. The focus on families in contrast to individuals is seen as "a profound shift of perspective for many professionals whose training and practice has equipped them to work primarily with children and whose role with families has been primarily an instructive one" (Johnson et al., 1989, p. 8).

As one begins to visit with families, it becomes clear that complex interactions exist between family members, and some of these relationships may be characterized by dysfunctional patterns. The relationship between mother and child needs attention when the mother fails to bond with a child and does not establish a caring relationship with the child. Complex and disruptive interactions can occur between siblings and a child with disabilities. The marital relationship may be strained. When visiting in the home, the question of who the client is becomes complex. At one time it may be an individual in the family, and at other times it may be the family unit itself. Thus, in addition to focusing on a child with specific needs, one may focus on other family members, dyadic interactions between any two family members, or the entire family as a system (Bailey, 1988).

When considering the needs of multiple clients within the framework of home visiting, one can see the possibility of professional dilemmas. An intervention designed to help one family member could have a negative influence on another member. A program designed to help a woman complete her education and become employed will face barriers if the woman's husband and culture do not support her gainful employment. Potential conflicts between individual goals and family values need to be carefully addressed.

Consistent with the shift in working with the child as a member of the larger family, a parallel shift toward viewing the family as part of a larger network of extended family, neighborhood, and community has occurred. This view is supported not only from a systems theory position but also by empirical data showing the effects that the immediate social support in a person's life has on his or her mental and physical health. Weissbourd (1983) captured the importance of an ecological approach and noted,

> We are no longer "child savers." We realize that concern for the child's well-being means focusing not just on the child and his development, but also on the child in the context of his family, the community in which he lives, and the social institutions and government policies which affect family life. (p. 8)

This shift to considering the family's larger environment has a direct implication for home visitors and the programs for which they work. Both the program administrators and the home visitors have responsibility for interacting with other community agencies. At times, the causes of family issues reside within the community, and an advocacy role may need to be assumed. In some professions, such as social work and public health nursing, client advocacy and working with community agencies have had a long history.

As seen in Table 2.2, another consideration in answering the question, "Who is the client?" is with offering universal versus targeted services. This consideration addresses whether the concept of "client" is limited to a child or adult who is disabled or has specific needs in contrast to providing services to all families at specific times. Services to clients can be classified under the following three headings: (a) programs serving families with existing difficulties or established risk, (b) programs serving families and children with specific characteristics that place them at risk for later problems, and (c) programs serving all families during times that are judged to be universally stressful. Programs addressing these three objectives date back to the beginnings of formal home visiting and can be seen in current national and international efforts, as noted in Chapter 1. There is, however, increasing interest in programs designed to serve all families during common times of stress, with prenatal care and the birth of a first child receiving the most attention in home visiting services. One of the strongest advocates for universal home visiting was Kempe (1976), who addressed the right of all children to protection and health care.

Answers to the question, "Who is the client?" in more general terms were seen in responses to the family-focused home visiting survey of programs serving families (Roberts & Wasik, 1989). A detailed survey was mailed to directors of home visiting programs in the United States, and more than 1,900 completed surveys were included in the analysis. Program directors who completed the survey were asked to identify the primary and secondary child and parent characteristics of the population they served. The range of primary populations included children who had been maltreated (12%), children at risk for school failure (13%), children with physical (12%) or developmental (12%) disabilities, and other children without specific disabilities (25%).

Survey data also identified the primary characteristics of the parents involved in home visiting programs. The largest category was low-income families (who represented 30% of the program participants), followed by general population parents (20%), and then by maltreating parents (abusing or neglecting children) and parents of children with physical disabilities (10% each). Fewer programs focused primarily on drug or alcohol abusing parents (5%), single parents (4%), teenage parents (3%), and parents of low birthweight infants (3%). From these data, poor families appear to be of primary concern, as reflected by the number of programs that target this population.

The survey data also showed increased interest in providing services to younger children. The age of the child served was related to the primary parent characteristics. Programs that identified low-income as the primary characteristic of their families more frequently served children aged 3 to 5 years rather than infants or toddlers. Of programs serving other populations, 85% reported services for children as infants and toddlers. Programs for children at biological risk generally began serving families as soon as the children were diagnosed with a disability or disease, usually shortly after birth. Since this survey, a proliferation of programs such as Healthy Families America and Parents as Teachers has occurred, increasing the number of families with infants and toddlers being served.

How Is the Client Served?

Theories and beliefs about best practices affect how programs serve clients. Traditionally, home visiting services have consisted of treatment or intervention for specific problems and have often been restricted to the predefined needs of children or adults. As noted in Table 2.2, a shift from a restrictive approach to a more broad-based approach has occurred. Another shift has been from a predetermined to a more negotiated service, which allows the family involvement in specifying needs, priorities, and preferences for service procedures, and individualized services are now more emphasized than standardized services. These three shifts all have in common a recognition of the preeminent role each family should have in the determination of the services they receive.

Although there is a trend toward offering more comprehensive services for families, the family's right to negotiate services as well as the need to individualize services implies that not all families will want or need a broad-based approach. In some situations, especially in private home visiting services, a specific contract will be written between the visitor and the family specifying the services that will be provided. Also, some families may want help only with a specific concern, such as the care of a chronically ill child. Broader or more intensive services are not better services if they do not meet the family's needs.

Interest has also increased in interventions for problems that could be prevented rather than intervening in these situations after problems have developed. This interest is reflected in the development of services beginning when the child is in infancy rather than in the preschool or early school-age years, as well as the interest in providing support to all families during the prenatal and early infancy period. Interest in prevention is also reflected in the focus on parents who are at risk for abuse and neglect, and youth at risk for delinquency. Other programs focus on young, single, and poor parents who may have difficulty in child rearing and whose children may be at risk for a range of health, social, and education difficulties.

Another direction in services is building on family strengths rather than taking a deficit model based on what families are missing. To take a strengths model, one helps families look for patterns of success and accomplishment in previous situations, using their knowledge, skills, and attitudes to help define actions that will be successful in the present. One also helps families identify their social, family, and individual resources that can be used in new ways to address family or individual dilemmas and everyday problems. Building on strengths helps assure sensitivity to issues of diversity and culture, recognizing the uniqueness of each family and using those unique features to facilitate effective coping and problem solving. For us, taking a strengths approach does not mean closing one's eyes to limitations in an individual or family. Rather, it means positively accepting and affirming those skills and abilities the individual or family has and using these as a foundation for new skill development as needed.

Programs for individuals with disabilities are also placing emphasis on the most natural way of helping families, from promoting support networks to helping families learn how to include family members with disabilities in the family's ongoing routines and activities. This shift in direction reflects the principles underlying IDEA, namely, that services should be "provided in as normal a fashion and environment as is possible" and such services should "promote the integration of the child and family within the community" (Johnson et al., 1989, p. 9). These principles promote natural social supports and are consistent with the views described earlier on the need to consider the family as part of a larger community of extended family, friends, and community.

In summary, current views of how the client is served reflect a change from narrowly focused interventions for specific disabilities to a broader conceptualization of family services with a focus on individualized services, prevention, and family strengths.

What Is the Role of the Helper?

The role of the helper is determined by the goals of the helping process. As part of our philosophy of home visiting, we believe that the helper's role is to assist clients in addressing situations in their daily lives more effectively. A second goal is to help clients generalize to future situations in their lives what they gain from the helping process. These goals can be accomplished in various ways. For most of this century, the home visitor has been the "expert," whether he or she was a professional or paraprofessional. With presumably more knowledge or experience than the client, he or she came prepared to solve problems and make decisions. Families are now no longer seen as passive recipients but, rather, as active participants in the helping process, encouraged to define their own needs, decide on priorities, and state preferences for services. Thus, the visitor must be a collaborator, a facilitator, and a negotiator. Although these roles have not been as prominent in the past, they are now necessary to help assure successful family-focused interventions as well as respect for the family.

Describing the role of the helper as a collaborator implies that the client must also be a collaborator. Egan (1998), in elaborating on the nature of the helping relationship, wrote, "Helping is not something that helpers do to clients; rather, it is a process that helpers and clients work through together" (p. 41). These changes in the role of the visitor do not imply the need for less competence on the part of the visitor. Indeed, to be a collaborator, the visitor must be an expert in helping skills as well as being competent in the program's intervention procedures. The need for competence and knowledge on the part of the home visitor is also essential given the complexity of families and the societal changes reflected in the lives of families. The shift from the "expert problem solver" means that the visitor engages the family in active problem solving, encouraging them to identify their concerns and goals, and ways they could help resolve their own difficulties. The shift in focus is not on less competence on the part of the visitor but on incorporating families as active participants. The visitor needs to bring his or her own knowledge and expertise to the helping process and use these as appropriate to facilitate family progress.

Principles for Providing Home-Based Family Services

From our own experience with many home visitors in a wide range of programs, we articulate seven principles that are useful in focusing the work of the home visitor. These principles address the need for (a) individualized services, (b) responding to the family as a system, (c) establishing a collaborative relationship between the helper and the family, (d) remaining flexible and responsive to family needs, (e) promoting coping and problem-solving skills, (f) facilitating generalization of new skills and knowledge to future situations, and (g) ongoing assessment to determine progress and modify services as necessary.

1. *Home-based intervention should be individualized, whether focused on an individual family member or a particular family.* This individualization needs to take into account relevant social, psychological, cultural, educational, economic, and physical or health characteristics of the individual or family. The visitor must begin with the family where the family is. The family may or may not be emotionally ready to address concerns; their resources may be limited or extensive. Each person and each family is unique. Beginning where the family is will reduce frustration for both the helper and the client and will promote progress. Wide variations occur among families in their abilities to cope with their own life circumstances. Some families may benefit from extra assistance at particularly stressful times, but their general coping skills may be very strong. Other families will require help beyond the skills of the home visitor or of the program resources. A strength of home visiting lies in its capacity to facilitate individualized interventions to meet each family's needs.

2. *The family is a social system where changes in one individual in the family can influence other family members and the overall functioning of the family.* Knowledge about family dynamics and relationships is fundamental for assisting individuals or families in their own homes. As a part of home visiting, a visitor needs to remain attentive to the interactions in a family regardless of whether he or she is providing help to an individual or to the family as a whole.

3. *A helping relationship is best conceptualized as a collaboration between the home visitor and the family members.* This collaborative concept is a relatively recent one in the practice of home visiting. Although earlier writers such as Richmond (1899) talked about the importance of discussing needs with families, many programs have been based on a philosophy that others in society knew what was best for the families. This approach can be seen across the history of home visiting regardless of the profession involved. A collaborative relationship emphasizes the importance of families working cooperatively and actively with home visitors. Although each family has a responsibility to actively participate, the home visitor has the responsibility for making a collaborative relationship possible.

4. *A home visitor must be flexible and responsive to the immediate needs of families as well as to their long-term goals.* A sick child needs

medical attention. An abused woman needs support and possibly shelter. Respite care or homemaker services may be more important at a particular time than focusing on long-term goals. The home visitor must be able to assess such needs and know when to provide direct services, call for assistance, and help a family secure needed services through their own efforts. The program's responsibility is to help home visitors assess such situations and make appropriate decisions.

5. *Home visitors need to be able to encourage effective coping and problem-solving skills.* Home visiting is offered because individuals or families are currently struggling with some event or situation in their lives or because there is a risk of poor social, educational, or health outcomes. In either situation, there is strong evidence for the important role of effective problem-solving skills. Home visitors can prompt effective problem management and coping by helping families identify and discuss options for addressing their needs, desires, and challenges; build on their strengths; learn new skills; and take action as necessary.

6. *The home visitor should remain attentive to future needs of families and help them consider ways that new skills or attitudes might be generalized to later situations.* Helping families plan for generalization to new situations needs to be a part of the home visitor's work. Providing direct services for immediate needs may help alleviate present stresses, but it does not necessarily help clients become better able to deal with future stresses in their lives. Visitors need to remain continually aware that their objective is to help families become more independent over time.

7. *The home visitor needs to continually evaluate family strengths, limitations, and progress and use that knowledge to modify interventions as necessary.* Attentiveness to the family's current status and progress is essential for effective home visiting. We recommend that visitors assess their work with families on a continuous basis to assure that the family is engaged and participating in the helping process. When progress is not occurring, a number of variables need to be considered that may be hindering progress, ranging from personal characteristics to social support. As progress does

occur, visitors can help families celebrate and learn from their successes.

Summary

In this chapter, we have discussed philosophical shifts over time, noting that some shifts bring us back to positions held at the beginning of the century, especially the renewed focus on the entire family. Such shifts should help us keep in perspective our current views and remind us of the need to learn from and build on the work of others in the field. The recommended shifts in roles should not conflict with good practice. Overall, however, the current philosophical views appear to be grounded in an appreciation of the importance of each individual, a recognition of individual and family beliefs and values, and a commitment to promoting family participation in all aspects of the helping process.

3

Illustrative Home Visiting Programs for Children, Youth, and Their Families

As we enter the new millennium, tens of thousands of home visitors work throughout the United States. Many of their services are provided within the structure of programs that focus on specific child or family characteristics. A number of issues are common across many programs, such as the effects of poverty on families, but programs may differ in significant ways, such as the main clientele they serve, staffing patterns, and intervention procedures.

In this chapter, our purpose is to illustrate the diversity in the field by presenting information on several home visiting programs. We have included programs with different funding sources, including state, federal, and private foundations. We have included services offered across family income levels and across a variety of family needs as well as programs that employ professionals and those that employ paraprofessionals. We also selected programs that illustrate restrictive versus universal inclusion criteria. These programs are among the more empirically documented home visiting interventions, and each has produced written materials on its procedures.

This chapter is organized into three sections. In the first section, we describe the Head Start Home-Based and Early Head Start programs to illustrate federally supported family-focused home visiting programs. Representing programs that are national in scope and supported by national nonprofit groups are the Parents as Teachers Program and the Healthy Families America program as well as the Hawaii Healthy Start program, Homebuilders, and the Home Improvement Program for Preschool Children. The third section includes several exemplary research programs, including Project SafeCare, the Nurse Home Visitation Program, the Infant Health and Development Program, and the Multisystemic Therapy for delinquent youth.

Federal Programs

To illustrate home visiting programs funded at the federal level, we selected the home-based option of Head Start and the newly funded Early Head Start (EHS). The federal government offered the first widespread funding for a home visiting program by providing a home-based option for Project Head Start. This option became available following the positive evaluation of a demonstration program indicating that a home-based program, referred to as Home Start, had the same benefits as the center-based Head Start program (Love et al., 1976). Head Start home-based programs are seen as facilitating continuity between center-based programs and the actual conditions of family life (Zigler & Freedman, 1987). Also, when center-based programs cannot be established in communities, home-based programs provide an alternative way to reach families. Communities now determine which type of program best fits their needs, and they may select a center-based program, home-based program, or a combination of programs (Boyd & Herwig, 1980; Wolfe & Herwig, 1986).

The philosophy of the Head Start home visiting program is based on parent participation and focuses on establishing a positive interpersonal relationship between the home visitor and family so that there can be an effective exchange of information. The program philosophy also emphasizes that parents have the primary responsibility for their children's development. The Head Start staff assumes a secondary role in the life of the child; their role is to facilitate the parent's role as the teacher of the child and promote confidence in parenting.

Head Start has described a number of advantages for providing services to a family in its own home, the first being that it facilitates learning in the natural environment. The visitor can directly observe the parent-child interaction, making it possible for the visitor to help the parents become better managers of their child's behavior. Such information may be particularly important when working with parents of children with disabilities. Home-based programs also have the advantage of intervening early in the development of problematic situations, potentially preventing more serious problems. Furthermore, they provide unique opportunities for involving the parents and other family members in the education of the child, and they can facilitate interactions between the parent and center-based programs.

Head Start home visitors are expected to perform a variety of activities in addition to working with parents in the home. These activities include assisting in recruitment, encouraging attendance at parent meetings, and, if necessary, providing transportation to medical and dental appointments. Several publications provide detailed information on conducting these visits and on materials and activities for young children and their families (see, e.g., Boyd & Herwig, 1980; Wolfe & Herwig, 1986).

EHS is a federally funded, community-based program for pregnant women and low-income families with infants and toddlers. It was designed by the Administration on Children, Youth and Families (ACYF) in response to the 1994 Head Start reauthorization that set aside 3% of 1995 funds for services to families with infants and toddlers. These funds increased to 8% in the 2000 budget. In 1999, approximately 40,000 children younger than the age of 3 and their families were served in about 500 EHS programs. EHS is designed as a comprehensive, two-generation program that includes intensive services during a mother's pregnancy and the child's first 3 years of life to enhance the child's development and support the family. Desired outcomes have been grouped into the following four domains: (a) child development (including health, resiliency, social competence, and cognitive and language development), (b) family development (including parenting and relationships with children, the home environment and family functioning, family health, parent involvement, and economic self-sufficiency), (c) staff development (including professional development and relationships with parents), and (d) community development (including enhanced child care quality, community collaboration, and integration of services to support families with young children).

EHS programs are to be individualized according to the strengths and needs of each child and family. Services include home visits (especially for families with newborns and young children) parent education (including parent-child activities), comprehensive health and nutrition services (including services to women before, during, and after pregnancy), and ongoing support for parents through case management and peer support groups. Programs are also required to provide quality child care if the family needs it, either by operating their own infant classrooms or through collaboration with local child care providers.

Home visitor training is handled locally, and the frequency and content of home visits vary considerably among EHS programs: Some use a published curriculum, and others use materials that are linked to the activities being conducted in the EHS child care center. A comprehensive evaluation of EHS is being conducted in conjunction with a number of local research and evaluation studies. It is designed to advance the field in determining program effects on children and families as well as examining the role of the program and contextual variables. The final impact report will be available in the year 2002.

National Programs

Several home visiting programs that were originally developed as local efforts to serve families have expanded into national and even international programs. These programs each have a national office that provides training and technical assistance to communities or agencies interested in implementing the program. In this section, we provide a brief description of family preservation services and the Home Instruction Program for Preschool Youngsters. A more detailed description follows of the Parents as Teachers program and the Healthy Families America program, as well as the Hawaii Healthy Start program on which Healthy Families America is modeled.

Family Preservation Services

Family preservation services are designed to prevent the out-of-home placement of children or adolescents. Out-of-home placement typically means foster care, group homes, residential treatment centers, psychiatric hospitals, or correctional institutions (Wells, 1995). Various models of family preservation services share the assumption that the family should be the focus of services, and needs should be addressed in the context of the family. These programs also assume that services provided in the home increase the helper's understanding of the family, facilitating his or her ability to help the family address its needs. Such programs emphasize an integrated approach to the concrete and social-psychological issues families experience. Finally, family preservation models assume that services need to be time limited to convey to families a belief in their own capabilities (Wells, 1995).

Homebuilders is among the better known family preservation programs. It is a crisis intervention model in which counselors (home visitors) are on call 24 hours a day, 7 days a week. Families are urged to call their counselors as needed. Crisis calls are seen as opportunities to respond to emergencies, teach, and gather new information on families. Counselors average between 8 to 10 hours per week of face-to-face interactions with families. A typical visiting pattern with a family might involve providing direct help to the family 3 hours each day for the first 2 days, a phone call the 3rd day, 2 hours in the home the 4th day, and then 3 hours every other day for the next week. The time is flexible to assure that counselors have adequate time to meet with families and respond to their unique needs. The Homebuilders' counselors model and shape new behaviors, watch families practice skills, and give families feedback on and support for their efforts. The Homebuilders model is described in more depth in the book *Keeping Families Together: The Homebuilders Model* (Kinney et al., 1991; see also Kinney & Dittmar, 1995).

Home Instruction Program for Preschool Youngsters

The Home Instruction Program for Preschool Youngsters (HIPPY) is a 2-year, home-based early education program designed to prepare 3- to 5-year-olds for kindergarten and the first grade. It was originally developed in Israel in 1969 to respond to the low educational achievement of minority children. Implemented in the United States in 1984, the program now has more than 120 sites in this country. HIPPY focuses on enhancing the home literacy environment, parent-child verbal interactions, and the ability of parents to help their children learn (Lombard, 1981). Visitors are paraprofessionals who live in the same neighborhood as the families they visit. Full-time visitors typically serve 20 to 25 families. Visits are made bimonthly, and group parent meetings are held on alternate weeks. HIPPY is a relatively structured program with 30 weeks of planned activities used for each year in the program. Home visits last approximately 30 to 60 minutes. During these visits, role-playing is used to help parents learn how to use HIPPY books and educational activities with their children.

Baker, Piotrkowski, and Brooks-Gunn (1999) have summarized findings from three studies of HIPPY. Among the 69 families in the first cohort of a two-cohort study using random assignment to HIPPY or a control group, the HIPPY children scored higher on several measures of school success and had a more successful beginning in kindergarten than did children in the control group. These findings were not replicated among the 113 families in the second cohort. In qualitative studies of program participation, results showed that few families actually participated at the intended level. Parents received fewer home visits and attended fewer group meetings than were offered, and they most likely did not spend the recommended 15 minutes per day in learning activities with their children. Being able to document patterns of parent involvement and link those patterns to child outcomes is important in any analysis of program effectiveness.

Since these research studies were completed, the HIPPY program has modified its materials and has extended the program from 2 to 3 years. Given the ever-changing needs of programs and client populations, such modifications of procedures and materials are not uncommon in home visiting programs. Although this poses a challenge for researchers, it is a sign of an active and forward-looking program.

Parents as Teachers Program

♦ *Background*

The Parents as Teachers Program (PAT) began in Missouri in 1972 when the Missouri State Board of Education adopted early childhood education as a priority. It was originally designed for all first-time parents of children from birth to age 3. The philosophy of the program was influenced by research in the 1950s and 1960s that called attention to the importance of the first years of life for a child's cognitive, language, and emotional development. The early education programs of the 1960s that had emphasized the importance of working with the family to improve the child's development also influenced PAT. The program was guided by the philosophy that a partnership between parents and the school during the early years could enhance the likelihood of school success for young children (Winter & McDonald, 1997).

The PAT program has grown considerably from its early days as a statewide effort in Missouri. It is now a national program and is currently used in 49 states and 6 countries. In all, 2,400 programs provide services to 500,000 families. In response to the growth of the PAT program, the Parents as Teachers National Center (PATNC), a nonprofit organization, was established in 1987 to foster continued program development, evaluation, and professional training (The Future of Children, Appendix B, 1999).

The Harvard University Preschool Project study of early development provided the original basis for the PAT curriculum (White, 1975). Language, curiosity, social skills, and cognitive skills were emphasized as the foundations of educational ability. The PAT program stressed the importance of the prenatal period for parents and conducted parent support groups and an individualized educational program for each family.

♦ *Program*

Home visitors, called *parent educators*, typically have backgrounds in child development, early childhood education, or related degrees and experience in the fields of education, social work, or health. Parent educators are required to have 1 week of preservice training by instructors who have been certified by PATNC. Annual updating of credentials is required of all parent educators through in-service training to help assure quality in program delivery. Emphasis is placed on selecting home visitors who are themselves parents and who can maintain a close relationship over many months with a wide variety of families. Home visitors are responsible for planning and making home visits, participating in recruitment and screening activities, and assisting in parent group meetings.

Home visitors use a set of comprehensive materials that describe objectives and procedures for visits made during the prenatal period and throughout the first 3 years of a child's life. Recent program modifications have resulted in the Born to Learn Curriculum™, incorporating new research about brain development. The curriculum includes home visiting plans, resource materials for parents and educators, and handouts for parents. Of particular note is a video series viewed by parents at home and coordinated with home visiting plans.

Home visitors provide information on child development and guidance before the baby is born to help expectant parents prepare for parenthood. They also provide information about what to look for and expect as the child develops, and they offer guidance in fostering the child's intellectual, language, social, and motor skills development. If serious problems are discovered, home visitors help parents seek assistance from other agencies or professionals. Monthly group meetings with other new parents are also provided for parents to share experiences and interests.

Home visits are generally 1 hour in length and are scheduled monthly, biweekly, or weekly, depending on family needs and local program budgetary restrictions. High-needs families receive more frequent home visits. PAT programs can be offered as stand-alone programs by school districts, hospitals, churches, and social service agencies or as part of a more comprehensive service delivery system, such as Head Start, Even Start, or family resource centers. Funding is generated from a combination of federal, state, and local dollars as well as private monies.

♦ *Empirical Support*

Several studies have been conducted on PAT, including both quasi-experimental and randomized experimental designs. These studies have demonstrated positive gains for children in several domains, and limited gains or no notable gains have been found in other areas. To evaluate the original PAT demonstration project in 1981-1982, a random sample of 380 families was identified, and a comparison group was selected to match as nearly as possible the characteristics of the families in the intervention program (Pfannenstiel & Seltzer, 1985). This study resulted in a number of important findings. First, children in the PAT program scored significantly higher than the comparison children on intelligence, achievement, auditory comprehension, verbal ability, and language ability as measured by the Kaufman Assessment Battery for Children. PAT children were also rated higher on positive social development. Additional findings showed that parent participation was positively correlated with a child's intelligence, achievement, and language ability. Parents who participated more frequently in home visits were more likely to have children who were rated higher on prosocial behaviors.

Two research studies designed to evaluate PAT's effectiveness were recently conducted with Latino families in Northern California and with teen parents (Wagner & Clayton, 1999). Both studies used random assignment of families to either the PAT group or other comparison or control groups. Most of the parent educators were Latinos who spoke both English and Spanish. PAT program participants received an average of 20 home visits over 3 years. Voluntary group meetings in English and Spanish were offered periodically by parent educators, during which time parents discussed issues with and received social support from the parent educator and other parents. Fewer than 15% of participant group families attended any group meeting.

The results of these two evaluations showed small, positive, but inconsistent effects on parent knowledge, attitudes, and behavior and no gains on child development or health when experimental and control groups were compared. Subgroup analyses in the Northern California program indicated that children in primarily Spanish-speaking Latino families benefited more than either non-Latino or English-speaking Latino families, with significant gains in cognitive, communication, social, and self-help skills. The children whose families received PAT services as well as the case management services to help mothers improve their life course benefited most. Subgroup analyses showed that children whose families received intensive services benefited more than children whose families received less intensive services. Results suggest that 10 home visits produced about a 1-month developmental advantage for participating children (Wagner Clayton, 1999).

The PAT curriculum and programming have changed in several ways during the past decade. Although originally designed to serve children at birth or prenatally to age 3, a new curriculum has extended the program to age 5. Also, in 1995, a specialized training and curriculum guide for teen parents was established. PAT continues to improve and fine-tune the model as it expands throughout the United States.

Healthy Families America

♦ *Background*

Healthy Families America (HFA) was initiated by the National Committee to Prevent Child Abuse in partnership with the Ronald McDonald Children's Charities and the Hawaii Family Stress Center. HFA is based on a belief in the importance of home visiting services for new parents as a child abuse prevention strategy. The program has been influenced by two decades of research and experiences of the Hawaii Healthy Start program, a home-based intervention program designed to prevent child abuse and neglect and to increase parent competence in high-risk families (Sia & Breakey, 1985).

The Healthy Start Project is based on several assumptions. The first assumption is that the most effective way to prevent child abuse or neglect is to intervene with parents at the birth of a new infant. The second is that children at risk for child abuse and neglect are also at risk for emotional and mental health problems and developmental delays. The failure of bonding between parent and child is seen as the most predictive risk factor for abuse and neglect. This belief led to facilitating positive parent-child interactions as part of the intervention. The third assumption is that services should be provided from birth to age 5 to successfully prevent child abuse and neglect throughout early childhood.

Healthy Start targets families at risk for child abuse or neglect by screening hospital records of mothers of newborns to assess demographic risk factors, such as being single or from a low-income background. If any of 16 different factors are present, a personal interview is conducted with the mother (and, often, the father) in the hospital. Information from the interview is used to complete the Family Stress Checklist. If the score is above an at-risk criterion, the mother is invited to be a part of the program. Home visitors, referred to as family support workers, are selected for their nurturing qualities and successful experiences in parenting. These home visitors offer support, advice, and information about child development and parenting.

A pilot study of the Hawaii program in the mid-1980s suggested decreased rates of abuse and neglect for participants. Families also scored lower on a stress inventory. In 1994, the Hawaii State Department of Health, in collaboration with the Hawaii Medical Association and Johns Hopkins University, initiated an experimental evaluation using randomized treatment groups: the Healthy Start Program group, the main control group, and a testing control group. The model called for 3 to 5 years of home visiting, but results summarized after the first 2 years of data collection have shown some positive effects (Duggan et al., 1999). The program was effective in linking families with pediatric medical care, improving maternal parenting efficacy, decreasing maternal parenting stress, promoting nonviolent discipline, and decreasing injury due to partner violence in the home. Positive results were not seen at the end of 2 years for other program outcomes, including well-child health care, maternal life skills, social support, child development, child's home learning environment, parent-child interaction, or child maltreatment. The outcomes seemed to differ depending on which of three agencies provided the program. These program-specific differences are being examined in more depth to provide information on those program or home visitor characteristics that might enhance program outcomes.

Based on the results of the research on the Hawaii Healthy Start program in the 1980s, the National Committee to Prevent Child Abuse developed a program using many of the procedures of the Hawaii program while refining elements of the program based on other research and experiences. The critical elements of HFA are intended to represent the field's most current knowledge about how to implement successful home visiting services. HFA believes that, to be successful in reducing child abuse and neglect, programs must be intensive, comprehensive, long-term, flexible, and culturally appropriate. HFA also emphasizes collaboration with service delivery systems already existing in a community.

In promoting this program, HFA has identified a set of critical elements central to all HFA programs. These elements can be grouped under the following three headings: (a) initiation of services, (b) content, and (c) selection and training of service providers. A standardized assessment tool is used to identify families who are most at risk. The assessment tool should measure variables associated with increased risk for child maltreatment or other poor developmental outcomes for children. Services should be initiated prenatally or at the birth of the child and should also be offered voluntarily with positive, persistent outreach efforts made to build trust.

Critical elements for service content include offering services intensively (at least once a week), with specified criteria for increasing or decreasing intensity of services. Services are to be culturally appropriate and reflect the diversity of the population served. Services include a focus on parent support, parent-child interactions, and child development. Programs should assure that all families are linked to a medical provider to assure timely health care. Depending on family needs, links to additional services such as social services or child care may be necessary. Finally, caseloads are limited to assure that home visitors have sufficient time with each family to meet the family's needs and plan for future activities.

Critical elements in the selection and training of service providers include selecting providers based on their personal characteristics, skills, and motivation to work with culturally diverse populations. Furthermore, service providers should have a framework for guiding their decision making within the objectives of the program. They should receive intensive training as well as ongoing supervision.

In 1999, Daro and Harding reported that there were 17 HFA program evaluations across the country with either preliminary or final results. They also reported that 18 additional evaluations were being implemented or were in progress. All 35 studies are part of the HFA research network. Of these studies, 8 are randomized designs, 11 are comparison designs, and the remainder are pretest-posttest designs. In their summary of the 17 studies with reported results, Daro and Harding (1999) noted several positive outcomes. First, 13 of the evaluations with data on child abuse and neglect rates have reported lower rates for maltreatment than generally occurs for children in comparable circumstances. However, in three randomized trials, no significant difference was found between the treatment and control groups on reports of abuse and neglect (Daro & Harding, 1999; Duggan et al., 1999).

Because HFA programs are designed to address child abuse and neglect, an expected outcome is lower rates of abuse and neglect in treated families than in control families. However, using such reports as an outcome measure may not be a valid way to evaluate success. Abuse and neglect is a low frequency event, even in at-risk populations. Thus, the limited sample size in many evaluations makes it unlikely that a significant difference between treatment and control groups will be observed. Second, abused or neglected infants are less likely to be identified and reported than older children, and HFA primarily serves infants and toddlers. Third, families receiving services tend to be reported less often than those who are not receiving services, but there is a higher likelihood that child maltreatment will be observed if there are visitors in the home. Data from many HFA evaluations have shown that the most frequent source of reports of abuse and neglect is the family's home visitor. This fact suggests that it is possible that these families are able to receive assistance earlier than those not in home visiting programs, thus possibly serving to prevent later abuse or neglect or more serious actions. Results from many of the HFA evaluations currently in progress will become known in the near future. These studies will shed new light on the effectiveness of HFA across a range of families and communities.

Research-Focused Programs

Some home visiting programs originated as research programs. In this section, we will describe the following four programs: (a) Project SafeCare, (b) the Infant Health and Development Program, (c) the Nurse Home Visitation Project, and (d) Multisystemic Treatment of Juvenile Offenders and Their Families. These programs have focused on maternal and child health, low birthweight infants, juvenile offenders, or abused and neglected children in the context of research studies.

Project SafeCare

Lutzker and colleagues (Lutzker, Bigelow, Doctor, Gershater, & Greene, 1998; Lutzker, Frame, & Rice, 1982, 1984; Lutzker & Rice, 1984, 1987) have developed an individualized approach to treatment of child abuse and neglect. Rather than implementing a more generalized program for all parents, they have implemented a highly individualized program that defines specific parent problems and considers solutions within a broad ecobehavioral framework. Their work began in the early 1970s in an intervention program called Project 12 Ways, so named because the program included 12 ways of helping families. Initiated in Carbondale, Illinois, this program was later replicated and expanded in an ongoing program called Project SafeCare in Los Angeles, California.

In reviewing the different theories of child abuse and neglect, such as those focused on interpersonal variables (i.e., lack of impulse control) or sociocultural factors (i.e., poverty), Lutzker has noted that they do not explain why the majority of families with these characteristics do not abuse their children or why families with other characteristics, such as middle class and employed, do abuse children. Theories that may offer more promise for guiding prevention and treatment approaches include developmental-ecological and transactional theories (Belsky, 1993; Sameroff, 1994). The developmental-ecological model emphasizes the sociological context in which child maltreatment occurs. In this model, risk factors can occur at the individual, family, environmental, and cultural level. Events and people within the four levels can change and interact over time, thus mediating the possibility of abuse or neglect (Ammerman, 1990).

Accepting the multifaceted nature of abuse and neglect, Lutzker et al. (1984) designed an ecobehavioral approach to address these societal concerns. Assessment and treatment are conducted in the setting in which they occur, such as private homes, schools, foster care, preschools, or other settings in the community. Treatment strategies include direct observation, behavioral assessment, behavior analysis and therapy procedures, and humanistic counseling proceures. Generalization of new skills is also addressed directly (Lutzker et al., 1998).

Project 12 Ways focused on a wide range of interventions, including parent-child interaction training, stress reduction, money management, home safety, home cleanliness, infant health care, nutrition, marital counseling, and basic skills training of the children. Results from numerous studies demonstrated the effectiveness of these procedures, with families participating in Project 12 Ways showing less abuse of their children after intervention than families who were matched on demographic characteristics and received other community services for child abuse and neglect (Lutzker et al., 1984; Lutzker & Rice, 1984, 1987).

Project SafeCare has refined the procedures of Project 12 Ways to focus on 3, rather than 12, areas of intervention. These areas include home safety, infant and child health care, and bonding and stimulation (i.e., parent-child training). In a 15-week intervention, each of these three components is addressed during a period of 5 weeks (Lutzker et al., 1998). Home visits take place once per week and last for approximately 2 hours.

Home safety focuses on hazards in the home as well as home cleanliness. Parents are taught to recognize safety hazards and to correct them by removing them or making them inaccessible to children. Assessments are made using the Home Accident Prevention Inventory—Revised (Tertinger, Greene, & Lutzker, 1984). Cleanliness is measured using the Checklist of Living Environments to assess neglect (Watson-Perczel, Lutzker, Green, & McGimpsey, 1988). The health care component trains parents to prevent illnesses, properly use reference materials, and follow the steps of a task analysis in identifying, treating, and reporting children's illnesses. This task analysis includes recognizing when a child is ill, seeking emergency treatment, calling a physician, and self-treating an illness (Lutzker et al., 1998). The third intervention component, bonding and stimulation, includes direct instruction, modeling by the home visitor, practice with feedback, and homework assignments as ways of helping parents interact more positively with their child.

The results of Project SafeCare and those of Project 12 Ways together have provided strong support for reducing parent behaviors associated with neglect and abuse. The careful examination of procedures provided in the research on these projects and their positive outcomes give empirical support for continuing to provide help through home visiting for families who abuse or neglect their children.

The Infant Health and Development Program

The Infant Health and Development Program (IHDP) was designed to study the effects of early intervention with low birthweight infants and their families. It was a randomized clinical trial that took place in eight U.S. cities between 1985 and 1989, funded by the Robert Wood Johnson Foundation (Gross et al., 1997). IHDP was based on theory and research related to the cognitive, medical, and social development of low birthweight infants (Ramey, Bryant, Sparling, & Wasik, 1984, 1985). The content of IHDP and the way in which it was delivered to parents and children were based on Project CARE (Ramey et al., 1985) and the Abecedarian Project

(Ramey & Campbell, 1984), which were research projects designed for low-income families that were initiated when children were in infancy. It was assumed that the transactions of greatest educational importance were the young child's social interactions with adult caregivers. For this reason, the focus of the IHDP intervention was on parent-child interactions in the home and teacher-child interactions in a center-based program.

IHDP families had infants born in 1985 whose birthweight was 2,500 grams or less. The ethnic composition differed from site to site, although overall, about 52% of the participants were Black, 11% were Hispanic, and the remainder were White or of other ethnic backgrounds. About 60% of the families were living in poverty at the time of the child's birth, and the average education of the mothers was a high school degree. Infants were randomly assigned to either an intervention ($n = 377$) or follow-up group ($n = 608$). Groups were balanced by birthweight, gender, maternal age, maternal education, and maternal race (Black, Hispanic, White, or other) at each site. Both groups received pediatric follow-up and social support services, but only the intervention group received the comprehensive early education program (IHDP, 1990; Ramey et al., 1992).

The program components consisted of home visits, attendance at a child development center, and parent group meetings. The content of the program included parent support and learning activities and play materials for children. Visitors also encouraged decision making and problem management through discussions, modeling, and support. Home visitors met with families weekly from the time the child was discharged from the hospital until the age of 1 year, when the child could begin attending the IHDP child development center. Home visits were then provided twice a month throughout the remainder of the program.

All home visitors had at least a bachelor's degree or an equivalent primarily from the fields of education, social work, and nursing. Basic clinical skills were part of the in-service training of home visitors provided through workshops, role-playing, supervision, and written materials. All home visitors from the eight sites attended annual 3-day training meetings at the Frank Porter Graham Child Development Center at the University of North Carolina and were supervised by an education director at each site. Several training materials were developed for use by home visitors, including a handbook on home visiting (Wasik & Lyons, 1984) and a handbook on teaching parents problem-solving skills (Wasik, 1984).

The training program focused on competence in basic helping skills and techniques as well as knowledge and skills on specific child and parent curriculum materials. The importance of providing supervision was stressed and supervisors across sites met periodically with the program developers to discuss the content and structure of in-service training.

Home visitors were guided by the following goals: (a) provide information on child development, (b) provide health care information and encourage parents to use community resources as needed to maintain the children's health, (c) provide emotional support to parents during stressful times, (d) help parents enhance their children's intellectual, physical, and social development, (e) encourage effective problem solving, and (f) help parents with positive ways of interacting with their children.

A curriculum for low birthweight infants, *Early Partners* (Sparling, Lewis, Neuwirth, & Ramey, 1995), was used in conjunction with an established curriculum for children from birth to age 2, *Partners for Learning* (Sparling & Lewis, 1984). Both curricula were essential components of the home visiting program and were designed to help parents encourage the growth and development of their children. Each child development center met the licensing requirements for each respective state as well as standards and procedures established as part of the IHDP. Children aged 1 to 3 years attended the centers.

The three major outcomes studied were children's cognitive development, social behavior, and health. The results of the children's cognitive development, measured at 36 months with the Stanford-Binet Intelligence Scale, showed that children in the intervention group scored significantly higher than the follow-up group. Additional analyses showed that higher scores were associated with being White, having a higher birthweight, and being relatively healthier at birth. Site differences were also noted, with seven of the eight sites having higher cognitive scores for the children in the intervention group than for the children in the follow-up group at age 3 (Gross et al., 1997). Child behavioral competence was measured by using the Child Behavior Checklist. Results showed that the mothers in the intervention group reported fewer behavioral problems for their children than did mothers in the control group.

Results of the follow-up study conducted when the children were 5 years old showed that the differences between the intervention group and the follow-up group on cognitive scores had become smaller and were no longer statistically significant. The follow-up group gained in scores, perhaps because more of them had entered some type of early childhood care. However, in the heavier birthweight group, the intervention children had significantly higher full-scale and verbal IQ scores as well as higher receptive vocabulary scores than did the follow-up children (Brooks-Gunn et al., 1994).

When the children reached the age of 8, similar results were found. Among the heavier birthweight children, modest intervention-related differences were seen in full-scale and verbal IQ, mathematics achievement, and receptive vocabulary. For the sample as a whole and for the lighter birthweight group, no intervention effects were noted (McCarton et al., 1997). Although the intervention ended when the children reached the age of 3, this finding at age 8 should not surprise us. Vulnerable children, especially those affected by both poverty and low birthweight, need ongoing support if longer term effects are to be expected.

The Nurse Home Visitation Program

The Nurse Home Visitation program is designed to prevent or reduce a number of maternal and child health problems. Three evaluations have been conducted in the past 20 years: first in Elmira, New York, then in Memphis, Tennessee, and currently in Denver, Colorado. The structure of the program has remained constant over time, while the curriculum has become more comprehensive and intensive with detailed plans for home visitors. The intervention focuses on improving prenatal health habits, infant caregiving skills, social support, use of community services, and informal community supports through nurse home visiting (Olds, 1988a; Olds et al., 1999; Olds, Henderson, Chamberlin, & Tatelbaum, 1986; Olds, Henderson, Tatelbaum, & Chamberlin, 1985).

Because the goal of the Elmira program was to prevent a wide range of maternal and child health problems, the mothers were recruited using the following three factors identified as being predictive of such problems: being a teenage parent, being poor, or being unmarried. The presence of any one of the three factors was sufficient to include a mother in the research sample because it was not clear whether one of these variables was more important than another. To reduce the possible stigma associated with a program that focused on young, single, poor parents, any first-time mother was invited to be part of the service delivery sample, including those without any of the three risk factors. Women were recruited early in their pregnancy, at less than 25 weeks of gestation. All three programs focused on first-time mothers because the developers thought that these women would be more receptive to help, and they would be able to use the knowledge and skills they learned in future pregnancies. The researchers also believed that there was a higher likelihood that the mothers would return to school or work if they had only one child to care for.

All three programs were designed as randomized clinical trials with families assigned to one of four groups. The first group served as a control group and received no treatment services, but at 12 and 24 months of age, these children were screened for sensory and developmental problems. The three remaining groups all received the same screening as well as one of three treatment conditions. Group 2 families received free transportation for prenatal and well-child visits at local clinics and physicians' offices. Group 3 families not only received screening and transportation but also had home visits by nurses every 2 weeks during pregnancy. Group 4 families received all the services of Group 3 plus home visits by nurses throughout the first 2 years of the child's life.

The frequency of home visits was designed to change with the stages of pregnancy and the mother's needs. In general, mothers began the program at the end of the second trimester of pregnancy and continued until the child was age 2. Women generally received 13 visits during pregnancy and 47 after the child was born (Olds et al., 1999).

The program content included educating the parent, involving informal support systems, and encouraging linkages with other health and human services. Parent education included both prenatal and infancy education. Visitors encouraged parents to make decisions concerning their own education or job training, employment, and future childbearing. When these topics were discussed, the woman's primary support person (e.g., husband, friend, boyfriend) was especially encouraged to attend. As examples of specific objectives, visitors were to help women improve their diets during pregnancy and monitor their weight gain; eliminate the use of cigarettes, alcohol, and drugs; learn the common signs of pregnancy complications; and prepare for labor, delivery, and the early days of infant care.

The primary procedure for encouraging social support was to have the mother identify family members and friends she could count on for help. Based on her discussions with the mother, the home visitor helped identify the mother's resources, which were most often their own mothers, husbands, or boyfriends. She then encouraged the mother to include these individuals in the home visits. When these individuals did participate, they were encouraged to be supportive of the mother by, for example, accompanying her to the hospital during pregnancy or helping with the infant's care. Home visitors encouraged contact as appropriate with the local health and human service agencies. One way the home visitor communicated with the medical care provider was by sending written reports to the obstetricians and pediatricians who were providing the care. Case conferences and phone calls were also used to facilitate communication.

The Prenatal/Early Infancy Project has been evaluated by comparing families in the different groups. The Elmira project families have been followed the longest. To obtain information on maternal and child health, assessments were made during pregnancy and at periodic intervals after the infant's birth. Although the program ended when the children reached age 2, the children and their families continued to be evaluated, with the most recent evaluation being a follow-up at age 15 (Olds et al., 1999). The results of the evaluations showed that during pregnancy, women who received home visits had more informal supports, improved their diets more, and smoked less. The very young mothers had significant increases in infant birthweight, and for those who smoked, there was a 75% reduction in preterm delivery. Of particular significance was that for those women with all three risk characteristics (poor, unmarried teenagers) there was a reduction from 19% to 4% in verified cases of child abuse and neglect.

In the Memphis study, the mothers were almost all unmarried and were all low-income. When outcomes on pregnancy were considered, no program effects were found for home visiting on women's use of standard prenatal care or obstetrical emergency services. Other pregnancy outcomes, including reduction of preterm delivery and low birthweight, were equivocal. More positive results were obtained for other goals. Participating families showed a reduction in the dysfunctional care of children and an improvement of some maternal life course outcomes, such as fewer second pregnancies (35% vs. 47%), but not for other life course variables, such as maternal educational achievement (Olds et al., 1999).

In a third major study underway in Denver, Colorado, home visiting by nurses is being compared with home visits by paraprofessionals. Preliminary analyses suggest some differences with, for example, nurses completing several more visits throughout the duration of the intervention than paraprofessionals and a higher turnover among paraprofessionals. Future analyses are to be conducted on a range of parent and child outcomes.

The research by Olds and colleagues has taken place within randomized experimental designs. A number of significant findings have been reported, but some anticipated positive outcomes did not develop. Also, some of the outcomes, although statistically significant, did not show large differences between families receiving nurse home visiting compared with other families. Results of this work are important for the field, and future findings from the Denver comparison should yield additional valuable information.

Multisystemic Treatment of Serious Juvenile Offenders

Is it better to serve juvenile delinquents in an institution or in their own homes and communities? This question has been debated over the past century with no definite answers provided by research. Multisystemic Therapy (MST) for serious juvenile delinquents is based on several theories that point toward home-based services. These theories include ecological theory, family systems theory, behavioral theory, and cognitive-behavioral theory—theories that are consistent with many of our own beliefs and that described in Chapter 2. Systematic treatment takes a comprehensive approach to treating antisocial behavior, encompassing family, peer, and school variables as well as the individual youth. Consistent with the tenets of ecological theory and behavioral theory, the intervention procedures focus on ensuring changes in the youth's natural environment (e.g., family, peer group, and school) (Henggeler, Schoenwald, Borduin, Rowland, & Cunningham, 1998).

This therapeutic approach does not have a unique set of treatment techniques; rather, procedures are drawn from the theories mentioned above and pragmatic, problem-focused models (Henggeler & Borduin, 1995). Generally, therapists in this program are mental health professionals with advanced degrees. Treatment typically lasts about 4 months, with a range of 2 to 6 months, and treatment plans are developed, specified, and monitored during weekly group supervisory sessions.

Home-based treatment is considered the cornerstone of MST, especially for families with multiple needs. Home-based treatment has several advantages for families with a juvenile offender. Although family members agree to treatment, they may have done so under some type of mandate or sanction. Consequently, they may be hostile or anxious about participating. Meeting in unfamiliar settings may also be troublesome for family members; meeting in the home helps put the family at ease because they are in familiar surroundings. Meeting in the home also has the same kinds of advantages noted in other parts of this book, namely that families do not have to schedule their own transportation or rearrange work times, and the number of missed or canceled clinic appointments is reduced.

A general outline for a home-based visit begins with the therapist helping each person relax and be a part of the session. Then the therapist focuses on a presenting problem, asking for input from each person. During this time, the therapist can address areas of agreement and conflict in the family. The visit ends with a focus on goal setting, with clear definitions of concerns and of problem behaviors that family members want to resolve. Future visits focus on the attitudinal and relationship changes needed to help the family reach "the conjoint goals of the family members and the therapist" (Henggeler & Borduin, 1995, p. 124).

Sessions may be as brief as 15 minutes or as long as 90 minutes. The timing differs as a function of the objectives of the visit. Sessions may be held daily or weekly. The family members in attendance may also vary, depending on the issues that are being addressed. Henggeler and Borduin (1995) describe this approach as using a set of guidelines that are common to many approaches, not as having a set of specific "techniques." They note that interventions should be present focused and action oriented, targeting specific and well-defined problems. They also note that interventions should be developmentally appropriate, with different strategies for older adolescents and younger adolescents.

Evaluating the outcomes of MST has been a high priority since its inception. Although some of the earlier studies did not have the rigor of later studies, they helped define the characteristics of successful services for juvenile offenders, especially the advantages of providing therapy in the home (Henggeler et al., 1986). Some later studies have used randomized trials to evaluate MST. In one study with maltreating parents, outcomes showed that those in the MST group were more effective in managing their children, their children were more compliant, and the parents were more responsive to their children (Brunk, Henggeler, & Whelan, 1987).

In another significant study using randomized trails, home-based individual outpatient counseling was provided for almost 200 chronic juvenile offenders (Borduin et al., 1995). The in-home visitors were doctoral students in clinical psychology, and the outpatient clinic counselors were master's level health professionals. Improved functioning was found for the families in the MST group. Compared with the clinic-counseled group, results showed improved family functioning, such as increased supportiveness and decreased conflict and hostility during family discussions. In a 4-year follow-up, youth who received MST were arrested less often and had less serious offenses than individually counseled youth.

Other studies using MST have also demonstrated socially significant outcomes. One study was designed to investigate whether MST would be an effective alternative to incarceration for violent and chronic juvenile offenders and their families. Results from this randomized study found that it was effective in lowering individuals' subsequent arrests and number of weeks incarcerated when compared with youth who were receiving the usual services (Henggeler et al., 1998). Other studies are underway or planned, including a downward extension of MST for families with young children.

Summary

Significant program development and research efforts reported between 1985 and 2000 have sustained strong interest in home-based interventions. Interventions have addressed a wide range of family needs, and many of these programs have focused on infants or young children and their families. Program objectives generally include enhanced parenting skills and improved developmental outcomes for children. The results of these programs have shown positive outcomes, but the results are not consistent.

On the other hand, some interventions have demonstrated strong and relatively consistent positive outcomes, notably those by Henggeler's and Lutzker's groups. In both programs, home visitors are highly trained and closely supervised. Identification of problematic situations and goals gives clear direction for the intervention procedures. Both programs focus on children and youth at high risk for out-of-home placements, resulting in an urgency for these interventions that does not exist for other interventions in which families are not faced with such immediate consequences. These programs also seem to insist on more family involvement and cooperation.

It has been suggested that the goals for home visiting programs, in general, might be too ambitious and that more modest goals might be more appropriate (Gomby et al., 1999). However, the results of Project SafeCare and MST show that home visiting programs can be very effective. Their procedures should be considered by other home visiting programs. Research on programs for families with infants and young children should continue to be a priority because the empirical evidence of home visiting's effectiveness with this age group is not consistently positive.

4

Home Visitor Characteristics, Training, and Supervision

Competent home visitors are essential for effective home visiting, and consequently, their credentials, characteristics, professional training, and supervision all require serious consideration. In this chapter, we will discuss these personnel issues as they relate to the employment of home visitors. We will also discuss guidelines for the hiring process. Although some home visiting services are part of larger administrative units and may have existing personnel procedures, others do not have such links and need to develop their own personnel procedures. Even within large organizational structures, such as local and state government or universities where relatively comprehensive personnel guidelines usually exist, procedures often need to be modified to recruit people with the necessary characteristics and to provide for their ongoing professional development.

Home visitor credentials, professional development, and supervision are closely interwoven not only with each other but with other aspects of home visiting such as program goals, resources, and program evaluations. Questions about whether to hire professional or paraprofessional visitors or to have a paid or volunteer staff are issues directly related to program goals, resources, populations served, and the complexity of services offered.

Some programs require a home visitor who is particularly skilled in encouraging child development and supporting families. Others need individuals with specific knowledge and skills related to medical conditions or children with disabilities. As a result of these different program needs, no single set of specific credentials is appropriate for all home visitors; rather, each program must match its needs with the criteria it sets for home visitors. Nevertheless, there are fundamental skills and knowledge all home visitors need to establish working relationships with families.

The credentials of the individuals who are recruited and employed will influence the amount of required training and supervision. Visitors who have graduated from professional training programs will need less preservice and in-service training and supervision than those with little or no educational preparation for home visiting or experience with families.

Sometimes an inappropriate match between program needs and home visitor competence results from a lack of financial resources to pay for qualified home visitors. An agency may have a well-developed program, but if salaries and benefits differ significantly from the expectations of qualified applicants, the program is likely to have trouble filling positions with capable visitors.

Results from program evaluations can influence the hiring and training of home visitors. Program directors who have established an ongoing evaluation of the home visiting program may have information on effective services. If a program is not reaching its objective in a particular area, administrators need to consider possible factors that might be interfering with successful home visiting: Are the goals unrealistic for the resources? Is additional training necessary for the home visitors? Are family needs more complex than had been anticipated? Because the effectiveness of home visitors is essential for the success of any program, information from evaluations can lead to revisions in hiring credentials or to the implementation of additional in-service training.

In the following sections, we will discuss home visitor qualifications, professional development, and supervision. We will then discuss hiring procedures and make suggestions for the employment process. Attentiveness to these staffing considerations can increase the quality of services.

Qualifications for Home Visiting

What educational credentials are considered essential for effective home visiting? Does one have to be a professional or can a paraprofessional provide home visiting services? If a professional is desired, does it matter what profession? What kinds of personal characteristics are desirable in home visitors? The next two sections address these questions.

Educational Credentials: Professional or Paraprofessional?

According to the respondents in a national survey of family home visiting programs by Wasik and Roberts (1994b), more than 50% of programs reported a requirement of at least a bachelor's degree for employment as a home visitor. Of the public education agencies conducting home visiting programs, 75% reported a bachelor's degree as the minimal educational requirement. These educational levels reflect the general 4-year degree requirements for entry into teaching, nursing, and social work. Some programs require specific professional degrees such as nursing for the Nurse Home Visiting Program (Olds et al., 1999) or a master's degree in counseling for the MST program (Henggeler et al., 1998). Other programs, such as the Infant Health and Development Program (IHDP), require at least a bachelor's degree but accept a range of educational backgrounds, including education, nursing, and social work (Gross et al., 1997).

Many programs choose not to require a bachelor's degree. For instance, 2-year degrees in early childhood development are available from many community colleges. The Council for Early Childhood Professional Recognition offers a Child Development Associate (CDA) credential especially tailored for home visitors. CDA home visitor requirements include 480 hours of experience working with families in a home visitor program and 120 hours of classroom education in specific content areas, such as strategies to enhance parents' skills and to establish productive relationships with families. Competence must be demonstrated through a portfolio demonstrating the candidate's work, an interview, feedback from parents in the candidate's caseload, and other records and observations. Both a 2-year degree and a CDA credential are evidence of coursework or experience beyond the high school level, but they are not as extensive an education as that represented by a 4-year degree.

Some programs prefer lay or paraprofessional home visitors. For example, the U.S. Advisory Board on Child Abuse and Neglect (1991) proposed a system of paraprofessional neonatal home visitors for reducing child maltreatment and improving maternal and child health. The question of whether to employ degreed or nondegreed, professional or paraprofessional (lay) home visitors is possibly the most frequently asked staffing question.[1] The question is more relevant to home visiting than to other services because professionals and paraprofessionals have served as home visitors throughout the 20th century. Furthermore, many programs employ a combination of professional and lay workers, making the more relevant questions for these programs one of how to capitalize on the unique skills of staff with different backgrounds and how best to meet their professional development and supervision needs.

Decisions about the qualifications of home visitors are critical to each program's overall success and must be carefully considered. Some programs strongly recommend professionals (e.g., Henggeler et al., 1998; Kinney et al., 1991; Olds, 1988b), and others, such as the Resource Mothers Program (Heins, Nance, & Ferguson, 1987), Healthy Start in Hawaii (Daro & Harding, 1999), and the Home Instruction Program for Preschool Youngsters (Baker et al., 1999), recommend paraprofessionals. This debate has been prevalent for many years and across a range of family services (see, e.g., Curtis & Miller, 1976; Umbarger, 1972). The determining factor is usually the program's specific goals, but other variables considered are family complexity, the role of the home visitor in the agency, and whether the home visitor has responsibility for coordinating services among agencies. At the present time, hiring decisions are most often made based on the need for specific training (e.g., nursing) or a commitment to hire people from the community. The former decision typically results in hiring professionals; the latter often results in hiring paraprofessionals.

Researchers have considered the different merits of professional and paraprofessional workers (e.g., Carkhuff & Truax, 1965; Durlak, 1979; Hattie, Sharpley, & Rogers, 1984), but very little research exists to guide practice. A review of 42 research studies by Durlak (1979) suggested that paraprofessionals and professionals were equally effective in working with families (see also Hattie et al., 1984). However, the studies in these reviews had several limitations, including a focus primarily on adults, and did not provide a basis for drawing conclusions for young children and their families (Hiatt, Sampson, & Baird, 1997).

There is some evidence of a trend toward hiring home visitors with higher educational levels, and evidence of this is seen in the hiring recommendations for Head Start. In the past, Head Start hired many paraprofessionals. Their new performance standards call for at least a 2-year postsecondary degree.

Olds et al. (1999) conducted one of the most important studies on this topic. In this study, both nurses and paraprofessionals were employed to staff a research study comparing professional and paraprofessional staff. Although the results of this major study were not available in time to include in this book, conceptual and pragmatic issues that emerged in this study have been described (Hiatt et al., 1997).

At the present time, the best answer to the question of whether to hire professional or paraprofessional home visitors is "it depends." It depends on program goals and on the knowledge and skills the home visitor will need to implement those goals. Regardless of the set of credentials used to employ home visitors, we need to remember that the roles and responsibilities of home visitors have increased over time, with the expectations placed on many of them being similar to those placed on individuals with professional degrees. As a result, we need to remain vigilant about the match between roles and responsibilities and a person's training and abilities. We need to be cautious about making demands beyond those that can be met. If professional credentials are not required, the service program has an increased responsibility to provide training and sufficient supervision. The program also has a responsibility to remain attentive to concerns that may arise between their professional and paraprofessional staff, such as scope of responsibility and access to confidential information (Goldstein, 1978; Hiatt et al., 1997).

Personal Characteristics

A number of personal characteristics are taken into consideration by home visiting programs when determining the criteria for hiring home visitors. These characteristics include interpersonal and communication skills as well as experience, age, gender, ethnicity, and bilingual skills.

Interpersonal and Communication Skills. Home visiting is demanding work that is best carried out by mature individuals who have had life experiences that enhance their own capacity to help others. The Resource Mothers Program, an organization that employs nonprofessional women to reduce the hazards associated with adolescent pregnancy, describes the Resource Mothers as women who combine warmth, successful parenting experience, and knowledge of community resources in their work (Heins et al., 1987). The importance of interpersonal and communication skills and maturity and good judgment appear continually in the literature on home visiting. When asked about the essential home visitor characteristics for their program, respondents to a national survey of home visiting programs identified communication and interpersonal skills as well as maturity, warmth, and acceptance of others (Wasik & Roberts, 1994b). The need for home visitors to be nonjudgmental, objective, and reflective is also very important. It is through the use of such abilities that home visitors are able to establish a productive working relationship with families. Because these characteristics are so essential to the success of the home visiting process, selection of individuals who already possess basic competencies in these areas is important. Training after a person is employed to compensate for insufficient skills in these areas is not only difficult but often unsuccessful.

In Chapter 5, we will discuss ways of improving interpersonal and communications skills as well as specific clinical or interviewing skills. However, we believe that home visitors should have positive interpersonal skills at the time of employment. Otherwise, training will become excessively lengthy and intense and still may not be able to achieve the level of skill required of home visitors. Later in this chapter, we will discuss procedures that can help in the selection process.

Experience. Relevant previous experiences of applicants should also be a major consideration in evaluating credentials. Such experiences serve several functions. For instance, they allow the applicant to make decisions about his or her own work objectives and determine whether there is a good fit between personal objectives and work in a helping profession. Previous experience also provides an opportunity for an employer to consider the applicant's performance in similar work situations. Such experience need not be limited to paid employment. Volunteer work in community, government, religious, educational, or health organizations can be relevant and beneficial. Home visitors themselves who work in family-focused programs have stressed the need to have considerable prior experience in working with children as well as experience in implementing intervention procedures.

Age. The age of an applicant is also relevant. Setting a minimum age can be one way of assuring a minimum acceptable level of maturity. Programs that require a bachelor's degree will find that almost every applicant is at least 21 or 22 years old. With few exceptions, we recommend that 21 be the minimum age for employing home visitors. We recognize that reaching a certain age does not assure maturity, but we also know that quality home visiting calls for mature judgments and the ability to keep life events in perspective. The success of home visiting also depends on the family's ability to have confidence and trust in the visitor, a situation more likely to develop if the visitor is perceived as a competent, knowledgeable, and reasonably experienced individual.

When would hiring a younger home visitor be desirable? It may be that young men or women could be employed if their youth served to open doors and facilitate communication with young clients, as in a program for school dropouts. A program designed for pregnant teenagers or young mothers might also choose to employ women who are similar in age to or slightly older than the clients, such as young women who have successfully handled adolescent motherhood.

Although there are some programs in which youth might gain some advantages, in general we believe that younger home visitors have not had the opportunity for the breadth of experience or the time to develop the maturity and judgment needed in home visiting. We urge programs that do employ very young home visitors to provide them with frequent and close supervision.

Gender. Almost all of the home visiting positions in this country are filled by women. In one program we directed, women were the only applicants for the home visitor position. In another program, a women-only hiring rule was created because the program focused on maternal and child care.

Should men be home visitors? Does it matter? We believe gender is an important consideration, although, like age, it may be a more relevant issue in some programs than in others. For certain programs, it may be advantageous to hire women. These situations may include single women with young children and women in programs focused on prenatal or postnatal care. On the other hand, programs serving male school dropouts or teenage fathers may be more effective with male home visitors. Sometimes a team with a male and a female home visitor may be desirable.

Regardless of whether the home visitor is male or female, occasions exist in which their role might be misunderstood in the local community. When a male home visitor provides home visiting services for a woman on a regular basis in her own home, misunderstanding can occur in the community. Programs need to take steps to reduce any possible misunderstandings. They may have a person known in the community accompany the home visitor on the first few visits. The goal is not only to provide services but to do so in ways that are sensitive to local values and traditions. Both men and women visitors face circumstances that could be uncomfortable because of their gender. This topic is addressed in more depth in Chapter 6, when we discuss the personal safety of home visitors.

Ethnic Background. Ethnicity in relation to service providers has been defined as an umbrella concept that includes both cultural characteristics and social and racial distinctiveness (Jenkins, 1987). Religion, nationality, kinship patterns, and language can all be a part of ethnicity. Jenkins (1987) noted that ethnicity has particular relevance for those who work with families. Prior to more formalized home visiting, home care was provided by family members, friends, and members of a person's immediate community. Consequently, the characteristics of helpers were similar to the characteristics of those who received their services. As support services became formalized and professionalized, home care began to be provided by individuals who may have had no commonality with their clients. This situation could increase the likelihood that the professional may not be sensitive to family culture and ethnicity.

Jenkins (1981) proposed a typology to suggest how, when, and where ethnicity needs to be addressed in human service programs. These are the individual, group, and society levels. She noted that there are no simple formulas or general prescriptions by which one can make decisions but, rather, there is only a framework for evaluating decisions about ethnicity and the need to remain sensitive to family needs. Jenkins (1981) described several programs in which matching the helper and the family on similar ethnic characteristics was perceived as an important part of program success.

Programs need to balance advantages and disadvantages of hiring individuals from specific ethnic groups just as they should for other characteristics such as age and education. In selecting between two applicants with equivalent education and experience qualifications, many programs will generally hire the person most similar to their clients. The harder decision arises when the applicant who is most similar to the families being served is qualified for the position but has fewer qualifications than an applicant of a different ethnic or cultural group. In making hiring decisions such as these, new programs might review the effectiveness of procedures used by other programs serving similar groups. Existing program staff could discuss these issues with current home visitors.

Programs are concerned with the question of ethnicity in hiring because of the desire to be sensitive to family values, beliefs, and traditions. However, as Gambrill (1997) has observed, we need to be willing to examine common assumptions about multiculturalism, including the assumption that "better services are provided by helpers who match clients" (p. 33). We should incorporate a range of criteria in our employment decisions to assure that clients receive quality services.

Bilingual Skills. Since the first edition of this book in 1990, the demographic characteristics of the U.S. population have changed considerably. There has been a decline in the percentage of the White, non-Hispanic population, while the Black and Hispanic populations have increased (Day, 1996). Of special importance to home visiting services are the number of non-English speaking families. As a result, bilingual skills have become essential when visiting many families. The largest demand is for individuals who can speak and read Spanish. Even among Spanish-speaking families, there are variations from different countries and regions. The ability to speak and understand dialects within a language can be essential for communication. Families who speak languages other than Spanish are also increasing in number in the United States, a situation that makes the ability to read and converse in other languages an increasingly important skill for home visitors, just as it is becoming increasingly important for other professionals. For those who work with families who do use a different language, several options exist. Visitors can learn the language of their families or they can use translators. Programs should hire bilingual staff when possible. We need to remember that being able to converse directly with families in their own language helps increase communication (Gambrill, 1997).

Professional Development

A responsible program provides for continual professional development for its visitors. In-service training is particularly important because few educational institutions provide specific training in home visiting (Weissbourd, 1987). Basic preparation of professionals is typically under the auspices of colleges and universities, but there are few formal educational experiences that specifically address the needs of home visitors. Weissbourd (1987) noted that training programs related to the family support movement generally lag behind the demands of current practice. The same can be said when speaking specifically of family support services in the home.

The training of paraprofessionals or lay visitors has almost always been the responsibility of the employing organization. For organizations that employ some combination of professional, paraprofessional, and lay helpers, responding to the needs of these various groups can make training a complex activity. Individuals enter home visitor positions with different educational backgrounds, helping skills, and content area knowledge, such as child development or nursing. At the professional level, a home visitor could have a 2-year early childhood or nursing degree, a bachelor's degree, a master's degree, or a doctoral degree. At the paraprofessional level, he or she could have completed the 11th grade or could have attended college for 2 years. Furthermore, both salaried and volunteer helpers can have either professional or nonprofessional backgrounds.

Decisions about training need to consider a person's experience, knowledge, and skills, and individualize the training as necessary. For example, a teacher may have a relevant degree in education but may not be knowledgeable about the specific curriculum used in a program and may have had very little preparation for interacting with families. A social worker may have had considerable experience in interacting with families in a clinic but may need to gain knowledge about interacting with families in the home. A home visitor may have been a very successful mother herself but may know little about helping parents who have abused their children.

In providing for professional development activities, home visiting programs can consider existing educational opportunities in their community, including programs in technical schools, colleges, and universities. Home visiting programs can either seek educational opportunities for their staff or require such educational experiences before employment. Because most program administrators will need to provide program-specific or content-specific training activities, using other professional resources for more general training should be considered when available and appropriate. One creative program (i.e., Parents as Teachers) has teamed with a community college to provide relevant coursework. It has encouraged students already enrolled in the community college to take the courses and then apply for employment with their agency after graduation.

One resource for the training of home visitors who work with young children and provide parent support is the CDA credentialing program administered by the Council for Early Childhood Professional Recognition (1998) in a national effort to provide training, assessment, and credentialing of child care providers and home visitors. The program is competency based, defining the skills needed by caregivers who work in center-based programs serving infants, toddlers, and preschool children; family day care settings; and home visitor programs. In the CDA credentialing process, home visitors are trained to provide home visits to families with children 5 years old or younger and to support parents in meeting the needs of their young children. Training is available at numerous colleges and universities as well as by day care and Head Start centers. This credentialing process serves as an initial entry level for many individuals, but we caution that the demands of many programs will necessitate more extensive training in general skills and program-specific objectives.

Professional Development Procedures

Training programs need to be designed to provide home visitors with the skills and knowledge necessary for their work. The procedures used in such training should maximize adult learning processes of the trainees. In this section, we will present recommendations for staff training and for content in a basic home visiting training curriculum. Ideally, the trainees will be active participants in defining the specific content areas and procedures that may best serve their training needs.

We strongly recommend the following procedures in the training of home visitors: (a) opportunities to observe skilled home visitors both in person and through video tapes, (b) role playing, (c) experiential learning, (d) ongoing professional development, and (e) supervision. The first four procedures are discussed in this section; supervision is discussed later in this chapter. Providing opportunities for new trainees to accompany experienced home visitors provides a very effective way for a new trainee to observe how a home visit is managed, how the visitor interacts with the family, and how family and program goals are included in the home visit. Such visits should be preceded by meetings between the new trainee and the experienced visitor to discuss the goals for the home visit and should follow the home visit with an opportunity to discuss the visit with the trainee. Many good training tapes are now available and can provide an additional source of models using good practices in the role of home visitor (see Wasik, Thompson, Shaeffer, & Herrmann, 1996).

Role playing allows the trainee to take turns being the helper, helpee, and observer. We have found role playing to be an effective part of our procedures for teaching clinical skills and have seen role playing prompt home visitors to provide feedback and encouragement to their peers. Role playing allows supervisors to gain information about trainees' strengths and limitations that can be used to individualize further training. In one program serving families with a history of abuse and neglect (McGimsey, Greene, & Lutzker, 1995), graduate students were first taught to apply behavioral procedures with parents through role playing. However, simply knowing how to apply these procedures was not sufficient to assure that the students could teach these skills to parents. Using role playing a second time, students were taught how to be effective behavioral consultants, learning how to use modeling, rehearsal, correction, and reinforcement. This explicit training in consultation skills was essential for the graduate students to be able to help parents. This intensity and specificity of training is not often included in professional development programs but may be essential for success in some situations.

Home visitors also learn by actively trying new procedures or behaviors in their own lives. This experiential learning is especially important for helping others learn a problem-solving process, an approach we used in two home visiting programs. As part of their training, home visitors first learned the problem-solving processes and then had opportunities to practice these processes on professional and personal levels in a supportive training environment. Only then did they engage in problem solving with clients. Egan (1975) elaborated on the importance of such training, noting that because trainees "are eventually going to place demands on others to live more effectively, I believe that they should begin by placing these kinds of demands on one another" (p. 155).

The fourth important training procedure is ongoing professional development. Professional development has been defined as "an ongoing process through which an individual derives a cohesive sense of professional identify by integrating the broad-based knowledge, skills, and attitudes with one's values and interests" (Ducheny, Crandell, Alletzhauser, & Schneider, 1997, p. 89). Professional development has become an integral part of many service agencies because of changes in the field, new procedures, and increasing demands on helpers providing services to families with multiple needs. Adult growth depends on interactions between people and the environment. When adults take on new roles or ways of functioning, it is very important for them to receive support from others and be able to practice these new roles or behaviors over a period of time (Reiman, McNair, McGee, & Hines, 1988).

One innovative model for implementing professional development is to organize activities within a definable service area, such as a county or region of a county, and invite public and private agencies and organizations to participate. Coordination between the agencies could result in a comprehensive, ongoing training effort with activities planned on a regular, predictable schedule. Such an arrangement could reduce redundancy in training, provide more specialized training across agencies, improve professional collaboration and coordination, and enhance the quality of services throughout a geographic area. Peer groups could develop from such an organization, providing an opportunity for visitors to meet with other visitors on an ongoing basis to share experiences and learn from each other.

Several training procedures have been stressed as especially appropriate for paraprofessional training, including on-the-job training, active participation rather than a lecture approach, and a team approach to provide a supportive learning environment. For home visitors, Gambrill and Stein's (1978) 20 components of effective training programs are particularly relevant (see Table 4.1). Often, staff may present training programs on particular topics, such as child management, spouse abuse, or substance abuse, that include excellent coverage of content but that do not focus on specifying the objectives of the training, identifying the skills required to attain the objectives, or determining ways to monitor new skill acquisition. Use of a guide such as Gambrill and Stein's (1978) can help assure that training is relevant and presented in ways that are easy to master. The guide prompts a focus on mastery of objectives, and it can also serve as a basis for evaluating the outcome of training.

Basic Knowledge and Skills

In developing training programs, administrators should assure that they build on the existing knowledge and expertise in the field. Although training of home visitors needs to be individualized according to program goals, family characteristics, and home visitor credentials, we also believe fundamental knowledge and skills about home visiting needs to be a part of all home visiting programs. Our recommended topics are given in Table 4.2 and discussed below.

History. The knowledge of the history of one's field of specialization can help provide a sense of pride and professionalism. We have found home visitors to be interested in the historical aspects of home visiting and in learning about other home visiting programs else-

TABLE 4.1 Components of Effective Training Programs

_____ 1. Outcomes to be achieved through the use of new skills are clearly described.

_____ 2. Skills required to achieve these outcomes are clearly described.

_____ 3. Intermediate skills are described.

_____ 4. Clear criteria are identified for assessing whether each skill is present and for monitoring progress.

_____ 5. Each trainee's initial repertoire is evaluated in the situation in which the skill will be used.

_____ 6. Objectives are directly related to required on-the-job tasks.

_____ 7. A step-by-step learning format is used.

_____ 8. More advanced material is withheld until mastery of earlier steps is achieved.

_____ 9. Models of effective performance are presented.

_____10. Models of inappropriate behavior are presented.

_____11. During model presentation, desirable behaviors are clearly identified.

_____12. Trainee attention to modeled behavior is arranged.

_____13. Practice opportunities are offered.

_____14. Immediate feedback on performance is offered based on previously identified criteria on each trainee's initial skill levels.

_____15. Constructive feedback is provided in which progress related to specific behaviors is first noted (see Chapter 9).

_____16. Opportunities for model presentation, practice, and feedback are offered as necessary.

(*Continued*)

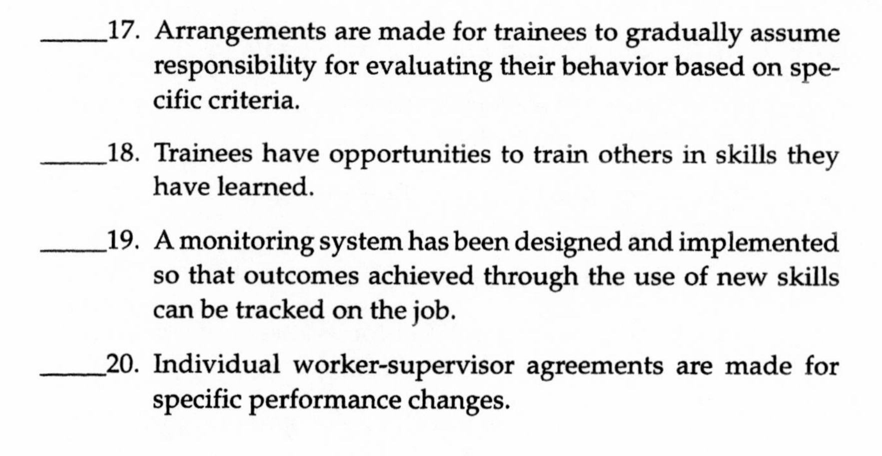

_____17. Arrangements are made for trainees to gradually assume responsibility for evaluating their behavior based on specific criteria.

_____18. Trainees have opportunities to train others in skills they have learned.

_____19. A monitoring system has been designed and implemented so that outcomes achieved through the use of new skills can be tracked on the job.

_____20. Individual worker-supervisor agreements are made for specific performance changes.

SOURCE: Gambrill & Stein (1978, p. 209).

where in their country. Making this type of information available during the early weeks of employment helps visitors place their work in a larger perspective. Those who come from professional areas such as social work or nursing may know the history of their own field but will not likely know of the history and breadth of home visiting across disciplines. Those who do not have a professional background in a particular area are often especially interested in the history because it helps them see their work in relation to other efforts in society while providing a sense of professional identity. Additional information on the history of home visiting beyond that presented in Chapter 1 of this book is available in Holbrook (1983) and Hancock and Pelton (1989) on social work, Buhler-Wilkerson (1985), Monteiro (1985), and Donahue (1985) on nursing as well as Levine and Levine (1970), who present information on the history of visiting teachers and social workers. Accounts of home visiting in Europe have also been discussed in books by Wagner and Wagner (1976), Glendinning (1986), and Kamerman and Kahn (1993).

Philosophy. If the philosophy and goals of a home visiting program are stated clearly, expectations for home visitors and reasons for specific program policies and procedures will be more quickly understood. Of particular importance in program philosophy is the

TABLE 4.2 Basic Content of a Home Visitor Training Program

I. History of Home Visiting

II. Philosophy of Home Visiting

1. The goals of the specific program
2. The role of the home visitor

III. Knowledge and Skills of the Helping Process

1. Basic and advanced clinical skills
2. Professional and ethical issues

IV. Knowledge of Families and Children

1. Prenatal/perinatal development
2. Child development
3. Child management
4. Family systems theory
5. Health and safety
6. Special issues (e.g., child abuse and neglect, alcoholism, drugs, spouse abuse, chronically ill child)

V. Knowledge and Skills Specific to Programs

1. Program goals and procedures
2. Record-keeping and documentation
3. Curriculum

VI. Knowledge and Skills Specific to Communities

1. Cultural characteristics
2. Health and human service resources
3. Other pertinent community resources
4. Transportation issues

role home visitors are to play. In Chapter 2, we noted that, historically, many programs promoted an authoritarian role, one in which the visitor was the expert who typically worked with one family member. This approach is now seen as interfering with active client participation and, consequently, many programs have shifted to an approach in which the visitor is a collaborator and facilitator. To accomplish this shift, home visitors need to learn new skills. Role playing, observing videos, and supervision of home visitor-family interactions are all ways of learning how to use a collaborative approach.

Directors of programs that are guided by specific philosophies should give their home visitors written information that describes those philosophies. In the IHDP, our philosophy of helping families was presented to home visitors through workshops and was described in a training manual. The *Head Start Home Visitor Handbook* (U.S. DHHS, 1993) is a good example of material that describes a program's philosophy. Writings on the philosophy of parent support relevant for home visitors include the summary by Johnson et al. (1989) on the implementation of P.L. 99-457 and two edited books on family support programs by Kagan, Powell, Weissbourd, and Zigler (1987) and Zigler, Kagan, and Hall (1996).

Knowledge and Skills of the Helping Process. Regardless of the specific content of a home visiting program, several areas of knowledge and many skills are needed in all home visiting programs, including knowledge of professional and ethical issues and basic and advanced helping skills. Chapters 5, 6, and 8 can serve as an introduction to these areas or as a general review. Training programs will need to supplement these materials with additional discussions, readings, and supervision. Additional resources on helping skills include books by Gambrill (1997), Egan (1998), Sue and Sue (1999), and Srebalus and Brown (in press).

Knowledge of Families, Children, and Their Environments. Knowledge of families and children is essential for those who work in family support programs. Home visitors in family-focused programs require knowledge about the needs, strengths, and values of families. Helpers also need knowledge and skills specific for interacting with parents and with parent-child dyads. Knowledge about the stages of family development and basic information on family systems theory are also essential for understanding family needs and the implications of intervention programs.

Knowledge that can help a visitor be most effective includes prenatal/perinatal development, child development, child management, health and safety, life-span development, and special family needs such as alcohol or drug abuse, spouse or child abuse, or children with disabilities. Home visitors will not become experts in all these areas, but they need sufficient knowledge to respond appropriately when visiting a variety of families. Their knowledge should allow them to recognize situations that call for additional services and be able to make referrals as necessary.

For example, visitors will undoubtedly notice symptoms of depression among some of their clients. The support they provide through home visiting may help alleviate some of the causes of the depression and help the clients cope more effectively. But a home visitor also needs to be able to recognize severe depression and know when to call on other professionals or, when necessary, seek emergency assistance. In Chapter 7, we describe in more detail issues in working with families with special needs.

Knowledge and Skills Specific to Programs. The directors of home visiting programs need to assure that home visitors receive an adequate orientation to their program, becoming familiar with goals, procedures, record-keeping, documentation, and curriculum. Written materials provide an extremely valuable resource for informing home visitors of essential program procedures. Such materials can provide step-by-step instructions for what to do in specific situations, particularly those that might be dangerous. Because the development of written training materials is so expensive, we recommend that programs examine materials developed by others before undertaking this process. To make information on existing training available, two guidebooks for home visitors have been developed: one describing written training materials and one describing audio training materials. *A Guide to Written Training Materials for Home Visitors* (Wasik, Shaeffer, Pohlman, & Baird, 1996) reviews materials on maternal and child health; child abuse, neglect, and injury prevention; early intervention; family support; and health promotion and home health. For each set of training materials, information is presented on the content, presentation, writing and literacy levels, and how to obtain these materials.

A Guide to Audio-Visual Materials for Home Visitors reviews 58 videotapes relevant to one or more aspects of home visitor training (Wasik, Thompson, et al., 1996). The content of these videotapes covers a wide range of topics including basic skills of home visitors, family-centered concepts and skills, early intervention, explanations of family support, nurturing, child abuse and neglect prevention, and home health visiting. Using videotapes for new home visitors is an efficient way to provide them with an overview of the variety in home visiting.

Many programs have developed specific training materials and detailed guidelines for home visitors to use. For example, Sparling and Lewis's (1984) *Partners for Learning* curriculum has been used with mothers of children from many different ethnic and social backgrounds as well as with mothers of low birthweight infants, infants with cerebral palsy, and infants at risk for abuse and neglect. When used in the IHDP, Partners for Learning was implemented through a combination of child care centers, home visiting, and parent groups. It had a positive effect on low birthweight children's IQ at age 3 (IHDP, 1990). This study also showed that the intervention effects are stronger when higher numbers of the Partners activities are used (Sparling et al., 1991) and when the family and the child have more active experience with Partners (Liaw, Meisels, & Brooks-Gunn, 1995).

The *Partners for a Healthy Baby* curriculum (Graham, Powell, Stabile, & Chiricos, 1998) is a set of three programs for home visitors to use with families before a baby arrives, during the baby's first 6 months, and during the baby's second 6 months. The curricula include detailed, user-friendly manuals, colorful and informative handouts for parents, and record-keeping sheets. The program is designed to be used by visitors who are supervised by a professional in a health or early childhood-related field in a multidisciplinary setting.

Another excellent example of written materials in the health domain is *Child Development, Health, and Safety: Educational Materials for Home Visitors and Parents* (Cohen, Shaeffer, Gordon, & Baird, 1996). This book is a set of materials focusing on childhood injury and child abuse and neglect prevention. The unit on safety addresses a wide range of topics, including car seats, fire escape plans, poisons, space heaters, and stairs and windows. The unit on visit ideas contains 20 sections describing ways to add injury and child abuse prevention to a home visitor's other duties; each visit idea includes a rationale, when the idea should be implemented, the home visitor's role, parent learning objectives, and resources. A trainer's manual provides information to help program directors and trainers prepare home visitors working with new mothers to use the book (Shaeffer et al., 1999).

Another set of written training materials, the *Resource Mothers Handbook,* has been prepared specifically for community workers to help identify and mentor at-risk pregnant women (International Medical Services for Health, 1994a). These materials have been prepared by the International Medical Services for Health for the National Commission to Prevent Infant Mortality. The curriculum sourcebook is designed for people who train resource mothers (International Medical Services for Health, 1994b). Topics address home visiting as well as communication and relationship-building skills, problem solving and decision making, pregnancy and prenatal care, labor and birth, postpartum care, breast-feeding and infant nutrition, child growth and development, and interacting with other agencies in the community. It also gives recommendations for trainers on teaching strategies and group processes. These are but a few examples of the many existing training resources that we encourage program directors to review before developing their own.

Knowledge and Skills Specific to Communities. Communities vary considerably along many dimensions that may influence home visiting, including ethnic composition, income, employment rate, cohesiveness, values, resources, and safety. Business and civic groups as well as staff members of other public or private service agencies can often provide very useful information about a community's characteristics that might help locate services more strategically or focus on particular pockets of need. One or more agencies in a community may produce an annual guidebook of services and programs available for children and families, including contact and cost information. These resource books can broaden the visitor's knowledge of what is available in the community and, if copies can be obtained free or at low cost, the guidebooks can also be given to families.

Training as an Evaluation Opportunity. Training also serves as an occasion to assess the beliefs, skills, and abilities of a new employee. Regardless of how carefully one conducts the hiring procedures, some individuals who are employed may not be appropriate for the job. Reasons for this can range from their initial misunderstanding of job demands to their inability to implement program procedures. Supervisors can use training as an opportunity to observe new home visitors and make alternative plans for trainees who do not exhibit the necessary skills and knowledge during or following training. Perhaps the person could fill a different role in the program or perhaps the person should not continue in the program. The High/Scope Parent-to-Parent Early Intervention Program noted that it was not always possible to make an accurate assessment of an individual's potential as a home visitor during a short interview. Consequently, they used the training process itself as a framework in which the supervisory staff and potential home visitors could make judgments about an individual's potential for the home visiting role (Evans, 1978). The Parents as Teachers national training program uses its basic training not only to train but also to identify individuals who do not appear able to carry out the program objectives. Making such decisions during training reduces the likelihood of assigning an ineffective or inappropriate home visitor to families.

Supervision

Supervision is a relationship with an experienced service provider who gives feedback, advice, and support to foster professional growth and enables visitors to better serve families. Supervision must have a prominent role in home visiting programs. A strong program provides supervision regularly for all visitors, although its frequency and intensity will vary as a function of needs. Home visiting can have many rewards associated with seeing families grow and develop. Yet it is a front-line, stressful position that can be lonely and at times frustrating. Visitors generally work alone and away from coworkers during a normal day and thus do not have frequent contact with peers. The work itself can be physically tiring and emotionally draining because families can face many of life's most pressing problems. Being able to discuss specific concerns about families and receive input and advice from other knowledgeable people is not only very productive for home visitors but can also serve as a stress-reduction process.

In describing the important role of supervision in social work, Kadushin (1976) made a similar observation: "There are few professions that come close to social work in developing in the worker the need for support, encouragement, reassurance, and restoration of morale—a need met by supportive supervision" (p. 35). In addition to being critical for morale, supervision has also been described as essential for maintaining objectivity and professional competence (Hardy-Brown, Miller, Dean, Carrasco, & Thompson, 1987). In research programs, such as the IHDP, supervision also served to prevent "program drift," a situation in which home visitors tend to drift away from the specified program objectives and goals.

The following definition of supervision is very relevant for home visiting:

> Supervision exists to provide a respectful, understanding and thoughtful atmosphere where exchanges of information, thoughts and feelings about the things that arise in one's work can occur. The focus is on the families involved and on the experiences of the supervisee. Depending on discipline, content may vary enormously, but it is not possible to work on behalf of human beings to try to help them without having powerful feelings aroused in yourself. It is the place to understand the meaning of your work with a family and the meaning and impact of your relationship with the family. (Pawl, 1994-1995, p. 24)

Because programs vary in their goals for supervisors and to reduce ambiguities concerning expectations during supervision, both the supervisor and the home visitor should understand the supervisor's roles. Ekstein (1972) described the supervisor's roles as administrator, teacher, and therapist. We believe that the nature of home visiting calls for supervision that includes support, teaching, program management, and evaluation. If the supervisor is mainly an administrator, then supervision may be focused solely on caseload, transportation concerns, or working conditions. A supervisor who views his or her role primarily as a teacher may focus on teaching specific techniques or content the visitor needs. A supervisor who sees his or her role primarily as a therapist may provide emotional support and emphasize the home visitor's feelings and satisfaction with his or her own work.

Gambrill and Stein (1983) suggested that the many separate tasks of supervisors—administrative, educational, and supportive—are really closely related and that information gained from one task is relevant for carrying out another task. No one role is inherently more appropriate than another. Some programs, however, have divided certain supervisory roles from the evaluation roles to enable home visitors to express their opinions or feelings during supervision without being concerned that these opinions or feelings could jeopardize their jobs.

We recommend that all home visitors have professional supervision. The nature and intensity of supervision will differ, but all visitors should have a trusting, knowledgeable person or persons with whom they can discuss their experiences and receive feedback and support. Those who practice independently or privately can seek out professional peer support groups to provide constructive opportunities for discussing day-by-day issues and to provide a resource for professional growth. Pawl (1994-1995) observed, "I don't think that it is possible for any of us to do what we do without some good place to tell our tales" (p. 26). Sharing our stories with others during supervision and receiving supportive, constructive feedback is a powerful learning process.

Supervisory Formats

Supervision can take place individually, in a group, or in the home. Each format has its advantages and limitations: (a) Individual supervision can be more intensive, respond more fully to an individual's needs, and be more personal. (b) Group supervision provides opportunities for learning from peers and sharing one's own experiences. It is also an excellent setting for role-playing and peer teaching activities. Group supervision can be lead by the regular supervisor or by another individual, including a home visitor. (c) On-site or field-based supervision in which the supervisor observes the visitor while meeting with a person or a family in their home allows the supervisor to observe and provide direct feedback on the visitor's performance. The supervisor also obtains firsthand knowledge of the home and family situation and uses this information to inform the supervision.

Some programs provide supervision in several formats. The most commonly reported supervision in family-focused programs is weekly individual supervision followed by weekly group supervision (Wasik & Roberts, 1994b). On-site or field-based supervision is the least frequently used supervision format, possibly because it is the most time-consuming and, hence, expensive. Programs may consider providing supervision in each of these formats because each has advantages. A program could, for example, provide weekly individual supervision, monthly group supervision, and bimonthly on-site supervision. The format and frequency should be responsive to the needs of the home visitors and may change over time.

An example of a program that uses several supervisory formats is the Families Facing the Future project in Pittsburgh in which individuals with no prerequisite skills or experience were employed. All visitors had three weekly opportunities for supervision: The first was with their direct supervisor in a one-to-one conference in which personal issues, quality and quantity of work, or case discussion took place. Second, a group session was held with the program coordinator to discuss program policy, roles, and responsibilities. Other possible topics during group supervision included business issues or program problem solving. In addition to these supervisory sessions, the home visitors met with a mental health professional in the community as part of a weekly process group. This professional, selected by the home visitors themselves, helped the visitors discuss interpersonal issues among themselves, with other staff members, or with their clients (Mulvey, 1988). The supervisory variability in this project not only matched the purpose of supervision with its format but the attention to supervision illustrated the value the program placed on supporting home visitors.

Evaluation in Supervision

Evaluation of visitors is a professional responsibility that may be a part of supervision and is usually at least a yearly requirement of staff members in many organizations. Assuring that individuals know what is expected of them and on what criteria they will be evaluated can reduce the stresses typically involved in evaluation. If the evaluation occurs in a supportive environment and in a timely manner, it can give helpful feedback to home visitors and serve as an opportunity to improve their performance. Written evaluation forms that identify the visitor's responsibilities, program expectations, and the evaluation procedures help home visitors understand the evaluation process clearly. Visitors especially need to know how evaluation information will be used. For example, in some agencies, evaluations influence salary raises from one year to another.

The Home Visit Assessment Instrument (Wasik & Sparling, 1998) has been developed to serve as a guide for supervision. It allows for systematically recording the observations and impressions of the supervisor when accompanying a home visitor on a scheduled visit with a family or families. This instrument can also be used by home visitors to evaluate their own performance, and it can be used by research programs to assess how closely the home visits match the program protocol. The instrument begins with a previsit interview between the supervisor and visitor to clarify the goals and plans for the visit and to discuss aspects of the family that the supervisor needs to be aware of to make an informed observation. The instrument is divided into the following 10 sections: (a) greeting and engagement, (b) assessment of current family/child status, (c) child focus, (d) parent-child focus, (e) family focus, (f) health/safety, (g) parent coping and problem solving, (h) case management and coordination, (i) closure and planning for next steps, and (j) clinical and interviewing skills. These areas are all observed during a visit. A postvisit session is then held between the supervisor and visitor to review the visit. This session provides an opportunity for the supervisor to validate effective work and make suggestions for change as needed. These are often productive sessions because the supervisor has gained more direct knowledge and can often offer more specific feedback.

In Table 4.3, the items from the first section of this instrument on the greeting and engagement of families are provided to illustrate this instrument. The purpose of this first set of items is to provide information on setting a positive tone, establishing rapport, and creating a supportive framework for the home visit.

Supervisory Models

Several supervisory models have been proposed as ways of helping supervisors carry out their responsibilities. For social work-

TABLE 4.3 Home Visit Assessment Instrument: In-Home Observation (One of 10 domains assessed)

A. GREETING AND ENGAGEMENT (7 items)					
Visitor arrives on time	3	2	1	0	NA
Visitor uses the parent's name in greeting	3	2	1	0	NA
Visitor warmly greets the child	3	2	1	0	NA
Visitor asks about parent/family well-being since last visit	3	2	1	0	NA
Visitor establishes rapport with the parent(s)	3	2	1	0	NA
Visitor facilitates constructive home visiting environment (e.g., helps reduce distractions)	3	2	1	0	NA
Visitor discusses purpose of visit	3	2	1	0	NA
Comments:					

SOURCE: Reprinted by permission of the authors: Barbara H. Wasik and Joseph J. Sparling, Center for Home Visiting, UNC-CH, Chapel Hill, NC. ©1995.
Note: 3- Excellent; 2- Good; 1- Fair; 0- Not Observed; NA- Not Applicable

ers, Gambrill and Stein (1983) proposed a decision-making approach to supervision based on the decisions supervisors have to make and the decisions they help others to make. To facilitate the supervisor's decision-making role, Gambrill and Stein (1983) presented a detailed guide for supervisors. In some areas, the supervisor may be discussing issues in assessment and intervention. At other times, supervisors will be involved in decision making related to service coordination, staff competence, and training programs.

Another model of supervision uses a problem-solving approach (Wasik & Fishbein, 1982). In this model, the process of problem solving is viewed as synonymous with the responsibilities of the supervisor and supervisee. Specifically, supervisors and supervisees collaborate on identifying goals and problems in the supervisee's work, generating solutions, evaluating consequences, and making decisions. Together, the supervisor and home visitor evaluate the work of the home visitor. This model serves as a very effective one for modeling with the home visitor the kind of collaborative relationship he or she will have with families. Supervisors can help home visitors evaluate their own strengths, limitations, and activities to foster professional growth.

It is important for supervisors to select a model or philosophy to guide their work. It is also important that the model or philosophy chosen be compatible with those the home visitors are expected to use with families. Doing so provides consistency in the organization as well as role-modeling the program's philosophy. (For additional sources on supervision, see Fenichel, 1992, and Holloway, 1995.)

Hiring Procedures

Employment procedures should involve, at a minimum, a review of the applicant's résumé, an interview, and information from references. Because the interview is so important in the employment decision, specific recommendations for the conduct and content of the interview are provided here. Although we have identified a number of areas about which the interviewer needs to obtain information, the interviewer should make sure he or she does not dominate the interview. Rather, the interviewer needs to assure that the applicant has ample opportunity to describe his or her background and experiences and ask questions about the position.

Interviewing

A well-conducted interview should provide information to help program directors decide whether they want to employ the applicant. Interviews also serve to provide the applicant with an opportunity to find out enough about the position to determine whether he or she wants the job. We recommend that the personnel interviewer (a) assure that all important program goals are explained and understood by the applicant; (b) assure that a home visitor's specific work responsibilities are identified; (c) assure that all expectations concerning supervision, evaluation, and professional development are identified; (d) provide information about staff benefits, working conditions, and salary range; and (e) assess the interpersonal characteristics of the applicant. Providing interviewees a packet of information covering some of these topics in advance reduces the amount of interview time that needs to be devoted to this basic information, thus allowing more time for discussion of the applicant's knowledge, beliefs, and experiences. Each of these areas is discussed in the following sections.

Program Goals. The goals and objectives should be made clear in the interview. Even when program directors are very knowledgeable about the goals and objectives of their program, it is easy for another person to misunderstand what the program is trying to accomplish and what his or her role will be. Because many programs serve families with many needs, it is also important to identify areas that are excluded from program responsibility.

Visitor Responsibilities. Discussing specific home visitor responsibilities provides essential information for the applicant. As one example of what can happen when responsibilities are not initially defined, we worked with home visitors who became concerned when they learned *after* they were employed that they would be responsible for providing their own transportation to the homes of clients. The implications of this expectation were too important for it to have been omitted in the interview.

The following areas of visitor responsibility or work conditions are also areas that should be discussed during an interview. In addition, programs will want to add items specific to their situations.

1. *Work setting.* Information about office space and working conditions for those times when the home visitor is not in the field should be specified. Because visitors are often out in the community, programs may assign them limited space or may assign several visitors to one office. Although there are understandable reasons for this practice, information on the office space conditions should be provided; ideally, the facilities would be shown to the applicant during the interview.

2. *Report preparation.* Information should be provided on the expectations for report preparation or program documentation. A program may show an applicant examples of the types of written reports and data collection required by the program. For programs expecting a home visitor to complete reports or case notes or prepare other written materials, the program may want to ask for a writing sample as part of the evaluation.
3. *Work hours.* The home visitor needs information on the program expectations for general work hours and for work at other times, such as attending evening parent group meetings or making weekend or evening home visits. Many programs expect some evening hours, and this expectation needs to be clear during the interview process to reduce future misunderstandings.
4. *Work expenses.* On-the-job expenses of the home visitor that are reimbursed by the program need to be identified. In particular, information should be provided about mileage, car insurance, or other transportation expenses, including items such as cellular phones.

Supervision, Evaluation, and Professional Development. The degree of autonomy for the visitor in assisting families needs to be described in the interview, and the program expectations for the home visitor's involvement in supervision should be described. This explanation should include information on the frequency and type of supervision. If on-site supervision is part of the program, the home visitor should be made aware that his or her field performance will be observed and by whom.

Program evaluation procedures for home visitor performance need to be specified, particularly if the program has a probation period. The applicant should be told what work will be reviewed and the criteria for evaluation. The applicant also needs to be informed of the evaluation procedures, when evaluation will occur, and how he or she will be informed of the evaluation results.

Any expectations for ongoing professional development, including costs and time, also need to be identified. If the program requires attendance at weekend or evening professional training sessions, applicants should be informed during the interview so that

TABLE 4.4 Interpersonal Rating Scale for Interviewing Home Visitor Applicants

	Not Adequate	Adequate	Good	Excellent
Rapport	1	2	3	4
Warmth	1	2	3	4
Motivation	1	2	3	4
Self-confidence	1	2	3	4
Tolerance	1	2	3	4
Flexibility	1	2	3	4
Maturity	1	2	3	4
Calm/reflectiveness	1	2	3	4
Cultural sensitivity	1	2	3	4
Empathy	1	2	3	4

they can determine whether the job requirements are ones they are willing to accept.

Salary and Other Staff Benefits. The interviewer needs to describe the salary and staff benefits, including vacation time, sick leave, and any other benefits (e.g., health insurance, life insurance, retirement, tuition fees for continuing education). If written policies exist, these should be made available.

Interpersonal Characteristics. As we noted earlier in this chapter, good interpersonal and communication skills are imperative for a home visitor. The personal interview is a prime method for evaluating these characteristics. We have constructed an interview rating form (see Table 4.4) to record judgments on the applicant's interpersonal characteristics and to facilitate a comparative evaluation of multiple applicants. In this rating form, we have included interpersonal skills identified most often in the field as important characteristics for

(*Continued on p. 110*)

TABLE 4.5 Sample Interview Questions

Children and Families

Directions: The interviewer should lead into these questions with an appropriate introduction so that the applicant does not feel like this is a test in which they must give one "right" answer. For example, as a lead-in to some attitudes questions, the interviewer could ask, "Our current home visitors have different backgrounds in their work with families. What experience have you had?"

Have you had experience with unwed mothers? Teenage mothers? What did you think about the experience?

How do you feel about mothers of infants who are on welfare?

What do you believe about the number of children a person should have? Could you elaborate?

What kind of person makes a good mother?

Should a baby be picked up if he is crying or should he be left alone?

What do you think about the timing for toilet training children?

What do you think is most important for fathers to do when caring for infants?

What do children need most from their families?

Home Visiting Situations

Directions: As a lead-in to this area, the interviewer might say, "Many home visits proceed in a fairly routine manner, but sometimes problems occur. What would you say or do if you arrived for a home visit and found the following:"

- The mother had a number of noisy friends visiting her.
- No one was there.
- No one was there for the third visit in a row.
- The whole family was watching television and you could not hear the parent talk.

(*Continued*)

TABLE 4.5 *continued*

- The parent was drunk.
- The mother had lost the materials you had left her and did not remember what you had done the last time.
- The mother was sad and crying.
- The father had left the baby alone with a 7-year-old child.

How would you handle the following situations?

- The baby has a runny nose and the mother hands him or her to you for a hello kiss.
- The baby's older brother and sister want you to play with them.
- You must miss a visit, but the family has no telephone.
- The mother gives her children soda pop and potato chips for lunch instead of nutritional foods.
- The toys you had left on loan are broken.

The Home Visiting Position

Directions: These questions are designed to obtain information on values related to home visiting and whether there is a good match between the applicant and the position. The interviewer should select two or three questions that best fit the particular interview situation.

What would your ideal job be like? Could you tell me why this job interests you? Are there some parts on the job that you would not like?

Could you tell me why you think you would be good for this position?

What do you think the benefits of this program might be for the clients? For you?

What would you do if the program director asked you to convey some information with which you disagreed?

home visitors. Directors of programs may also want to have more than one person conduct interviews with the same applicant. The collective judgments of the interviewers should facilitate accuracy in hiring decisions.

We also recommend that, during the latter part of the interview, information be obtained through interview questions on the applicant's attitudes and beliefs about children, families, and providing services in the home. In addition, information about how the applicant might respond in difficult situations related to home visiting should be gathered. What a person says he or she might do in a particular situation is not always consistent with what he or she would actually do, but these questions will help assess an applicant's beliefs, ability to problem solve, ability to respond under stress, and resourcefulness.

Table 4.5 contains several sample interview questions that could be used to obtain information about an applicant's potential effectiveness as a home visitor. Several interview questions are listed in the following three categories: children and families, home visiting situations, and the home visiting position. All of the examples would not be used in an interview; rather, they are illustrative of the kinds of questions that can be asked. Interviewers may want to substitute examples that are directly pertinent to their own communities, population, or program content.

Interviewers need to know how to interpret an applicant's responses to hypothetical situations. The interviewer is not looking for one right answer because several different responses could be acceptable. In listening to the applicant's responses, the interviewer may want to consider reasonableness, potential effectiveness, and sensitivity to the family in addition to whether the responses suggest knowledge, resourcefulness, and willingness to consider alternative options.

Summary

We have discussed visitor characteristics, including educational credentials, experiences, personal characteristics, professional development, and supervision. We have also made suggestions for the hiring process. Because the question of whether to employ professionals or paraprofessionals has been so salient in the field, we addressed several aspects of this question. This issue is grounded in the traditions and history of home visiting, in which both professionals and paraprofessionals have provided family support in the home. We do not recommend one professional level over another; rather, we strongly endorse a philosophy of matching educational and training credentials to program goals and procedures.

Home visiting is a process used by many different professional groups and service agencies and serves a multitude of needs. One strength of home visiting is its diversity in goals and services. Although we endorse such diversity, we also strongly endorse rigor in selecting, training, and supervising home visitors. To assure the most effective services, careful attention must be devoted to all aspects of the employment, training, and supervision of home visitors, and future research efforts should direct attention to improving these processes.

In this chapter, we have outlined what we believe are valuable components of any training program, but we need to underscore that the most important guideline for training is that it should fit the program's goals and home visitor needs. A second guideline is that training should be of sufficient duration and intensity to assure that home visitors are competent to meet the program objectives and obtain confidence in their skills in doing so. Such training needs to be an integral part of program budgets so that the necessary time and materials can be available.

Note

1. For our purposes, we have defined *professionals* as those who have earned credentials in a recognized field, such as education, nursing, social work, psychology, or counseling. We will use the term *lay visitors* interchangeably with the term *paraprofessionals*, consistent with some of the literature in the field (e.g., Larner & Halpern, 1987). We are aware, though, that in some volunteer programs, lay visitors may be a cross-section of community members and include individuals with a wide range of education and experience.

5

Helping Skills and Techniques

At the heart of home visiting is the relationship between the home visitor and his or her client. This relationship, established to provide help over a period of time, serves as the foundation for the help that is offered. It is through a trusting, respectful relationship that the visitor is able to engage the family in a working alliance. Through this process, the visitor can provide support and encouragement, convey information, help families identify priorities, resolve difficulties, reach goals, promote self-reliance and effective coping, and be an advocate. The importance of the helping relationship has been supported in research, showing a strong, highly significant correlation between the outcome of treatment and the quality of the helper-client relationship (Beck & Jones, 1973). Hollis and Wood (1981) have described it as a powerful tool in the field of social work, noting that "successful treatment depends heavily on the quality of this relationship" (p. 284). De la Cuesta (1994) found the relationship between health visitors and clients to have an enabling and mediating function for their work together.

Almost every approach to helping others stresses the importance of the relationship between helper and client to the helping process (Corey & Corey, 1998; Egan, 1998; Gambrill, 1997; Young, 1998). Even therapeutic approaches that have not traditionally emphasized relationships have documented the importance of therapist characteristics such as warmth and humor (Alexander, Barton, Schiavo, & Parsons, 1976). The helping relationship itself can be defined as having the following three basic elements: a person seeking help, a capable or trained person willing to provide help, and a setting that permits help to be given and received (Cormier & Cormier, 1991; Hackney & Cormier, 1979). The goals of this relationship are to help the clients find ways to manage or resolve problem situations in their lives (Haley, 1987) and to be able to generalize what they learn to future situations (Egan, 1998).

Many synonyms exist for the helping relationship, among them psychotherapy, counseling, casework, crisis intervention, and education. Because of the diversity among home visitors and the diversity of family concerns that are addressed, any one of several intervention approaches might be employed. Some researchers have distinguished the procedures of the helping process from crisis intervention and psychotherapy (Brammer & Shostrom, 1982; Cormier, Cormier, & Weisser, 1984). Crisis intervention is an action-oriented effort to provide immediate help in an emergency situation and is usually time limited. Almost all home visitors may be involved in crisis intervention at some time; we have seen the need for crisis help arise in every program we have conducted. Some home visiting efforts may be specifically designed to address specific urgent situations, such as school suspension, truancy, or child abuse. On the other hand, psychotherapy is often defined as an intensive introspective analysis that may focus on self-understanding, behavior problems, emotional difficulties, or personality characteristics. It has traditionally been of long-term duration, although short-term or time-limited psychotherapy is also a prevalent intervention. Although traditional psychotherapy most often occurs in clinical settings, it also takes place in home settings. Over time, many of the synonyms for the helping relationship have come to be used interchangeably (Young, 1998).

The helping relationship has also been referred to as a *working alliance* (Bordin, 1979; Egan, 1998; Greenson, 1967). This terminology highlights the responsibility of both the helper and the client in making a commitment to work together in helping the client become more effective in reaching goals and resolving problematic situations.

A number of skills and procedures are essential to be an effective helper. The home visitor must be a competent clinician. That is, he or she must be able to listen carefully to what the family says, ascertain feelings and meanings about what people say, and understand verbal and nonverbal communication. He or she also must be able to assess difficulties the family is encountering that interfere with effective problem solving, assess their strengths in problem resolution, and promote the skills, knowledge, attitudes, and environmental conditions that contribute to effective coping.

In this chapter, we will first discuss the following four sets of characteristics and skills essential for effective helping relationships: (a) helper characteristics, (b) basic helping skills, (c) specific helping techniques, and (d) behavioral change procedures. We will then describe a problem-solving approach advantageous for guiding the home visiting process.

Helper Characteristics

Most home visitor programs identify communication and interpersonal skills as essential characteristics for their home visitors; program directors speak of a warm, caring person when describing desired characteristics of home visitors. Although these terms are general, one can identify specific behaviors that define these characteristics.

One of the more generally accepted and useful descriptions of helper characteristics was proposed a number of years ago by Rogers (1951, 1957) and has been used by Truax and Carkhuff (1967), Egan (1975, 1982, 1998) and Cormier et al. (1984). These characteristics are considered to be the critical abilities needed to establish an effective helping relationship: (a) empathy, (b) respect, and (c) genuineness. *Empathy* is the ability to understand and relate to another person's feelings and actions as though they were one's own. *Respect* is the ability to regard another person with worth and dignity. Respect involves a commitment to the client, nonjudgmental attitudes, and warmth. *Genuineness* is the ability to convey sincerity and to be congruent in one's words and actions.

Cormier and her colleagues (1984) have elaborated on these three characteristics in a clear and instructive manner. Because their presentation seems particularly helpful for home visitors, we have incorporated it into Table 5.1. For each characteristic, they have presented a definition, described the purposes of the characteristic, and made specific suggestions for the type of helper behaviors that can convey these important elements.

The information in Table 5.1 describing helper behaviors has multiple purposes. It can be used during training, for self-evaluation, for supervisory feedback, and for suggested areas to observe and discuss during role-playing experiences. One guideline for empathy is to use language that is similar to that used by the client. This guideline is particularly important for conveying to the client that one understands what is being said to him or her. The helper should not try to sound like the client, but he or she should modify his or her language to adjust to the client's characteristics or needs. Including client expressions and phrases in responses to a client conveys attentiveness and respect.

For training purposes, listening to an audiotape of a home visit allows the home visitor and supervisor to determine how responsive the visitor is to the client. Audiotapes can be used to improve many of the other behaviors listed in Table 5.1.

Fundamental Helping Skills

Fundamental skills include verbal and nonverbal communication that sets the tone of an interaction and that help one person assist another to accomplish a goal or address some difficulty. Many people attracted to the helping professions often have skills in these areas, but to be most effective, they need to build on their existing strengths by developing competence in the techniques and strategies described below. Such practice needs to occur in their personal lives as well as in their work. It is desirable, for example, for a home visitor to strive to be a good listener in his or her own daily life as well as in his or her professional life. Supervision from a skilled individual is also essential for the visitor to become more proficient.

Good communication skills enable visitors to interact with families in constructive, supportive, and effective ways. Visitors who have poor communication skills cannot establish the necessary relationships needed to help families. Visitors who are not sensitive listeners will not know what their clients' real needs are. Home visitors who cannot support, encourage, model, or prompt cannot help families reach their goals. Also, visitors who are not knowledgeable of basic behavioral change procedures cannot be effective in helping clients deal with day-to-day concerns.

Another critical aspect of helping or counseling relates to counseling those culturally different from the visitor. In a comprehensive book on this topic, Sue and Sue (1999) have addressed in detail many beliefs and assumptions about therapy for the different cultures.

TABLE 5.1 Fundamental Helper Characteristics

Condition	*Purposes*	*Guidelines for Use*
Empathy		
The capacity to respond to a client's feelings and experiences as if they were your own; the ability to communicate accurate understanding of the client	1. Establish rapport. 2. Show understanding and support. 3. Demonstrate civility. 4. Clarify problems. 5. Collect information.	1. Concentrate with intensity on the client's verbal and nonverbal messages. 2. Use silence to assimilate the material before responding. 3. Formulate and deliver a verbal response that is equivalent to a message expressed by a client. 4. Make a verbal response concise. 5. Use language that is similar to that used by the client. 6. Respond in a nonverbal manner that is congruent with a client's feelings.

(*Continued*)

TABLE 5.1 Fundamental Helper Characteristics *(continued)*

Condition	*Purposes*	*Guidelines for Use*
Respect		
The ability to see a person with worth and dignity; consists of commitment, understanding, nonjudgmental attitude, and warmth.	1. Communicate a willingness to work with a client. 2. Communicate interest. 3. Communicate acceptance of the client. 4. Communicate caring to the client. 5. Provide an outlet for and to diminish a client's angry feelings.	1. Reserve a specific amount of time and energy for client's use. 2. Interact with client without "hurrying." 3. Indicate respect with questions or comments. 4. Convey understanding of client without overt approval or disapproval. 5. Comment on positive aspects or attitudes of client. 6. Express differences of opinion with comments that support rather than criticize a client's ideas. 7. Support verbal expressions with appropriate nonverbal behaviors of respect and warmth.

Condition	*Purposes*	*Guidelines for Use*
Genuiness		
The ability to be yourself without presenting a facade.	1. Reduce the emotional distance between interviewer and client. 2. Increase the identification process between interviewer and client, thereby providing rapport and trust.	1. Be congruent; make sure verbal messages, nonverbal behavior, and feelings are consistent. 2. Be aware of any inconsistencies in your messages and behavior. 3. Avoid overemphasizing your role, position, status, or authority. 4. Be spontaneous—do not constantly ponder what to say and yet at the same time be tactful. 5. Express genuineness and supporting nonverbal behaviors, such as direct eye contact, smiling, and leaning toward the client.

SOURCE: Cormier et al. (1984).

They provide knowledge about different cultures and ways to be responsive to the needs of individuals from different cultures. Those who serve diverse populations need to have the knowledge and skills necessary to provide quality services. Behaviors as seemingly simple as eye contact and physical distance between the helper and client differ in meaning for clients from different cultures. We strongly recommend visitors have opportunities to learn from skilled trainers, supervisors, and peers in addition to individuals from different cultures (Ho, 1987, 1997; Lee, 1997; Okum, Fried, & Okum, 1999; Srebalus & Brown, 2000; Sue & Sue, 1999).

The essential helping skills we will discuss are the following: (a) observation, (b) listening, (c) questioning, (d) probing, and (e) prompting. These skills help assure clear communication between the visitor and client and allow information to be obtained that is essential for developing intervention programs. More advanced clinical skills, such as interpreting and confronting, are addressed in other sources (see, e.g., Cormier & Cormier, 1991; Egan, 1998; Gambrill, 1997).

Observation

Through observation, one gains information essential for understanding and collaborating with clients. Home visiting provides unique opportunities for observation. In contrast to a clinic, hospital, or school setting, homes provide knowledge about living conditions, families, and communities. From the time the home visitor begins a trip to the client's home, she is able to learn about the broader environment in which the client lives. The visitor gains information on community services, including transportation, medical and educational agencies, safety of the neighborhood, and recreational and cultural opportunities. Such information enables the home visitor to put into perspective interactions with the clients and provides a knowledge base for making suggestions about resources.

The organization of the home and the resources available for daily living enable one to understand more about an individual's or family's strengths and coping strategies, available supports, and limitations imposed by the home environment. When assisting parents of a developmentally delayed child, the visitor may note that very few child materials are in the home and may wonder about the parents' knowledge of the child's needs. The visitor may find that the initial hypothesis that was drawn from her observation of the home was supported in interviews with the parent. The visitor could then have discussions with the parent different from those that would have occurred if the visitor found the home equipped with many books, toys, and play equipment.

Assessing the resources through observation in the home is particularly important for those providing medical assistance. Being aware of physical barriers in the home may help the visitor understand why a person may have difficulty complying with a medical routine. A broken refrigerator would help one understand why a mother was not keeping milk available for her children and could alert the home visitor to other potential health and nutrition problems.

Through home visits, one can see how family members contribute to each individual's overall well being and can help families build on their strengths. Even simply validating for parents the level of support for each other can be very encouraging and motivating.

Information gained from in-home observations is covered by the same ethical guidelines for confidentiality and respect as other information provided by families. In fact, information gained from in-home observations must be handled with even more sensitivity than information provided directly by the client because visitors may observe events that were not intended to be revealed. Although this situation can also occur in a clinic situation, more opportunities exist for the visitor to obtain such information when in the home.

Listening

The ability of the home visitor to be an effective listener is critical to establishing rapport, building trust, and being helpful. It is important to listen not only to what the client says but also to the meanings and feelings associated with what the client says. Careful listening provides the home visitor with important knowledge about a person's emotional status and can help the visitor respond sensitively to current needs.

Several guidelines can be used to improve listening skills. First, the visitor can make sure that the client has been allowed ample time to discuss particular goals and concerns, talk about what has happened since the last visit, or describe other issues of importance.

Second, the visitor's own body language and words should convey a message of support and interest in what others are saying. Contradictory messages, such as acting restless while encouraging someone to talk, can discourage and confuse that person. Nonverbal communication such as body language and eye contact does not have the same meaning across cultures. Visitors need to understand the meaning of nonverbal language for the different families they visit and be able to change their behaviors as needed to be responsive and respectful.

Third, the visitor needs to remain mentally alert, sorting through what he or she is hearing so that the visitor can respond to spoken or unspoken messages as appropriate. Inattentiveness can be a frequent cause of misunderstanding. A home visitor needs to think while listening, asking him- or herself questions such as, "Is this concern similar to ones I have heard this father talk about before?" or "Is this reaction similar to the one his son had several weeks ago?" If so, the visitor might identify the similarities and ask the father what has helped him resolve similar situations in the past. The importance of listening is underscored by the evaluations of families who positively evaluate their home visitor by saying, "She really listened to me!" or "She heard what I said."

Questioning

Questioning, part of the verbal interchanges that naturally occur between individuals, can facilitate verbal interactions between the home visitor and family members. Long, Paradise, and Long (1981) have presented an excellent description of the role of questioning in the helping process, recognizing that there are advantages as well as disadvantages in using questions. Concerns about the use of questions include the overuse of questions by the unskilled interviewer and the possibility that questions can hinder the communication between the helper and the client. When misused, questions can take the form of an interrogation. When used appropriately, questioning can serve several purposes. For this reason, it is important for the visitor to learn the appropriate use of questions and avoid using questions in a way that interferes with good communication.

For our purposes, we selected a set of questions that seem particularly suitable for the home visiting process, namely those that help begin the interview (initial questions), open-ended questions, facilitative questions, clarifying questions, and focusing questions. Familiarity with these different types of questions and skill in using them will enhance the ability of the home visitor to be more effective with clients.

Initial Questions. A home visitor meeting with a new client needs to know how to begin the interview, including putting the client at ease; creating a comfortable, safe environment; establishing rapport; and building trust. The appropriate use of questions during this early time period can help make the client feel more at ease and can convey that the visitor is there to offer help in a nonjudgmental way. Questions asked during this time should encourage the client to talk about topics of his or her choice. To facilitate the initial visits, the home visitor may suggest topics related to the nature of the visit. For example, in a program providing visiting for parents of low birthweight babies, many home visitors found that asking questions about the birth of the baby was a good way to engage a mother during the first interview. The home visitors found questions such as the following to be valuable: "This is your first child. What have the first few weeks been like for you?" "How has your life changed since becoming a mother?" A mother who is somewhat nonverbal might respond more easily if she is asked to tell about a typical day with her newborn.

Open-Ended Questions. Open-ended questions are especially useful during the initial interview because they can help solicit information on family needs, concerns, wishes, and longings. These questions do not restrict the kinds of responses the client can give to the visitor. Using the example of the visitor with the parent of a low birthweight infant, the visitor might ask, "What are some ways our program can help you?" or "Are there particular concerns with your baby you would like help with?"

Open-ended questions also allow the visitor to learn from the client what events and feelings are important to him or her and allow the client to influence the content of the interaction. Through open-ended prompts, a parent may respond with examples from daily life that provide valuable information for understanding his or her needs and goals.

Facilitating Questions. Facilitating questions require active listening, and they are most often asked for a specific purpose. A good facilitative question can solicit missing information or clarify previously discussed material: "A facilitative question communicates understanding and respect. Most importantly, it helps the client better understand him or herself" (Long et al., 1981, p. 73).

Facilitative questions attempt to focus on the important element of what is being said while avoiding details that might detract from the main point. If a caregiver for a physically ill person were to tell a health visitor, "I am so confused by all the equipment, I don't know what to do," the visitor could encourage the caregiver by possibly asking, "Can you tell me more about what is confusing to you?" In this way, the home visitor can learn directly from the individual what is troubling him or her. The visitor may find out that the concern is not actually the equipment but, rather, the difficulty in following a schedule for using the equipment. If the visitor had responded, "This equipment is really very simple to operate. Let me show you how," he or she would be missing what the individual is trying to say and would not be respectful of the client's needs and feelings. Later in the same visit, it may be desirable for the visitor to demonstrate how to use the equipment, but if the visitor were to respond too quickly with a solution to a perceived problem, the caregiver might be prevented from elaborating on the real concern.

Clarifying Questions. Clarifying questions facilitate communication by seeking additional information. These questions are particularly appropriate during the initial visits in the home and at any other time when a client is discussing situations that are open to different interpretations.

A clue to when clarifying questions may be in order is when a client uses vague words or words that can have more than one meaning. For example, if a Head Start home visitor is discussing learning activities with a child's mother and the mother says, "Things are all mixed up," the visitor might not know what "things" refers to or what "all mixed up" means. He or she could begin by asking, "Could you tell me what you mean by *things*?" Once the visitor understands the mother's focus, he or she may then want to explore what "all mixed up" meant to the mother. In this example, clarifying questions helped prevent the Head Start visitor from jumping to conclusions about what "things are all mixed up" means. It could be that the child development materials were confusing to the mother, or it could be that she was concerned about changes in her child's transportation schedule to the Head Start center. The mother could also be referring to a major life event such as an unexpected pregnancy.

Visitors should be careful not to use clarifying questions in ways that interfere with what a person is trying to say. At times it is better to wait for clarification that may come as the individual elaborates rather than asking questions too soon.

Focusing Questions. Home visitors will find that it is often necessary to help some clients focus on specific concerns. Such individuals may feel overwhelmed with a number of problems or may not be able to identify on their own what is troubling about a situation. Focusing questions are particularly important in helping clients address problematic situations. Clients may need help in focusing when they identify many issues without seeming to prioritize them, use vague language to identify concerns, or are unable to say what is troublesome about a particular situation. An example of identifying many issues at once is a new mother who might say, "Nothing is going right. My baby cries, she stays up at night, and I'm tired. I miss my job." To help this mother begin to focus, the home visitor could encourage her to identify what she most wants to talk about by saying, "There are several things right now that seem to be bothering you," or "A lot seems to be on your mind." "What would help you most to talk about now?" If it seems too difficult for the mother to sort through her concerns, the visitor may offer a suggestion such as, "You have mentioned the baby's crying a couple of times before. Would you like to talk about that now?"

An example of the use of focusing questions with clients using vague language might be the father who is very punitive with his 10-year-old son and says, "He does everything wrong. Nothing is right. He keeps me upset." In this situation, focusing questions could help the parent identify particular times, situations, or behaviors that are troublesome as a way to help the father identify the specific concern. Questions such as, "What about his behavior upsets you?" might begin to help both the father and the visitor identify specific areas of concern. Once these areas are identified, it becomes possible to discuss how serious the situations are and to determine whether action should be taken.

Redirecting Questions. Redirecting questions can shift the discussion from one topic to another or to one aspect of an issue. Redirecting questions might be used when a visitor believes that a client has wandered away from his or her initial concerns and is discussing unrelated or tangential matters. These questions may also be used when a visitor believes that a client is avoiding a difficult issue. If, for example, a mother expresses a considerable amount of anger toward a child at the beginning of a home visit and then spends most of her time talking about other topics, a visitor may judge that the mother is intentionally avoiding the topic. The visitor may also know that this mother has few coping skills for dealing with her anger toward her children. The visitor may decide to return to this topic in a way that expresses support for the mother while helping her think about ways she can deal with her anger. This discussion could lead to talking about more effective child management procedures and learning different ways of dealing with anger. When a visitor redirects, he or she is making a judgment about the importance of certain feelings or events in the life of the client, so the use of redirecting questions, similar to any intentional strategy in therapy, should be used in a thoughtful manner.

In the examples we have given, questioning was generally used to obtain additional information. We are aware that in any one of the examples, depending on the circumstances, a very different response by a home visitor might have been called for. If the father in the example above, when saying everything about his son upset him, was very emotional and crying, showing empathy for the father's feelings and giving him an opportunity to talk about his feelings would most likely have been the more appropriate immediate response. Clarification about the son's behavior could come later.

Probing and Prompting

Probing is an attempt to seek additional information and is particularly important when there is insufficient information to understand client concerns or feelings or to help clients deal with problems. Probing could be used to help a client begin to consider the personal and family resources that might be available in times of stress. Parents of a child with disabilities may have been depending only on each other for support and relief. A home visitor could help the parents consider extended family members, friends, neighbors, and respite care as alternative sources of support by asking, "Who are some members of your family who could help?" or "Earlier you said your mother could not help because she was working. Have you talked with her about your need for some help with your baby?" Such questions help a client consider in more depth alternatives that may have been dismissed too quickly or not considered at all.

Prompting facilitates a particular behavior by either verbally encouraging it or through the use of physical prompts. Prompting is particularly useful when teaching new behaviors or when encouraging a person to try actions he or she might be hesitant to try. A home visitor may, for example, directly guide a parent through a learning game with a toddler. He or she may suggest that a family carry out an activity they have been planning to do together but may have needed encouragement to get started. Prompting a client to try something new can convey the home visitor's confidence in the client's ability while helping the client learn new skills.

Summary

The basic helping skills presented above—observation, listening, questioning, probing and prompting, and reflecting—are skills that all home visitors need to use home visiting time constructively and productively. Interactions with families are not simply social exchanges; a home visitor must know how to use verbal and nonverbal communications in clinically meaningful ways. Advanced helping skills are also important and can be pursued once the basic skills are mastered (see Cormier & Cormier, 1991; Egan, 1998; Gambrill, 1997).

Specific Helping Techniques

A number of specific techniques are also available to home visitors in their interactions with families. As with basic clinical skills, these techniques are common across the helping professions. In this section, we will discuss the following four techniques that we believe are particularly useful in home visiting: (a) modeling, (b) role playing, (c) use of stories and examples, and (d) homework. These techniques help a client become better prepared to deal with some event in his or her life.

Modeling

Modeling is actually demonstrating a specific behavior for the client. It is particularly advantageous when a person cannot visualize him- or herself carrying out some action or when he or she cannot think of how to begin an activity. It is also useful when a client seems to lack the necessary skills or when a client seems hesitant to try out a new behavior. Modeling could include showing how to respond during a job interview, how to ask a spouse to help with child care, or how to comfort a colicky child. Modeling is an ideal teaching technique in many parenting situations, from showing how to burp an infant to helping parents who are learning therapy techniques with a child who has cerebral palsy. It is a prevalent practice of nurses and physical therapists in demonstrating appropriate medical care.

After a home visitor has modeled a behavior, he or she can then encourage a person to perform the behavior. Observing a parent practice lets the visitor see whether the client understood what was modeled and can match the modeled behavior. Such practice not only helps assure that the client will remember the behavior but it also gives the visitor the opportunity to reinforce and encourage the client's actions.

Role Playing

In role playing, the home visitor acts out a real-life role and the client acts out another, usually to help the client gain skill and confidence for dealing with a difficult situation. This technique is particularly appropriate when a client has difficulty being assertive. For example, a mother may have been offended by the brisk manner of her child's physician, and she may be reluctant to ask the physician questions about her child's health. During role playing, the home visitor can take on the role of physician and let the mother practice what she would like to ask the physician. In this example, there are advantages for the mother in trying out both roles. She can be the mother and ask the physician what she would like to know, or she could be the physician while the visitor models some of the questions the mother could ask. In a role-playing situation, a home visitor will also be modeling behaviors. (For information on using the role playing technique to learn new behaviors, see Young, 1998.)

Use of Stories and Examples

Storytelling and using examples are common, everyday ways people explain, describe, or teach something to another person. Both are also pertinent for visitor-client interactions. In a helping situation, telling stories and giving examples should be relevant to needs of the client.

Examples can be used to accomplish many objectives. First, examples can help an individual see that others are experiencing similar difficulties. To a mother who was concerned when her child started kindergarten, a visitor might say, "Many parents have these concerns. I remember a mother who told me that even with her third child she was worried when he began kindergarten." Examples can be used to provide information on a possible way of dealing with a difficult situation. A visitor might say, "Once when I talked with a mother about a similar situation, she told me that she had tried letting her child take a nap in the afternoon. Does this seem like it would work for you?"

Examples can also be used to help another person feel at ease when something he or she tried did not work out. The visitor might say, "I remember a mother who tried three different ways to help her daughter learn how to use the toilet before the child was trained. Like her, you may find that the second or third approach will work, even though the first one did not."

Interesting stories told by the home visitor as examples can also be extremely valuable when helping others. They often not only teach some point but also may be remembered when other information is not. Stories can come from the visitor's professional work or his or her own life. When describing information from his or her own life, the visitor must keep in mind that the purpose is to help the client. The home visitor may share a story to help put a client at ease, express empathy, or help a client see that others deal with similar situations.

Homework

A fourth useful procedure for helping families learn new ways of responding is to give the family an activity to carry out between visits. This can also allow families to see how effective procedures from their past might be applied to a current situation. The homework task can often be practiced while the visitor is in the home, making it easy to discuss events that might interfere with the families' ability to practice on their own. As families become more adept at doing things on their own, the visitor can encourage them to be more independent in deciding on behaviors to work on and strategies to use. Homework also has the advantage of helping families see their responsibility for working on their own between visits.

As part of asking families to carry out some activity between visits, the visitor might find it helpful to have one or more family members observe the behavior and record what they observe. This practice has often been applied when helping parents learn to manage disruptive child behavior. Self-monitoring of behaviors between visits has also been used with parents and their adolescent children.

Behavior Change Procedures

The principles and procedures of behavior change are fundamental parts of a home visitor's repertoire of skills. The procedures of behavioral change are based on principles of behavior modification and social learning theory (Bandura, 1977; Mash & Barkley, 1998) that describe how behaviors can be increased, decreased, or maintained, and how new behaviors can be learned. Understanding these principles is essential for anyone who works with families. Home visitors who are not familiar with these principles and cannot use them in their work will not achieve maximum effectiveness. These principles are especially important when working with parents of young children (Chamberlain & Patterson, 1995) and parents of adolescents (Robin & Foster, 1989).

The basic principles of behavior analysis describe the effects of both the antecedents of behavior and the consequences of behavior. The antecedents of an action refer to what is going on in the environment before the behavior occurs. Physical changes in the environment can change the likelihood that a behavior will occur. For example, making a home safe for toddlers by making changes in the environment can reduce the likelihood of harm to young children (Cohen et al., 1996). We put fences around playgrounds to keep children safe, and we remove dangerous objects from their reach. Stairs can be blocked off, electrical outlets can be covered, and the hot water temperature reduced. A home visitor who brings toys or other activities for a very active child to play with while conversing with the parent is changing the environment to make his or her conversations with the parent go more smoothly. Antecedent conditions also include verbal behavior. What we say to each other can increase the likelihood that a behavior will occur. Parents who give clear, unambiguous directions, for example, will see more cooperation from their children than parents who give confusing, conflicting directions.

Behavior is also strongly influenced by its consequences. These consequences can be positive and reinforcing and can increase the likelihood that the behavior will occur again, or the consequences can be negative and punitive and can decrease the likelihood that a particular behavior will occur again. Many parents spontaneously use positive consequences; they praise and encourage a child who is learning to walk or talk. But as a child's behavior becomes more complex or problematic, some parents need help in knowing which behaviors to attend to, which ones to ignore, and which ones may need to be punished. Sometimes parents may pay attention to a child's inappropriate attention-getting behavior, resulting in even more such behavior on the child's part. Sometimes parents unintentionally become negative in their interactions with their child and often need help in learning to change these unpleasant interactions into more positive, enjoyable ones (Chamberlain & Patterson, 1995).

The guidelines we discussed earlier concerning home visiting in general are important when teaching parents about child management procedures. For example, the home visitor needs to keep in mind that parental needs may be interfering with their ability to respond to their child and may need to be addressed. Home visitors also need to consider intervention procedures from a systems perspective, considering the effects on other family members. This recommendation is compatible with the views of Wahler and Dumas (1984), who emphasized that a child's behavior is influenced by subsystems in which the child lives and that these system influences need to be considered when addressing parent-child relationships.

Another area of compatibility between our philosophy of home visiting and parent training is seen in the work of Blechman (1980), who emphasized the importance of problem-solving skills as a prerequisite for competence in parenting. In addition, Bijou (1984) and Embry (1984) stressed the need to conduct parent teaching and training in the parent's home rather than in a clinic or other institutional setting, a tenet completely compatible with home visiting.

Project 12 Ways is a home visiting program that has demonstrated the effective use of behavioral change strategies with parents of abused and neglected children (Lutzker, 1984). This project has successfully helped parents increase home safety (Tertiger et al., 1984) and the personal cleanliness of children (Rosenfield, Sarber, Bueno, & Greene, 1983). It has also helped reduce incidents of abuse and neglect (Lutzker & Rice, 1984). In a later version of this model, Project Safecare, additional support for the use of behavioral change strategies with parents who are maltreating has been found (Lutzker et al., 1998).

We have only briefly summarized the use of behavioral change strategies by home visitors. We strongly recommend that the reader obtain additional information elsewhere. Several excellent, comprehensive parent training programs have been developed to help parents deal with many child management problems. The procedures are especially important for parents of children with disabilities and parents at risk of abusing or neglecting their children. Additional resources on parenting skills include Dishion and Patterson's (1996) *Preventive Parenting With Love, Encouragement, and Limits.*

A Problem-Solving Model for Home Visiting

In this chapter, we have discussed the following four topics essential to home visiting: helper characteristics, basic helping skills, specific techniques, and behavioral change procedures. As important as these areas are, they are not sufficient to provide structure and guidance for the helping process. An overarching framework to the helping process can help visitors bring unity to their relevant knowledge and skills.

In the late 1970s, we included a problem-solving model as part of our intervention program in Project CARE, an early intervention program for young children and their families (Wasik, Ramey, et al., 1990). Since then we have continued to expand this model for the practice of home visiting. Our beliefs about this model are consistent with those of Egan (1998), who observed that combining a problem-solving or problem-management approach with communication and helping skills provides a foundation for and adds substance to any approach to helping.

The rationale for using a problem-solving model in helping relationships has been further articulated by Egan (1998) who noted,

> Problem solving is one of the most highly researched paradigms in psychology. It is not fad. It is not based on an unsupported theory. . . . Problem management and opportunity development constitute key dynamics underlying every form of helping. The reason for this is that the process focuses on the client's needs, not the assumptions of a theory. (p. xv)

Egan (1998) also noted that although the basic problem-solving process or model is universal, adaptations need to be made for cultural differences.

As we have worked with this model over time, we have developed a three-part training program. First, we have home visitors learn the problem-solving model themselves and become able to use it in their own professional and personal lives. We have started with personal use because we do not believe that one can help others with enthusiasm and integrity if one is not in agreement with and knowledgeable about the intervention model and procedures one is using. We help home visitors learn problem-solving skills by first telling them about the model and then providing them with opportunities to practice the model using real-life situations. They receive feedback on their progress and learn to self-evaluate. Second, we help home visitors use the model as a framework for structuring their work with families. In so doing, we help them identify a family's strengths and areas of difficulty in coping with day-to-day situations. Third, when home visitors are comfortable and proficient with their use of problem solving and are using it as a model for identifying strengths and needs, we help them learn how to teach parents a problem-solving approach that can be used in their own lives.

The problem-solving model has seven processes that can guide the work of the home visitors. These steps are like a road map for the visitor, reminding him or her of the purpose of the interactions and helping the visitor evaluate whether he or she is helping the client make progress toward the client's goals. The seven steps of the model were selected because each is an important part of the total problem-solving process and at any of these steps individuals can have difficulty proceeding with a problem solution (Wasik, 1984). The steps used in the model are listed and defined as follows:

1. *Problem definition:* describing a problem situation (a situation is defined as a problem when its resolution is not automatic)
2. *Goal selection:* describing what a person wants to happen
3. *Generation of solutions:* identifying a number of alternative responses that may address a problem or reach a goal
4. *Consideration of consequences:* identifying the positive and negative consequences of any solution in relation to time; money; personal, emotional, and social effect; and immediate and long-term effects
5. *Decision making:* weighing the proposed solutions and consequences and determining which one is best for the individual at that time (decision making includes consideration of a person's priorities and values)
6. *Implementation:* carrying out those actions called for by the decision
7. *Evaluation:* reviewing the outcome to determine whether it met the person's goals

Problem solving involves thoughts, behavior, and feelings. The first five processes in this model are primarily cognitive. One can think through these five stages without taking any action. One can also evaluate one's success while thinking, not acting. Implementation, however, requires one to act. Feelings are also an integral part of this process. Strong feelings are often the reason a situation is defined as problematic in the first place. One's feelings need to be considered at each stage in the process. Emotions such as sadness or anger often interfere with a person's coping skills at each of the problem-solving processes. It may be essential to help a person identify these emotions so that they can move forward. Through his or her interactions with a client, a home visitor may help a client see a situation differently. The home visitor can also help a person see that there are choices as to how to respond in a particular situation.

The problem-solving planning guide used in Project CARE (Wasik, Ramey, et al., 1990) and the IHDP (Wasik, Bryant, Sparling, & Ramey, 1997), as well as other home visiting programs is shown in

TABLE 5.2 The Problem Solving Guide

What is my problem?	
What do I want?	
What can I do?	**What will happen if...?**
What is my decision?	
Carry out my plan!	
How did it work?	

Table 5.2. This guide identifies each problem-solving process in everyday language. It provides space for a person to write his or her thoughts regarding each problem-solving process.

Each of the problem-solving stages will be described in sequence, but solving problems rarely proceeds in a step-by-step manner; rather, it is often circular. A person may be thinking about a solution and then decide to reorient his or her goals and directions. Or a person can try a particular solution only to have it not work out and start over with a different solution. Some families may have beliefs that interfere with their ability to recognize and define problems. Such families may believe that what happens in their lives is due to fate or luck and that their own actions are not important. Other families may readily accept problem-solving procedures, already having recognized their value in their own lives and having seen their relevance to daily living. Because beliefs can interfere with effective problem solving at any stage in the process, it is important to consider such beliefs when making decisions on how to help a client.

The helping relationship must begin with the development of trust between the helper and the client. A trusting, supportive setting makes it easier for clients to open up and be comfortable when talking about their needs and concerns. Helpers need to make it easy for clients to tell their story. It is through listening to these stories that home visitors gain information about how to help their clients.

Problem Identification

Problem identification is defining or describing the troublesome issue or situation. It answers the question, "What is my concern?" Identifying problems helps to focus on the relevant aspects of a situation, eliminating those things that are not of concern. One important part of identifying problems is deciding who "owns" the problem. Most of us at some time have probably worried about situations or events that were really the responsibility of other people and we may have become needlessly distressed about things we had no control over and no responsibility for. Talking with another person can often help someone differentiate between problems they need to deal with and those they do not.

The home visitor can help a client see that some problem situations do not really need to be addressed. Some situations will work out on their own; other situations may not need attention if a person begins to see them differently. This shift occurs in some child-rearing situations in which parents may change their expectations of their children when they have more knowledge of children's abilities at different ages.

When discussing situations that clients want to address, it is important to obtain information on the severity and frequency of the concern. To obtain such information, the visitor may ask questions such as, "About how often does this situation occur?" and "How serious is this for you?" Information on the duration and location of the problem is also important for making intervention plans. Visitors can prompt such information by asking, "How long has this situation been bothering you?" or "Where does the behavior usually occur?" One can probe for additional information by asking, "Does it occur during mealtime?" or "Is this also an issue at school or work?" Such information may serve as a basis for selecting behavioral change strategies or may help the person decide that the situation is not as serious as originally thought.

All problem situations do not need resolution, and furthermore, all problems cannot be resolved. But many problematic situations can be managed in a way that makes life more comfortable. Parents cannot change certain limitations of a child with physical disabilities, but they can find ways to make the care of the child less burdensome or to help the child learn things he or she can do successfully despite a disability. At other times, it may be possible to change a situation, but a client may have learned to accept the situation as it is and may not wish to change anything.

In helping a client identify what is bothering him or her, a home visitor can help a client describe how, when, and where the problem occurs. A home visitor can also encourage a client to talk about how he or she feels about a situation. At times, this process of talking about and thinking about a particular situation can help a person evaluate how important the situation is personally and can help a client judge whether he or she can or wants to do anything about it.

Goal Selection

Goal selection is clearly essential for problem solving. It helps a person answer the question, "What do I want?" and keeps the focus on positive actions. Through collaboration, a home visitor can help clients clarify or sort through goals as necessary. Goals come from a person's own needs and desires, not from a theory or from the values of a home visitor. In some problem-solving models, goal selection is a part of the problem identification phase. We have always described it as a separate process because it is fundamental to the purpose of the helping relationship.

We have found that even when people can describe what is troubling them, many still have difficulty stating just what it is that they would like to have happen in a situation. It is essential to have clients state what they want. Emphasizing the essential aspect of goal selection by identifying it as a distinct process helps assure that one does not skip over this process, going from a problem situation to resolution, without having a person or family members say what they really want.

A new mother may say that she is tired all the time because her baby is fretful throughout the night, keeping the mother awake. When talking with the new mother, a home visitor might find that at first the mother says that she wants the baby to sleep through the night, but then says she wants to feel more rested during the day. The home visitor could then talk with the mother about ways the mother may be able to get more rest herself. If she is home during the day, she may be able to sleep in the afternoon when the baby is napping, or she may be able to arrange for another family member to get up with the baby during the night so that she could get more sleep.

To change a problem to a goal, one can ask clients to think of what a problem will look like when it is resolved. A home visitor can also ask each member of the family what he or she would want to see happen. Prompts such as this make it easier for many clients to begin to focus on their wishes.

Generating Solutions

A person typically has a better chance of finding effective solutions to a problem if he or she thinks of more than one way of handling a situation. A second or third choice may be better than the first; later choices may cost less, be more effective, or require less work. They may also be more acceptable to the person. A person may find that combining more than one alternative to deal with a situation can lead to a better outcome.

One should be careful, however, not to persist in generating alternatives beyond the point of productivity. Thinking of six or eight alternatives would be confusing for many people. Also, it is important to remember that all the good solutions may not come to mind at one time. A parent may need time to talk with others, think on his or her own, or gather new information to come up with solutions. At times, a home visitor will find it appropriate to offer suggestions. A home visitor can encourage a client to think of solutions that have been helpful in the past and explore their possible use now. Are the circumstances sufficiently similar that it makes sense to try this solution now? On the other hand, many people experience difficulty in resolving current issues because they remain with old behavior patterns that do not work in the present. In these situations, different ways of responding are essential for clients to reach their goals.

Considering Consequences

Considering consequences focuses attention on answering the question, "What will happen if . . . ?" Many important reasons exist for considering the consequences of what one does before taking action. Thinking ahead about what might happen can allow a person to decide whether these are consequences he or she is willing to live with. Just thinking about the consequences can help a person decide whether to go ahead and accept the consequences or determine how to minimize any negative consequences.

A home visitor can help in this process by encouraging a person to think about how much time, money, and energy is involved; how the solution will affect the person; and how the solution will affect other people. A home visitor can encourage a client to think of short-term and long-term consequences and to evaluate the positive and negative features of different actions. Talking with a father, a home visitor may find that he does not want to suggest a possible solution because he might not be successful. Yet when the father talks about the situation, he may be more inclined to go ahead, deciding that he is willing to deal with possible negative aspects. Although one does not need to consider the possible consequences of each action, it is important to consider serious consequences of any action.

Decision Making

To answer the question, "What is my decision?" home visitors can help people weigh the consequences of different actions and determine resources that are available. They can also encourage family members to consider their values and priorities and determine which alternatives best fit their needs. A home visitor can help a person think about what is best for him or her in a particular situation.

Many individuals can think through a difficult situation, consider consequences, and discuss the pros and cons of different actions, but they may then have difficulty actually making a decision. They may be so concerned with some of the possible negative consequences that they avoid them by not making a decision. They may let others make important decisions for them. Through discussion, home visitors can help individuals see how important it is to make their own decisions and discuss the consequences of leaving things to chance.

As part of decision making, a person can evaluate each possible solution and decide whether it is one he or she would like to try. If a client has more than one yes, he or she can consider combining solutions.

Implementation

For some people, figuring out the best thing to do is not the difficult part of resolving a problem. Rather, they have trouble taking action to carry out their plan. Home visitors can help their clients see the advantages in taking care of difficult situations. People can reduce the likelihood that some situations will become worse by taking action early. They can increase the time to attend to other things by taking care of the problem situations. Home visitors can help by encouraging a person to arrange for the necessary resources and procedures to carry out a plan and can support the person as he or she takes action.

Evaluation

Once a person has taken some action to address a concern or reach a goal, it is important to evaluate how satisfied he or she is with the outcome. Carrying out an action without evaluation does not allow one to learn from the occasion or see the need to try something else. To learn from our experiences, we must evaluate our actions. Unless we can gain knowledge of whether we were successful, we remain in the dark about our effectiveness. Finding out what does not work enables an individual to move on to other possible actions.

When a person tries to deal with a difficult situation and accomplishes a goal, that person needs to be able to feel proud of doing so. If it is a situation a client has struggled with, a home visitor can offer encouragement and praise. Even small successes need to be acknowledged. Sometimes the effort itself needs strong acknowledgement, especially if no solutions were found.

Strengths and Barriers to Problem Solving

Each person and each family system have both strengths and limitations related to problem solving. Strengths include emotional well-being, strong communication skills, strong marital relationships, social supports, knowledge about parenting and parenting skills, motivation, and good health. Barriers to effective coping are also numerous and vary considerably from person to person (Wasik, 1984). These barriers can fall under any of the following categories: cognitive, cultural, educational, emotional, informational, social, language, communication, physical, or environmental. Examples of barriers include an inability to read or write, lack of basic health care information to respond appropriately to a sick child, or depression so severe that a parent cannot act in his or her own best interest. Some barriers may be more complex and stressful than others, such as low educational levels, unsafe neighborhoods, or chronic illnesses.

In general, one would begin talking with families about less complex and less emotional situations in the earlier home visits, moving to more complex, more emotionally laden situations after families have some success with the problem-solving process. Over time, a helper can prompt families to take on more responsibility during discussions and to practice at home (Foster & Robin, 1998). In this way, a home visitor helps to move family members toward more independence and toward using these skills as part of their lives after home visiting ends.

Implications for Home Visitors

For a home visitor to implement a problem-solving approach, several conditions are important. First, a home visitor must recognize problem solving and problem management as important procedures for coping effectively with day-to-day difficulties. This recommendation addresses a home visitor's own orientation toward life events. It is not easy to use or teach something that one does not accept or believe in, and problem solving is no exception. A home visitor's problem-solving skills influence his or her ability to help families. If a home visitor believes that no matter what one does in life, some people will always have things work out poorly for them, he or she may be disinclined to promote effective problem solving.

Second, a home visitor must be knowledgeable about the problem-solving process. The more familiar a home visitor is with a problem-solving model, the more likely it is that he or she will understand a client's problem-solving strengths and limitations. We believe that knowledge of problem solving helps a home visitor become adept at recognizing when a client might be having difficulty reaching a goal.

Third, home visitors must be able to use a problem-solving approach in their own professional and personal lives. Experiences in doing so can be gained during training and supervision. Working with other home visitors in a group setting is also a good way to become more sensitive to and improve one's own problem-solving skills.

Fourth, a home visitor must be knowledgeable about individual and family strengths and barriers to problem solving. He or she needs to be able to help others build their strengths, looking for ways these strengths can be used to address current family concerns. Visitors also need to recognize barriers to effective coping and be able to use this information to help others better understand how to address difficult situations.

With the above as background, a home visitor can use problem solving as a way to guide planning with families. He or she can also go beyond helping family members address current situations to helping them understand how they can apply what they are learning in the present to future situations. Many parents are very responsive to learning the problem-solving process as a way of addressing both personal and parenting concerns.

Summary

In this chapter, we have discussed the following four sets of characteristics and skills important for home visitors: (a) helping characteristics (e.g., empathy, warmth, genuineness), (b) basic helping skills (e.g., observation, listening, questioning, prompting and probing), (c) techniques of modeling (e.g., role playing, use of examples, homework), and (d) behavior change procedures. We described problem solving as a framework for guiding home visiting. This approach is consistent with the goals of the helping process and compatible with the philosophy of most home visiting programs. Problem solving can be a strategy for focusing home visits and can serve as a guide for the home visitor. The important skills and techniques summarized in this chapter cannot be learned solely through written materials. Home visitor training should also incorporate extensive and appropriate practice and supervision.

6

Managing and Maintaining Home Visits

Successful home visiting takes planning, persistence, patience, and skill in getting along with people. It also requires a home visitor to have a thorough understanding of the objectives and materials used by his or her individual program. In this chapter, we will first discuss some of the practical aspects of home visiting, including scheduling and timing, materials, safety, special circumstances, and confidentiality. We will then focus on the following three stages of home visiting: the initial home visit, ongoing home visits, and final visits. Salient issues involved in these three stages will be explored as well as practical suggestions and philosophical approaches. Home visiting is a complex profession involving changing dynamics and requiring multiple skills. We have selected for discussion those skills that are fundamental to the management and maintenance of home visits over time.

Managing Home Visits

Scheduling and Timing

The scheduling of home visits is an essential part of a home visitor's work. Factors to be taken into account when scheduling visits include the purpose of the visit and its urgency, the planned content of the visit, the location of the family's home, the ease or difficulty in contacting and assisting the family, and the anticipated duration of the visit. Setting a schedule for visits is often convenient for home visitors and their clients. Home visitors will probably find that scheduling on a weekly or biweekly basis provides sufficient lead time for their planning and for families. Frequency of visits, however, will depend on the goals of the program, needs of clients, and responsibilities of the home visitors. When scheduling visits, home visitors need to allow time for other responsibilities, such as parent group meetings, supervision, community liaison and advocacy work, documentation of services provided, and other record-keeping tasks (Wolfe & Herwig, 1986).

Scheduling home visits requires flexibility. Well-made plans can be interrupted due to factors beyond the control of either the family or the home visitor. Home visitors need to build enough space into their schedules to adapt to changing situations and remain flexible enough to handle these changes without undue stress. A useful approach is to plan carefully but anticipate that events may interfere with one's plans and necessitate rescheduling.

Sufficient travel time should be built into a home visitor's schedule. It is helpful to make a trial run to a client's home prior to the first home visit to ascertain the time needed to get there and the most efficient route to take. Making this practice run will help assure a timely arrival for the first home visit. It will also help to orient the home visitor to his or her client's neighborhood, which can be very useful in preparing the home visitor for the circumstances in which he or she will be working (Berg & Helgeson, 1984). This procedure is also an important step in assuring the visitor's personal safety, a topic discussed later in this chapter.

Sometimes the time and distance between clients' homes will be the major consideration in scheduling visits. In fact, home visiting programs that cover large catchment areas will sometimes assign home visitors to families based on geographic location to reduce excessive travel time. (At times, other considerations in matching visitors and families will take precedence over travel time.) Allowing enough time between visits ensures that a delay in finishing one visit will not cause delays of subsequent visits the same day.

Many programs require that each visit be documented before beginning the next visit. This procedure is a good practice, although the time and place for accomplishing this task must be taken into account when setting the daily schedule. Many home visitors, looking for suitable places to complete their documentation, become regulars at coffee shops, libraries, and other convenient spots located between their clients' homes. Many reports are often completed in the home visitor's car. (Be sure the car is not in traffic; one of us once had a major accident while driving and jotting notes about a just-completed visit!)

Another aspect of timing is becoming knowledgeable about local traffic—the pattern and duration of rush hours, construction delays, bridge openings and closings, one-way streets, and other situations that have a bearing on travel time. For home visitors who work in congested urban areas, planning visits according to traffic patterns may become the deciding factor in arranging schedules. Keeping a current city or county map at hand is important because even home visitors who are working in familiar surroundings may not know alternative routes when changes are necessary.

In addition to environmental considerations, the timing of home visits should also reflect the needs of home visitors and their clients. For example, home visitors should be aware of their own energy levels at specific times of the day and try to maximize visits during their more productive hours. Home visitors may also want to consider the optimal time for scheduling visits with their most difficult clients. Some visitors may want to alternate between visiting clients who require more energy and time and clients who require less. Other home visitors may prefer to schedule all of their most challenging clients during one part of the week. We know visitors who choose to schedule all their most difficult clients early in the week when they feel they have the most energy. Others try to schedule these clients first in each day, seeing their easier clients later in the day. Scheduling is a highly individual matter. Home visitors need to aware of their own preferences and needs so that they can arrange their schedules to maximize their effectiveness and promote their own well-being. Handling a difficult caseload on a very inconvenient schedule can contribute to burnout. In addition, an exhausted home visitor will not be in optimal condition to provide the quality of services that his or her clients deserve.

Families, like home visitors, have preferences for visit times, and their preference will likely be a key factor in scheduling. Family members will vary widely in their life circumstances. Some will have predictable schedules and home lives that will easily accommodate regularly scheduled home visits. Others will have less organized lives, some even chaotic, so regularly scheduled visits may not be possible. Learning clients' preferences, habits, and lifestyles very early in the home visiting program will help the home visitor plan visits accordingly.

Because home visits take place in a client's personal living space, a home visitor should show respect for his or her client's privacy by accommodating family needs as much as possible. For example, some clients may not want visits scheduled near meal times. Some mothers may not want visits when children are napping; others may specifically prefer the visit while their children are asleep. The dedication of some family members to specific television programs, particularly afternoon soap operas, is another variable worth considering when scheduling home visits. It is wise not to interrupt these or other favorite activities. Visitors who arrive at these times may be welcomed to come inside, but they may be expected to wait until the end of a television program before beginning visit activities or discussion. On the other hand, some home visitors have found that briefly watching certain television programs with their clients prior to engaging in program activities provided a useful common ground for building rapport, particularly with clients who did not interact easily. In some homes, the television may always be on and the home visitor may ask if it is okay to turn down the volume or turn off the television during the visit. What to say and how to say it depends on a home visitor's knowledge of a family and the visitor's relationship with them.

For parents who work, scheduling an optimal time for a home visit becomes more complicated. After a day's work, both the parent and home visitor may be tired, and each may be feeling the pressures of impending evening activities. Neither parent nor home visitor may want the home visits in the evening. If this situation occurs, other acceptable options might be arranged, such as weekend visits or lunch time visits at the parent's workplace. Across the eight IHDP sites, 10% to 25% of home visits took place after 5:00 p.m. Most home visitors found this proportion to be manageable, both for themselves and for parents.

It is necessary for home visitors to find a reasonable balance between achieving specific program goals on every visit and responding to their client's immediate needs. Even after a home visitor and client have arranged a good schedule, the planned purpose of the visit may not be accomplished. On some days, a client may simply not be able to benefit from the planned purpose of the visit. The client may be concerned with the threat of eviction, loss of employment, or a child's illness. Under such circumstances, a home visitor should attend to a client's concerns and discuss possible solutions to the situation. The home visitor may need to help the client access other service agencies; he or she may need to listen to the client's problems and offer emotional support. In some situations, the visitor may need to take direct action, as in contacting other resources, or the visitor may need to encourage active problem solving. Trying to impose a home visitor's purposes on a client who is clearly not receptive may jeopardize the continuation of the relationship. As one home visitor phrased it, "Flexibility is the key. That was what kept me sane, remembering that nothing was cast in stone, and that I could really trust my instincts."

Materials

Being well prepared for a home visit enables home visitors to optimize their time with their clients. In programs focused on parenting and child development, a number of curriculum materials may be used during the home visits. Having all materials prepared ahead of time allows the home visitor to concentrate on planned activities. Materials may include activity cards, pamphlets, toys, and books; items that the visitor makes; and written materials such as recording forms, evaluation measures, or referral forms. Any form that requires prior completion or materials that need to be organized should be fully prepared before the home visit. Sometimes planning for the visit can take as long as the actual visit, especially if materials must be gathered or made. For some families, it is a good idea to bring copies of materials used during the most recent visit in case the materials have been misplaced or damaged.

Materials should be organized so that they can be located and used easily. Because home visitors may use many different sets of materials for several clients when traveling from home to home, and must keep other forms or materials organized at their agency office as well, the need to maintain an adequate organizational system is clear. Devising an organizational system suitable to the requirements of the program, the home visitor's preferences, and the protection of materials is a practical and important aspect of home visiting. Neglecting this task can result in loss of time, missed opportunities for effective visits, and considerable frustration for home visitors. We have seen visitors keep a cardboard file box in the car trunk for case-by-case storage of recent and current paperwork. They then transfer older materials to the main office files and add new materials for upcoming visits to their current file box.

Special precautions should be established to protect confidential materials from being lost, damaged, or inadvertently combined with other materials. A separate container or secured system for confidential materials must be maintained both en route to and during home visits as well as in the home office. A small, portable, metal file box that can be locked is very useful for this purpose.

Children in the Home Visit

Family systems theory helps visitors of families with children remember that all members of the family will be affected by factors that directly affect one member. The birth of a child with disabilities, for example, could profoundly influence the parents' interactions with their older children and with each other. The diagnosis of a condition such as autism or cancer will bring about major changes in family needs, interactions, and schedules. The siblings of sick children need opportunities to talk about their feelings and have their questions answered. Home visitors must be sensitive to the dynamics of the entire family and incorporate their needs into the home visits. Because of the diversity and complexity of family needs, decisions about when to involve children in home visits require attention.

In family support home visiting programs, children will often be the focal point. For many of these programs, home visits are initiated because of the needs of one child. Even when the home visit program is targeted to one child, additional children may often be present. If so, home visitors may have to consider these children's needs as well. Home visitors should involve a parent when devising a basic strategy for dealing with children during visits. This plan might include special activities for young children to occupy their attention such as coloring materials or games. Involving all children in the visit activities can also be a strategy, depending on the goals of the visit and the age of the children.

Home visitors have used a variety of approaches with young children during home visits. For example, they have agreed with children on a specific time period during which the children will occupy themselves, either with their own activities or those brought by the home visitor, while the home visitor had time with the adult. They have given children a timer and rewarded them for entertaining themselves for an agreed period of time. In especially difficult situations, another home visitor has accompanied the regular home visitor and kept the children occupied during the visit. Other supportive family members can also be called on to help.

Handling Special Circumstances

Although most home visits occur in a smooth, orderly fashion, home visitors should be prepared for those that do not. Blaring televisions, children's friends, and curious neighbors may all be part of the home milieu. Home visitors have worked with parents to find creative ways of handling diverse situations, such as meeting on the front stoop or at a restaurant or having an older sibling agree to entertain the younger children. If distractions and chaos persist over a long period of time, the home visitor and the family need to discuss these impediments to the home visiting program and find a reasonable method for resolving them.

Frequent mobility of clients is another reality of home visiting. If a family's move is planned and the home visitor is aware of it, the visitor she may only have to adjust the visiting schedule. However, some families move suddenly and without notifying the home visitor. At the beginning of the home visiting program, visitors may want to obtain from the family the name, address, and telephone number of a relative or neighbor who will always know where the family is living and can serve as a contact person. Frequently updating this contact information and maintaining a tracking plan can save home visitors many frustrating hours.

Safety

Knowing how to maintain personal safety is essential for home visitors. Home visitors will not be effective if they are anxious or fearful. Part of their responsibility is to create a comfortable and emotionally safe setting in which the visit can take place. If they are uncomfortable, they will not be able to create a comfortable atmosphere for others. In addition, they may be placing themselves at risk. To ensure the safest conditions for home visiting, we recommend that home visitors follow guidelines to protect themselves. Because home visitors work in diverse settings in all areas of the country—rural, isolated areas; urban settings; suburban areas—and because the populations that home visitors serve are diverse, safety concerns will vary in and across programs. However, several basic safety guidelines are applicable to all home visitors.

The first, and perhaps most important, safety guideline is that home visitors should use common sense and follow their instincts. If a home visitor feels unsafe, he or she probably is, and the visitor should take whatever action is necessary for self protection. Sometimes home visitors feel guilty about being suspicious of their clients' friends or feeling uneasy in their clients' neighborhoods, and this may lead them to ignore their personal sense of feeling threatened. Ignoring their own emotional reactions, however, puts them at risk and is not advisable. On the other hand, if the home visitor is merely unfamiliar with the client's setting or is visiting in a cultural milieu much different from his or her own, the source of the uneasiness should be examined before concluding that one is unsafe. A home visitor needs to be familiar with the neighborhoods and families being visited to be better able to discern real danger.

The second safety guideline is that home visitors should always make certain that their supervisor or other responsible staff members know their visit schedules. This schedule should include the name of the individual or family, the date and time of the visit, and the expected time of return. If home visiting is taking place in particularly dangerous environments, programs may devise a monitoring system such as having the home visitor call in when a visit is complete.

We strongly recommend that all home visitors be provided with cellular phones. These phones afford an immediate means of communication for both emergency and program needs. Mobile phones are too reasonably priced for cost to serve as a barrier to their use by programs, and the security they provide outweighs the financial considerations.

A third guideline for safe home visits is to know the neighborhoods where home visits take place. As home visitors become familiar to the people who live in the neighborhood, their sense of safety will increase. Learning the layout of the immediate area surrounding each client's home and the usual types of activities that occur there will provide the home visitor a baseline for judging unusual circumstances. Obtaining maps of the home visiting areas and knowing how to find information in them quickly is an important preparation for home visiting. Some police departments will provide advice about safety concerns in the neighborhoods of a program's service area.

A fourth guideline is to avoid dangerous neighborhoods at night. If this is impossible, arrangements should be made for an escort. One program with limited resources hired an escort who was available during specific late afternoon and early evening hours. Home visitors could then schedule certain visits when the escort could accompany them. Another option in this situation is to ask a client to meet the visitor at a previously agreed on location and time to accompany the home visitor into the home. Two visitors going together for a visit is also a frequently used procedure during the evening hours.

The fifth safety guideline is to learn the safest route to and from the client's home. If the most direct route is not on the most well-lighted or patrolled streets, the choice should always be safety first. Parking in clients' neighborhoods may also present safety problems. The only available parking may be at a distance from the client's home or in an area where vandalism is likely to occur. If safe parking cannot be arranged, home visitors need to consider other alternatives. One program hired a driver who took visitors to the homes of families where parking was a safety problem and then picked them up when the visit was over. Another home visiting program serving a high-risk urban community hired a full-time driver who escorted home visitors to all of their visits. Visiting in other settings is also an option that can be considered.

Other safety factors are related to the automobiles that most home visitors use for their work. Maintaining an automobile in good condition is clearly a necessary safety precaution for home visitors who must travel long distances and for visitors who must travel through potentially dangerous neighborhoods. Simple safety measures include having enough gasoline, keeping the car doors locked at all times, and parking in lighted areas. Because program materials, including confidential ones, may be kept in automobiles, it is imperative that they are secured against theft as much as possible. One program bought steering wheel locking devices for visitors to use when needed.

The security of personal possessions also should be considered when home visiting. Home visitors should limit carrying or wearing valuable possessions at work. Carrying more money than is necessary to get through the day is usually inadvisable. Accessories such as expensive purses and jewelry are generally not appropriate for home visiting. Although it is a rare event, the theft of money or other items from home visitors has occurred, and a great deal of effort was necessary to overcome the ill feelings that ensued. It is desirable to prevent such incidents from happening rather than to deal with them once they have occurred.

If a home visitor feels frightened during a visit, he or she should assess the gravity of the immediate situation and leave if the situation is perceived as dangerous. Circumstances that may require this response include violence in the home, drug use and drug dealing, evidence of firearms, or the presence of acutely intoxicated or otherwise out-of-control individuals. If the home visitor is encountering any of these circumstances during visits, there should be discussions with supervisory staff and explorations of alternatives for ensuring safety. In some circumstances, home visits may be discontinued or changed to a site safer than the client's home.

Another precaution is related to the presence of illness in the home. If the home visitor discovers that a family member has a contagious disease, he or she should exercise judgment about becoming exposed to this illness. When confronted by potentially serious communicable illness such as influenza or tuberculosis, home visitors should seek medical consultation about the advisability of visiting in the home. Home visitors will sometimes need to reschedule a visit due to illness in the client's family. Learning universal health precautions and having health safety materials available also helps to reduce health risks for the visitor (U.S. DHHS, 1993).

Many home visitors have questions about the presence of animals in or around the homes they visit. Several procedures may be helpful. The visitor can ask in advance whether animals will be present. One can also request the family's help in managing the animal so that the visit can be conducted. If a pet has caused a problem on one visit, insist that the animal be closed in another room during the next visit. In the past, when confronted by a threatening animal that the family could not restrain, home visitors have told the family that they would return to visit at a later time.

Sometimes visitors face situations that are uncomfortable because of their gender. A female home visitor may face a male client acting in a seductive manner. A male home visitor may encounter a woman client inappropriately dressed for a visit. In general, these are situations that need to be addressed immediately through direct discussion, if the visitor judges this the appropriate action, or the visitor may leave the home, saying that he or she will return at a more convenient time. The visit could be rescheduled at a later time. Future visits to such a home might need to be made by a team of two visitors.

In this section, we have summarized several issues relating to safety that should be addressed in any home visiting program. The basic guidelines underlying our suggestions about safety are that home visitors should use common sense and trust their own judgments, try to prevent dangerous situations from developing, and keep supervisory staff aware of the conditions under which they are visiting. At the end of any visit that has raised issues of personal safety, the visitor needs to make note of the circumstances and discuss the situation with a supervisor or colleague to obtain advice and other perspectives.

Dress

Each community and client population has its own standards of dress, and the home visitor should be sensitive to these standards during work hours. Remembering that how they dress can influence their relationship with their clients will help home visitors avoid looking overdressed or wearing clothing that is obviously costly. Clothing should be professional, although the degree of formality can vary. Dressing appropriately for the activities planned for a specific visit is a useful guideline. For example, if the visit requires home visitors to play on the floor with children or conduct physical therapy, clothing should be appropriate for these activities. Home visitors who are nurses or other health professionals may wear uniforms as part of their work.

Maintaining Contact

It is important to establish reliable methods of communication to facilitate scheduling and maintaining home visits. Home visitors must make sure that their clients know how to reach them and that they know how to reach their clients. Such communication is facilitated if a client has a home telephone, but some clients will not. For these families, a home visitor will need to devise another method for contacting the family. This may involve the use of neighbors' telephones or a system of leaving notes at the client's home. One home visitor, after many failures, found that supplying her client with addressed, stamped envelopes and stationery to inform her of cancelled visits or unanticipated moves was an effective method to stay in touch. If agency policy allows, it may be appropriate in some situations for the home visitor to give his or her clients home telephone number. Because this practice might lead to more frequent contact than is appropriate, home visitors need to consider their own limits and discuss this practice with their supervisors.

Confidentiality

Home visiting offers professional services to families on a potentially more personal level than other service delivery systems and, consequently, maintaining appropriate confidentiality is critical. The initial goal home visitors must achieve to be successful in their work is to gain the trust of their families. Conveying to a client that the information the home visitor learns about the client and his or her family will be kept confidential is a part of this process.

Every program will have its particular policies and procedures to ensure confidentiality. These policies and procedures will depend on the nature and purpose of the program. However, some guidelines will help describe the general extent and nature of the confidentiality that home visitors are expected to keep. Home visitors should not discuss clients by name unless they are doing so with their supervisor or in a conference with other professionals who have some responsibility for this family. They should always make certain that the setting in which they discuss clients is appropriately private, and they should never discuss clients in public places.

If home visitors are engaged in helping to link one of their families with other community services, they must obtain the family's permission to do so beforehand. If a family has given permission for a home visitor to share confidential information with specific agencies or individuals, a home visitor should limit the information to what is essential for the specific situation involved. Issues concerning confidentiality are among the most difficult dilemmas with which home visitors contend, and they will be further discussed in Chapter 8 as part of professional ethics.

Stages of Home Visiting

The First Home Visit

The first home visit is the beginning of what may become a long-term relationship between a home visitor and a client. This relationship may extend over a period of months or years or for a relatively brief duration. Whether of short-term or long-term duration, this relationship is the heart of the home visiting process. The first home visit requires special attention because it is the first step in establishing a working relationship between home visitor and client (Berg & Helgeson, 1984). The home visitor needs to engage the client and begin to establish the rapport that is crucial to the home visitor's continued presence in the home.

The first home visit should be focused and relaxed. It should also cover the six objectives essential to a first visit. These include (a) establishing rapport and a good working relationship, (b) becoming acquainted, (c) reviewing program purposes and goals, (d) defining the home visitor's role and the client's role, (e) clarifying client's expectations, and (f) scheduling the next visit. Although we discuss these objectives sequentially, some (e.g., establishing rapport) are an ongoing process.

Establishing rapport between the home visitor and client is a process that will develop over the course of home visiting. A home visitor can enhance the development of rapport by expressing sincere interest in a client's needs and conveying a willingness to help. With some clients, the development of rapport can be achieved quickly; with others, it may take considerably more time and effort, depending partly on the purposes of the program, the personality of the home visitor, and the personality and life experiences of the client. The development of a trusting relationship will not be consistently progressive. Gains made one week in developing trust can be lost the next week if events have intervened in the meantime that threaten the trust. These factors may or may not relate to the home visitor per se, but they may be events in a client's life that could lead him or her to feel suspicious of others' motives. For example, if a mother has been visited by a caseworker from a children's protective services agency for suspected neglect of her children, even though the home visitor's role has nothing to do with her children, the client may still generalize her anxiety, distrust, and fear to the home visitor.

In this first visit, as well as in later ones, home visitors should be sensitive to the privacy of the family and not ask intrusive questions that violate that privacy. During the first visit, a client may be eager to share information with the home visitor, but most likely he or she will not. Should a client choose to talk about very personal matters, a home visitor can listen and respond supportively. At the end of this visit, a home visitor may assure the client about confidentiality.

Becoming acquainted with a client is a specific objective of this first visit. This can consist of several simple exchanges between home visitor and client, including information or conversations that would be normal for any first dialogue between two people. Conversational talk about everyday happenings is appropriate here. This brief social interchange is an important part of establishing a helping relationship, especially in terms of allowing a client to see home visitors as the persons they are (Leahy et al., 1982). Another way in which home visitors can facilitate getting acquainted is to share their own enthusiasm about the home visiting program. This sharing often has the effect of inspiring more interest in the program for a client.

Reviewing the purpose of the home visiting program and the nature of the activities that will be completed to carry out the program is another major objective of this first visit. For this and for subsequent home visits, a focus on program goals is important in structuring visits in a purposeful way (Wolfe & Herwig, 1986). In the time between a client's agreement to participate and the first home visit, he or she may have forgotten the specific details of the program. Reminding a client about these details and about program benefits may also help to stimulate enthusiasm and interest.

Home visitors need to explain thier own role clearly; responsibilities and any limitations to their role should be defined (U.S. DHHS, 1993). Knowing the limits and structure of the relationship can be reassuring to families and can help foster a productive working relationship. This clarification of a home visitor's role may be necessary throughout the course of the home visiting program. Some home visiting programs have narrowly defined roles for home visitors; other programs may permit or encourage home visitors to be flexible and independent in creating their own role boundaries. In either case, clarifying a home visitor's responsibilities will help increase a family's understanding about what to expect.

The role of the client in the program should also be clarified. Enlisting the client as a partner in the home visiting venture rather than as a consumer will establish from the beginning that this is a collaborative relationship to which the client will be making important contributions (Wolfe & Herwig, 1986). The most important contributions of the client are availability and commitment.

What the client expects from the program should also be explored during this first visit. Sometimes clients' expectations are not realistic; perhaps they misunderstood the program content or were misinformed. Finding out exactly what the client expects and correcting any misperceptions during this first visit can help eliminate barriers to a productive working relationship.

The final component of this first visit is the scheduling of the next home visit. Encouraging the individual to choose a time that is convenient for the next visit will increase the chances that the visit will take place. The first home visit with a client may last 30 to 45 minutes, depending on program content. As soon as the home visitor believes that the visit has accomplished its purpose, he or she should begin to finish the visit. If the visitor judges that the client needs more time, the home visitor may extend the visit briefly to bring appropriate closure and indicate that the discussion can continue at the next visit. Leaving a client feeling comfortable and looking forward to the next visit is a primary goal of this first visit. If the home visitor accomplishes this, he or she should consider the first visit to be successful.

Ongoing Home Visits

Home visiting can be envisioned as a process in which a home visitor and client accept and respect one another, work together to achieve family or individual goals, and bring closure to and then end their relationship. The following five aspects of this process are particularly important: (a) focusing on the family's needs, (b) client self-determination, (c) supporting the independence of the family, (d) client motivation, and (e) the dynamics of the home visitor–family relationship. The rest of this chapter focuses on these aspects.

Recognizing that the home visiting program exists for the benefit of the client rather than for the benefit of the home visitor is crucial for developing a successful relationship. Home visitors engage in their work for professional reasons, and the experience will often produce personal feelings of satisfaction and pleasure. In the course of home visiting, home visitors will experience times when their self-esteem is heightened, their skills are improved, they gain insight, or they experience pleasure at the successes of their families. However, these outcomes emerge as a result of serving the client rather than being directly sought by the home visitor.

Sometimes focusing on the client is difficult, as when the home visitor may want to pursue some action that would be personally beneficial but that would not particularly benefit the client. A home visitor may be tempted to schedule a visit with a client at 4:00 p.m. so that he or she could end the work day by 5:00 p.m., but meeting at 4:00 p.m. would require the parent to leave work early and lose pay. Or, conversely, something that the client wants to do may be inconvenient for the home visitor or be at odds with the home visitor's beliefs. For example, one client once insisted on remaining with her drug-dealing boyfriend in a high-crime area instead of with her mother in a low-crime neighborhood because he was kinder to her than was her mother. The home visitor would have preferred to visit in a safer neighborhood but recognized that her client fared better with her boyfriend than she did with her mother.

The home visitor will need to continually evaluate client needs and her own. Unreasonable client requests clearly do not have to be accommodated, and reasonable adjustments on the part of the client can be appropriately requested.

Related to this focus on the client is a client's right to self-determination. Accepting a client as a valuable individual in his or her own right is widely considered to be the underlying basis for developing a helping relationship (Hollis & Wood, 1981). The home visitor's role is to encourage and sustain a client as he or she makes personal decisions. This facilitator role can be hard to maintain sometimes, especially when a home visitor recognizes a client's actions as self-destructive or futile, such as an unwillingness to leave a dangerously abusive relationship. Encouraging and enabling clients to make their own decisions increases their sense of competence and control over their lives. People learn by experience, and, unless a client has the opportunity to make his or her own decisions and try out plans (good or bad), a client will not develop new competencies. As one home visitor supervisor (who had previously been a home visitor) stated, "by supporting clients, providing them access to community resources and by continuing to help them improve upon their skills, clients become increasingly able to make appropriate [that is, better] decisions and to change destructive life patterns."

It is also helpful for a home visitor to remember to differentiate between personal values and a client's values and life goals, continually aware of the fact that the visitor's goal is to help clients reach their own objectives. Indeed, those in the helping professions are believed to be most effective when encouraging their clients' self-exploration and self-direction in the course of the helping process (Carkhuff, 1984). The home visitor also needs to frequently examine his or her own purposes as a home visitor, sorting out personal needs from those of clients. This self-examination can be greatly enhanced by talking with a supervisor.

A third aspect of home visiting is the issue of dependence and independence. In most professional relationships between two people, a dependency can develop; sometimes this dependency is temporary and appropriate, and at other times it is counterproductive (Hollis & Wood, 1981). In times of stress and crisis, for example, clients may depend on home visitors to help them make decisions in ways that would not be necessary in less stressful times. If a home visitor is at a client's home when a child is injured seriously while playing and the mother becomes very distraught, the home visitor may take both mother and child to a clinic, whereas ordinarily the client would take her own child to the clinic. In one case, a deeply depressed client told her home visitor that she wanted to obtain professional counseling but needed help in finding an appropriate therapist and setting up an appointment. The home visitor responded by devoting the remainder of the visit to phoning and scheduling the first session for her client; under other circumstances, she would have provided resources and information and encouraged the client to initiate contact.

Although occasional dependency may be acceptable, home visitors should avoid fostering unnecessary dependency. Home visitors who allow or encourage clients to become unnecessarily dependent can harm rather than help their clients. One home visitor left a family party when a client called her and asked her for a ride. This request was not an emergency situation, and the home visitor did not place appropriate limits on her own role. For this client, learning to find her own resources for transportation would have been more valuable than depending on her home visitor for transportation. During an ongoing home visiting relationship, the type and amount of dependence will vary, with the ultimate goal being for a client to function independently of the home visitor. Keeping this goal in mind helps home visitors judge what is acceptable dependent behavior and what is not. In making such a judgment, the following question might be asked: Whose needs are being met in the situation?

Another important aspect of home visiting is client motivation. Clients may not seem motivated to comply with a home visiting program's expectations or to work toward other life goals that the home visitor believes are important. Sometimes this behavior may seem like resistance or obstructionism. Whenever the home visitor is concerned by a seeming lack of motivation on the part of his or her client, the visitor can self-query, "Are these goals that my client wants to achieve or are they mine or the program's?" If they are not the client's goals, the home visitor can ask, "Why not?" Perhaps they are not culturally acceptable or personally meaningful to the client (Pedersen, 1981). If so, the home visitor needs to consider how the desired behavior will truly benefit the client. If in his or her judgment it will, the home visitor should try to find a way to present it to the client so that it is acceptable. If it does not appear to be of value to the client, the expectation should be dropped. Resistance is sometimes a message from a client that the process is moving too quickly to be comfortable or in directions a family may find unacceptable. At other times, resistance may be the client's way of not accepting responsibility for his or her actions.

When concerned about a client's lack of progress, a home visitor may ask the following, "What barriers may be preventing this person from moving forward?" Perhaps helping the client to problem solve to overcome or remove the barriers would enable the client to move toward the goal. Sometimes clients would like to pursue goals but are hampered by lack of resources. Home visitors can often help family members come up with new ideas for resources that may not have been considered before.

Home visitors have flexibility in how they respond to an apparent lack of motivation. If parents are not complying with the objectives of an involuntary program, such as one court ordered for child abusers, a home visitor's response will be influenced by program policy and legal procedures. If, however, the parents simply do not want to attend parent meetings that are part of a voluntary program, the home visitor can accept the parents' choice. The visitor may choose from time to time to tell the clients what topics are being addressed at the meetings while focusing closer attention on other aspects of the program to which the parents are more responsive.

The fifth important aspect of home visiting is the type of relationship home visitors have with their clients. As the home visitor–client relationship evolves, its quality and intensity may change. When strong positive feelings develop between the home visitor and a client, boundaries that define the relationship can become blurred. The professional relationship between the two individuals can begin to have the look of a personal friendship. Through his or her professional role of delivering services to a client, a home visitor may become truly fond of a client and deeply committed to helping the client. This positive regard, although important in developing a good working relationship, should not become confused with friendship.

There is a balance between a visitor's genuine concern for a client and maintaining professional distance that is difficult to define and more difficult to achieve. Maintaining this balance is important, however, for several reasons. The first reason is that a home visitor needs to remain objective and not overidentify with the client if the visitor is to be truly effective. The second reason is that a home visitor represents a specific area of expertise, and becoming personally too close can often diminish a visitor's role in the eyes of a client and thereby diminish what the client perceives as available expert help. A third reason not to become close friends is that a home visitor often serves as a role model for a client. There needs to be enough distance between client and home visitor that a client can see a home visitor objectively as a model to guide behavior.

Maintaining a professional rather than a personal relationship with a client serves as a protection for the home visitor. The circumstances of the client's life could become unbearable to a home visitor if he or she became too emotionally involved or assumed a level of personal responsibility for solving problems in a client's life. Focusing on understanding how a client may feel in his or her situation, rather than taking on the burdens of a client's life, will help a home visitor function professionally and effectively. When home visitors live in the community where their clients also live, they may know personally some of their clients. They may even be friends (e.g., when programs recruit mothers to visit other mothers in the community). In these situations, program supervisors have a responsibility to help visitors understand their roles and the need for boundaries in the home visitor–client relationship. When a home visitor has questions about his or her own role, it may help the home visitor to see oneself as a mentor who cares about a client, empathizes with a client's difficulties, helps a client identify and use personal resources, and delights in the client's success.

A client can also experience difficulty in understanding the nature of the relationship. We have known clients who felt pressured to be friends with a home visitor. Home visitors should be alert to this situation and help alleviate any pressure clients might feel to befriend them. They also need to assess their own actions to be sure they are not conveying this expectation of their clients.

A final aspect of maintaining home visits we would like to emphasize here is the primacy of the client's well-being. Home visitors need to recognize that family members can experience a visit in their home as placing them in a vulnerable position. They may take a long time to overcome a sense of inequity between themselves and their home visitors. Clients can feel overwhelmed by the expectations of a program and see these expectations as demands that they cannot fulfill. Although we stress the importance of encouraging family members, engendering hope, and conveying the expectation that they have strengths to cope with their lives, these ideas must be expressed realistically in light of the family's existing strengths and limitations. It is vitally important not to increase feelings of inadequacy that a client may have; rather, one needs to promote a sense of well-being (Gray & Wandersman, 1980).

In this section, we have discussed several aspects of ongoing home visits. Our final section will address issues involved in the termination of home visiting services.

Bringing Closure

The successful termination of a helping relationship requires considerable skill on the part of the helper. Although some home visitor–client relationships may end unexpectedly or abruptly, most often one can plan for closure. This phase should be planned carefully to help a client learn how to sustain what has been gained during the course of home visiting.

There are three reasons for ending the visits: when a predetermined time period has passed (e.g., when an infant reaches the age of 1), when the goals of the home visiting program have been achieved, and when a person no longer wants to participate in a program, as indicated by a verbal request or by uncooperative actions such as repeatedly not keeping scheduled visits. The decision to terminate home visits under such circumstances is discussed in Chapter 8.

Regardless of the circumstances for termination, many feelings may develop for the home visitor and the client. Home visitors may feel relieved to discontinue visiting in difficult circumstances. With other families, home visitors may feel sad and experience feelings of loss. Sometimes visitors may take delight in their successes. Home visitors need to be aware of the emergence of different feelings and, if necessary, seek help in addressing them.

Clients' feelings may range from pride and satisfaction by the time they terminate home visiting to anger, sadness, or regret. Clients may show negative feelings through words or behavior, such as denial or withdrawal. The home visitor needs to be sensitive to the possible occurrence of such behavior, for example, when a client begins to cancel appointments or miss visits. One home visitor tried to schedule her final visit with a client who cancelled three times in a row. Finally, the home visitor told this client that she was running out of available times to see her and wanted to say goodbye in person. At that point, her client said she did not want to say goodbye and end the visits, so she had been trying to put off the inevitable by canceling scheduled visits.

Home visitors can prepare themselves and their clients for bringing closure by taking specific steps. The first step is for a home visitor to discuss impending termination with the client, identifying as specific a time as possible for it. The second step is to review with the client what has been accomplished during the course of home visits. The third step is to talk about the future, helping a person see how he or she can apply new skills in future situations. Helping a client design a strategy for attaining future goals is an excellent method of helping a client generalize what has been learned to new situations.

The results of one study of termination are heartening (Fortune, 1987). For the majority of clients and their helpers, termination was experienced as essentially positive. Clients focused on their accomplishments, expressed increased self-confidence, and were eager to try out new skills acquired during the helping relationship. The helpers in this study felt that they had accomplished much with their clients, which increased their own self-esteem, and they expressed renewed energy to work with future clients.

Reviewing the accomplishments of one's visits with a particular family is part of a home visitor's self-evaluation. Often, home visitors will be able to note definite accomplishments of their clients. Success, however, needs to be judged not only in terms of client behavior but also in terms of the home visitor's professional development. With most clients, a home visitor learns something of value—a new skill or improvement of an existing skill. Self-learning for the home visitor might also be expressed as "I never gave up; I learned that I can be persistent" or "I have learned a lot about a different culture."

The difficulty of termination is exacerbated if a home visitor has not maintained a professional relationship with his or her client. For a home visitor who has become overly involved, ending the visits will be a painful experience. The visitor may miss the relationship on a personal level, may be worried about the client's welfare, and may feel the loss very intensely. Although all terminations may involve some of these feelings, a home visitor who has maintained professional objectivity will be able to deal with these feelings more effectively than home visitors who have not.

It is advantageous for home visitors to approach closure as a transition rather than an ending. Although this may seem to be an insignificant conceptual difference, in fact, many home visitors feel that viewing the completion of the program as a transition from one set of circumstances to a new set is helpful for themselves and their clients. It helps engender the sense of a new beginning as well as a recognition of all that had been accomplished. Although we are discussing closure, it is important for home visitors to let their clients know that the door is open to future services if their circumstances change.

Participating in a helping relationship requires a certain amount of faith—in oneself, in those we help, and in the process (Combs & Avila, 1985). Home visitors sometimes may not see clear or immediate evidence that they have helped their clients to change behaviors or achieve objectives. What may be of highest value in a home visitor's work may not be fully realized for a long time after the visits are over. Home visitors may have helped clients gain more self-confidence, new skills, or a shift in their feelings or way of acting that will positively influence their lives in significant ways (Schectman, 1986). Recognizing that clients continue to grow and learn and that they can take what they have learned and use it in new circumstances helps home visitors move on to meeting new families and offering what they have to them.

Summary

In this chapter, we have focused on various aspects of the process of home visiting, including the practical details of everyday practice and the stages of the process itself, from initiating home visits to ending them. Although home visiting encompasses a wide array of complex issues, being aware of these and preparing to manage them can increase home visitors' skills, self-confidence, and satisfaction significantly. In the next chapter, we will address several specific situations that many home visitors will encounter in their day-to-day work.

7

Visiting Families in Stressful Situations

Many families participate in home visiting. Some are functioning well and benefit from home visiting services designed to meet one specific need. Other families may not be functioning well. Unusual stresses, poor psychological or physical health, inadequate coping skills, insufficient social support, or lack of adequate environmental resources can negatively influence family functioning. Home visiting programs for such families may need to provide more specialized or intensive services, and home visitors who serve these families will need specific skills and knowledge to work effectively with them.

In this chapter, we identify some of the serious family problems that home visitors may encounter, including child abuse and neglect, family violence, and substance abuse and drug dealing. In addition, because adolescent parents present specific challenges to home visitors, we include information on visiting teenage parents in this chapter. For each of these family situations, we present information relevant to home visiting and suggestions for working with such families. Before doing so, however, we caution home visitors to remember that the existence of a problem in a family does not mean that the family accepts it or is ready to address it. Indeed, enabling a client to recognize the existence of a problem and encouraging work on it may be a more formidable task than subsequently helping a client address the problem. Lest home visitors feel overwhelmed with the situations they encounter, it is critical that they accept the fact that all problems cannot or need not be addressed, by either visitors or their clients. Furthermore, home visitors need to recognize that clients' progress may often be slow and incremental.

Child Abuse and Neglect

Relevant Theory and Research

Professionals do not agree on how broadly to define abuse and neglect, so statutory definitions and investigation policies vary from state to state (Lung & Daro, 1996). The National Research Council (1993) recommended using four areas of child maltreatment—physical abuse, sexual abuse, physical neglect, and emotional maltreatment—to define abuse and neglect. Leading researchers have recommended that the categories be further defined as to whether the abuse is maltreatment or violence (Emery & Laumann-Billings, 1998), but to date no national surveys have gathered data on the incidence and prevalence of abuse and neglect at such a detailed level.

Since 1976, when the first nationwide survey of child maltreatment was initiated, the number of reported cases has steadily climbed. By 1995, 3,111,000 cases of child abuse and neglect were reported nationally compared with 669,000 in 1976 (Besharov, Laumann-Billings, 1996). The estimates, though, are highly affected by the sampling strategy. Three studies undertaken in the mid-1990s arrived at annual incidence figures ranging from 1 million to 4.3 million U.S. children, depending on whether Child Protective Service reports, professional reports, or population surveys of parents were used (Emery & Laumann-Billings, 1998). The highest number came from Gallup poll data that included parent self-reported incidents of maltreating behavior such as aggressive spanking, hitting their child with their fist or an object, or kicking or beating up their child. Regardless of which national study most reflects reality, child maltreatment is a disturbingly common phenomenon.

The Third National Incidence Study of Child Abuse and Neglect (NIS-3) (Sedlak & Broadhurst, 1996) provided estimates of the proportions of different types of maltreatment. Of the 1.5 million incidents of child maltreatment, 20% to 35% of the children suffered a serious, long-term physical, mental, or emotional injury (i.e., broken bones, third-degree burns, the consequences of forced sex). The remaining less severe cases of maltreatment included educational neglect when parents failed to get their children to school (25%); moderate physical abuse in which a punishment produced an observable bruise, pain, or emotional distress for up to 48 hours but did not require medical care (20%); emotional abuse such as chronic ridiculing or belittling the child (10%); moderate physical neglect such as providing inadequate housing or other poverty-related conditions (8%); and sexual touching or fondling (7%). The national surveys do not address comorbidity, but many children are affected by more than one type of maltreatment.

An ongoing debate focuses on whether the incidence and prevalence of abuse and neglect are increasing or whether improved and mandatory reporting procedures, at least for child abuse, are simply bringing more cases to public attention. In the National Incidence Studies, the reports of moderate cases of child abuse remained steady from 1986 to 1993, whereas the number of serious cases reported quadrupled (from 142,000 to 565,000) (Sedlak & Broadhurst, 1996). If increased awareness was causing increases in reporting, one would think that all levels of abuse would increase equally. Consequently, it appears that the incidence of serious abuse is increasing. Increased drug use, worsening poverty, greater violence, and disintegrating communities may be contributing to this rise (Garbarino, 1995). The social systems set up to address child maltreatment have been overwhelmed by the scope of the problem. Providing supportive interventions should be their role, but monitoring families is often the best they can do (Besharov & Laumann-Billings, 1996).

♦ *Predictors of Child Abuse*

No single factor or constellation of factors invariably leads to child abuse. However, we have increasing knowledge about the relationship between social, environmental, and psychological factors and child abuse. Some of these factors will be reviewed here. Child abuse is most often associated with poverty, yet not all persons living in poverty abuse their children (Garbarino & Kostelny, 1992). Abusive parents were often victims of child abuse, but not every parent who was abused as a child in turn abuses his or her own child (McCloskey, Figuerdo, & Koss, 1995). Conversely, some parents with high economic and educational levels, who appear to function adequately and to have ample resources and social support, abuse their children. Because there are no clear causative factors that determine whether child abuse will occur, we caution home visitors not to hold preconceived ideas that abuse will always be found in one situation and never in others. Nevertheless, certain patterns of behavior and circumstances are known to be associated with child abuse, and home visitors need to be vigilant when these conditions exist in families they visit.

Several family factors increase the likelihood that a parent might abuse or neglect his or her child. These factors include low self-esteem, poor impulse control, a heightened response to stress, and a reluctance to seek or accept help (Fraley, 1983; Pianta, Egeland, & Erickson, 1989). A common belief about families prone to abuse is that they are socially isolated, but newer research does not support this assumption (Thompson, 1995). Alcohol and drug use play a role. In one study, alcoholism rates in abusive families ranged from 18% to 38% (Widom, 1992, cited in Emery & Laumann-Billings, 1998).

Abusive parents tend to have a poor understanding of child behavior and development, leading to unrealistic expectations of children (Steele, 1980). They are frequently ill-equipped to handle the daily stresses and decisions necessary to good parenting, and they often have poor problem-solving skills (Azar, Robinson, Hekimian, & Twentyman, 1984). Many abusive parents have a strong belief that punishment is the proper avenue for child discipline. They also have a strong aversion to "spoiling" their children (Fraley, 1983). Home visitors in programs with which we have been associated have also told us that parents in high-risk neighborhoods often sincerely believe that it is their responsibility to "toughen up" their children, who must survive in a harsh environment. To them, physically severe discipline seems the logical approach to achieving this goal.

Jackson (1984) described neglectful mothers as tending to withdraw from professionals and ward off relationships, which resulted in feelings of frustration and rejection among the professionals who tried to establish working relationships with them. One study of client characteristics found that although it usually requires between 7 and 18 months to treat abusive families, it is extremely difficult to keep such families in treatment for this long (Berkeley Planning Associates, 1982).

Characteristics of the social and cultural context of families also contribute to the development of family violence. Poverty, unemployment, social isolation, lack of family services, and community violence are factors that increase the family risk of child abuse (Garbarino & Kostelny, 1992). Among poor families, the degree of social cohesion seems to matter Neighborhoods with high levels of child maltreatment tend to be less socially organized, have fewer community resources, and little sense of solidarity. They also have higher rates of violent crime, drug trafficking, and juvenile delinquency (Coulton, Korbin, Su, & Chow, 1995).

Certain children are more likely to be abused than others (Finkelhor, Hotaling, & Yllo, 1988). Chronically ill, premature, or low birthweight infants; hyperactive children; and children with disabilities may present special problems for parents. Adopted children, unplanned children, and children in larger families are also at greater risk for abuse (Daly & Wilson, 1988).

♦ *Outcomes of Child Abuse*

The consequences of maltreatment vary a great deal depending on the nature and duration of the abuse, the relationship between the abuser and the child, and the presence of factors that can exacerbate or ameliorate the effects, such as family chaos or a supportive intervention. However, research has documented both physical and psychological outcomes. Clearly, physical injury, including death, is a possible consequence. An estimated 1,200 to 1,500 children, most younger than the age of 5, die each year as a result of parental physical abuse (48%), neglect (37%), or both (15%) (Lung & Daro, 1996). More than 18,000 children become severely disabled each year as a result of extreme abuse (Baladerian, 1991). Neglectful caregiving may result in a growth delay known as *failure-to-thrive* (Wolfe & McEachran, 1997).

Several studies have documented the existence of posttraumatic stress disorders in 25% to 50% of child victims of physical or sexual abuse (Emery & Laumann-Billings, 1998). Other psychological consequences of maltreatment include aggression or hostility toward others, anxiety, and depression. Sometimes young, abused children develop a behavioral pattern called *compulsive compliance,* an immediate compliance to adults to avoid abuse (Wolfe & McEachran, 1997). In the short run, this strategy may reduce the risk of abuse, but in the long run, compulsive compliance can hinder the development of interpersonal relationships. Other negative consequences of abusive parenting include the potential inhibition of a child's cognitive, social, and moral development (Dodge, Bates, & Pettit, 1990; Wolfe, 1999).

Implications for Home Visitors

Much of the research on child maltreatment presented above has clear implications for home visitors. Families who mistreat their children have difficulty establishing relationships and remaining in treatment, yet they are clearly in need of services. The obvious advantage of home visiting as a service for such families is that home visitors do not require or expect families to come to an agency or office. For families who need but do not seek support, such a service seems more promising of a positive outcome than agency-based services. Home visitors can diminish clients' isolation through their contact with them and can help establish the additional formal and informal support networks that families need. One striking example we know is of a mother who once abused her child, but through the help of her home visitor, did not repeat the abuse. Three years later, she told the home visitor, "You were the person who saved my life that first year, because I could count on your coming every week even when I saw nobody else."

The research on child maltreatment, even as briefly summarized above, clearly shows that home visitors will be challenged in their work with abusing families. We discuss the implications of this work for home visitors under two broad areas: dealing with one's own feelings about maltreating families and delivering the types of help that such families need.

Parents who abuse their children almost always elicit feelings of anger in those who interact with them. Home visitors may ask themselves, "How can I help this mother who has hurt her child when I find her behavior so detestable?" We suggest an approach that includes three major points. First, home visitors must consider the entire family as their clients in need of treatment. Conceptualizing the family as the client allows one to see the abuser and the injured child as part of the same system and serves to help the home visitor see that in order to provide help to the child, the visitor will need to help the parent. The goal is to strengthen the family so that it can become a more healthily functioning unit, enabling parent and child to remain together. For some families, this goal will be unrealistic. Second, home visitors must try to perceive the abusive parent as someone who needs help, not blame. The third point for home visitors to remember is to try to keep feelings separate from actions. By this we mean that although the abusive parent's action is not acceptable, his or her feelings that may have been behind the actions—frustration, fatigue, or helplessness—are legitimate feelings that the home visitor can accept. Likewise, home visitors must accept any of their own negative feelings toward the parent without translating these feelings into destructive or unprofessional behavior of their own. Although accepting people's feelings and recognizing their needs will not inevitably result in ease of communication and productive interaction, they are an important part of gaining the trust necessary to work with these families.

The research on maltreating families has other implications for home visitors regarding help that such families might need. Three areas of help seem particularly obvious: provision of knowledge, help with parenting skills, and referrals to other sources of support. As described previously, abusive parents often lack knowledge of children's development and needs, and have poor skills in managing their children's behavior. These parents may harm their children out of ignorance. Through educating parents about their children's real capabilities and needs at given ages, home visitors can help change parents' unrealistic expectations of their children. Conveying such basic information has been shown to help prevent child abuse (Garbarino, 1987).

Many intervention and prevention strategies seek to change parenting practices or the home environment. In fact, the goal of many well-known home visiting programs such as the Nurse Home Visiting Program (Olds et al., 1999) and Healthy Families America (Daro & Harding, 1999) (both described in Chapter 3) is to reduce child abuse by promoting positive parenting, providing family support, and reducing family stress. Other home visiting programs have more circumscribed goals, so it is important for home visitors to know their own program's philosophy regarding the level of intervention that they can and should provide regarding the prevention of child abuse and neglect. Even if home visitors can teach some new parenting skills, changing longstanding interpersonal behaviors and child management techniques is not an overnight process. It is not unusual for parents to have difficulty maintaining new behavior patterns and revert to old, more familiar, abusive practices.

The third area of potential help from the home visitor is referral to outside agencies. His or her knowledge of other community supports and recognition of children's or parents' needs for them can be a source of additional support for a maltreating family. Even if mental health support and child intervention are within the purview of the visitor's role and that of his or her program, referrals for additional services might also be helpful to the family. A home visitor might be able to convince a parent to enroll an abused child in an intervention program focused on the child's developmental needs. The visitor could encourage a mother or father to attend special parenting programs or enroll in Parents Anonymous.

♦ *Recognizing Child Maltreatment*

In this section, we have discussed the implications of research on child abuse and neglect for home visitors working with maltreating families. However, many programs serve families who have not mistreated their child but may be at risk for doing so. Visitors in those programs, and indeed all home visitors, should be able to recognize the symptoms of child abuse and neglect and know what to do when they suspect child maltreatment.

Home visitors need to be attuned to signs that child abuse or neglect may be occurring. These might include unexplained cuts, burns, or bruises or an unusual number of "accidents." Exceptionally timid or frightened children may also be an indication that abuse has occurred. One home visitor's suspicions were aroused when her client's young son became inconsolable when he spilled his milk. This home visitor subsequently discovered that her client had been severely beating this child whenever he had accidents with his food. In other cases, a child might appear malnourished or much smaller than other children of the same age, be inadequately clothed for weather conditions, or not receive health care when sick.

Because home visitors are in clients' homes frequently, they are more likely than other professionals to become aware of the possibility of child abuse and neglect. Unless some evidence of maltreatment is present, we urge home visitors to discuss their concerns with parents cautiously. If a home visitor has established the rapport and trust needed to interact with a parent over a period of time, the parent is less likely to want to disguise or hide what is happening, and discussions about child maltreatment can usually be accomplished without jeopardizing the relationship. The guiding principle here is to investigate and explore what is happening with an attitude of sincere concern rather than judgment. Most parents do not want to injure their children, and if help is offered to them in a nonaccusatory manner, most parents will accept it. Steady support from a patient visitor can be of great help.

How a home visitor handles a difficult situation such as suspected child neglect or abuse depends on the relationship that has been established with the family. Chalmers (1994) found that health visitors who thought they had a good relationship with their client were more direct in addressing a problem situation and believed that they had more options available to them. Visitors with a less than positive relationship had more difficulty raising safety concerns and felt more limited in their options.

Nevertheless, there are times when a report must be made. Home visitors should not mislead parents into believing that they will overlook parents' behavior because of their relationship with the family. We recommend that home visitors discuss with the parents their legal obligation to report abuse or neglect and explain the follow-up procedures that will likely ensue. A home visitor should emphasize his or her concern for the child and the parent, and the visitor should offer to continue to visit and assist the parent in ways that would be helpful. A successful outcome of an abuse report occurred in a program we supervised when a home visitor reluctantly reported her client—a single, professional father—for breaking his daughter's ankle when he angrily set her down too roughly. Although the father was very upset about being reported, he acknowledged that he needed help with the child. The continued support of the home visitor, including her identification of resources to assist the parent with child care, convinced him to continue his participation in the home visiting program. It is noteworthy that this home visitor needed much support from her supervisor and colleagues to see that her reporting of this client was not only mandatory but resulted in a better situation for everyone.

Knowing that the law typically requires the reporting of child abuse, most home visitors also know that only a small proportion of reported cases actually receive help. More than 3 million reports are made each year, less than one third are substantiated, and about 40%

of substantiated cases receive no services (Lung & Daro, 1996). The home visitor, who is already in a helping relationship with a family, is thus in the ironic position of potentially jeopardizing his or her relationship with the family to make a report that will not likely result in any more help for the family. Although we do not advocate civil disobedience (Melton et al.'s [1995] term for failure to report such cases), this dilemma does make obvious why home visiting programs must have written policies for compliance with state laws and clear procedures for discussing and deciding on such cases in supervision or team meetings. Home visitors should not have to make such decisions in isolation. An optimistic finding from the Infant Health and Development Program (IHDP) is that of the 44 cases of abuse or neglect that were reported by the IHDP staff (home visitors, nurses, social workers), only 2 clients severed all contact with the program (Bryant, 1991).

Although child neglect is more frequently observed than child abuse, it is less frequently reported (Trainor, 1983). One reason for this is the lack of a clear definition of what constitutes child neglect. We have cautioned home visitors who are concerned about neglect to first check whether what they are seeing is merely a difference in values orientation and cultural beliefs between themselves and their families. Child-rearing practices common in one culture may seem like neglect to those of another culture. In light of the broad range of cultures that home visitors may encounter, it is important that they remain alert to their own orientation and avoid judging clients according their own system of values. Scrutiny of the real consequences to children of the behavior in question should lead one to consider factors critical to health and safety, not style or other peripheral issues.

In summary, dealing with families in which child abuse or neglect has occurred or is suspected is difficult for home visitors. Where uncertainty or ambiguity exists, home visitors should seek consultation from supervisors, child protection agencies, and other appropriate sources to ensure fair treatment of parents as well as protection of children. Home visitors will need considerable support from supervisory and collegial staff when visiting maltreating parents. The challenges are great, but there can hardly be a greater reward than the prevention of harm to a child through the improvement of parenting knowledge and skills.

Family Violence

Just as home visitors may see or suspect child abuse in a family, they may visit in homes where other kinds of family violence occurs. In fact, the co-occurrence of partner violence and physical child abuse is as high as 40% to 75% (Layzer, Goodson, & DeLange, 1986; Straus, Gelles, & Steinmetz, 1980). It is not in the purview of most home visitors to offer intensive therapy for abused women. Nevertheless, home visitors need basic knowledge about partner abuse that can help prepare them to respond to it in constructive ways. (We are aware that men can be the victims in spouse abuse and that violence also occurs in gay and lesbian relationships. However, when medical severity rather than frequency of violence is measured, 94% of serious domestic assaults are male-to-female [Dutton, 1992], so we will focus on violence toward women.)

Relevant Theory and Research

Domestic violence is defined as a pattern of abusive behaviors consisting of physical, sexual, and/or psychological maltreatment against current or former intimate partners to gain or maintain power or control unfairly (American Psychological Association, 1996). In the United States, estimates of abuse against women range from about 4% (Sassetti, 1993; Straus & Gelles, 1990) to 12% of U.S. adult females (Wilt & Olson, 1996). The differences between studies involve whether one looks at crime records or obtains information through questionnaires or interviews of large samples of women. Violent episodes often also include sexual assault; 14% of ever-married women report being raped by a husband or an ex-husband, and more than twice as many are assaulted by strangers (Russell, 1982). In 1996, 30% of female homicides were perpetrated by an intimate partner (Federal Bureau of Investigation, 1997). In fact, American women are more likely to be assaulted in their own homes than anywhere else (Straus et al., 1980).

In recent decades, much research has been conducted on the subject of partner abuse. Older studies tended to propose theories about the abused woman's personality and past experience to explain who would be abused and who would not. These studies would often identify the woman as having been maltreated as a child, having low self-esteem and poor relationship skills, lacking education and coping skills, being immature and impulsive, being unable to express herself, lacking sources of support, and having learned to feel helpless (Fiedler, Briar, & Pierce, 1984; Roy, 1977; Walker, 1979). Recent research has revealed that it is not primarily the characteristics of the victim or her lifestyle that explain the abuse but, rather, the characteristics of the abuser.

Many of the same characteristics that predict child abuse predict partner violence. Many of the men who batter their wives or girlfriends were themselves abused as children or saw violence in their homes (Jacobson & Gottman, 1998). Hotaling and Sugarman (1986) discovered that in addition to the history of family violence that male batterers have often endured, they are also often poorly adjusted individuals with antisocial behavior, poor self-esteem and sense of personal efficacy, low levels of assertiveness, and frequently low educational, occupational, and income status. Severely abusive men are likely to have alcohol problems (Heyman, O'Leary, & Jouriles, 1995). Many studies have also found that abusive husbands are extremely jealous, suspicious, and possessive of their wives (Hilberman, 1980).

Although family violence occurs across the socioeconomic spectrum, it appears to be more frequently associated with lower socioeconomic status (Gelles, 1987). Unemployment, lack of family services, and community violence contribute to the risk (Garbarino & Kostelny, 1992). In addition, the patriarchal structure of our society subtly and overtly supports the physical dominance of men over women (Walker, 1983). Research, lobbying, and awareness raising in the past two decades have finally begun to change societal attitudes about abuse, but abuse will not be eradicated without looking carefully at the gender socialization issues that maintain or facilitate family violence (Walker, 1999).

The dynamics involved in violent relationships are complex. How do individuals come to hurt those they claim to love, and why do others seem to allow and endure it? Bowlby (1984) has conceptualized family violence as a disorder in the attachment and caregiving functions of family systems. As previously noted, many men who batter their wives or girlfriends were themselves abused as children or grew up in rejecting and violent households. Because children learn to treat others as they themselves have been treated, at some level, men's violence may be a repetition of what they learned in childhood. However, Bowlby (1984) believes that the mere repetition of a pattern of behavior does not sufficiently explain how these dynamics are perpetuated in many families. Looking more closely at the interaction between partners in abusive relationships, Bowlby (1984) identifies several patterns. Each partner appears to believe the other needs him or her while denying his or her own need for the other. Thus, threats of abandonment or actual abandonment may trigger violence. Each partner seeks the love and care that was denied as a child: the man through coercion, the woman through enduring pain. To each individual, the violent relationship seems preferable to the alternative: being alone.

The following inevitable question arises: Why do women stay? The answers to this question are varied and complex, and this highly personal choice may never be clear to an outsider. What outside observers may interpret as helplessness (not leaving, not pressing charges) may simply be the result of a realistic appraisal of the abuser's potential for even more serious violence toward the partner as well as the inability of our social systems to intervene in time to help. The research on abuse provides further understanding about why women stay.

Strube (1988) found that women who stay are those

> who lack the economic means to leave an abusive relationship, are willing to tolerate abuse so long as it does not become too severe or involve the children, and who appear to be very committed to making their relationship last. (p. 98)

Battered women often lack enough education or work experience to support themselves and their children independently; these women believe that poverty is the alternative to staying with abusive husbands (Fiedler et al., 1984). Other women may choose to stay because they have accepted the notion, internalized perhaps since their own childhood, that they are deserving of punishment or that this is simply the way it is (Walker, 1984). Others are reluctant to leave their home and go to a shelter out of fear that their children will be placed in foster care, a concern that has been empirically supported (Stark & Flitcraft, 1988).

Social isolation and economic dependence can create a deep sense of powerlessness and leave a woman feeling that she has no ability to extricate herself from a violent situation. One study found that most women who stay with abusive mates do so to have a relationship with another person, and some stated that they "needed to interpret their spouses' violence as intensity of caring or love because if they left their mates, there would be no one in their lives" (Duncan, 1982, p. 219). Other women may have profound beliefs regarding marriage and commitment, often derived from cultural beliefs or religious convictions, and may therefore accept whatever situation they find in marriage or another cohabitation arrangement, even if the relationship includes pain and danger (Snyder & Scheer, 1981). And there are those who, out of love, dependence, fear, or desperation, always hope that things will change.

♦ *Outcomes of Partner Violence*

The physical injuries resulting from partner violence range from bruises, cuts, and black eyes to burns, knife wounds, miscarriages, and even death. As traumatic as these physical injuries can be, the psychological trauma of abuse can be equally devastating, though it is often more difficult to quantify. Abused women's reactions to partner violence resemble posttraumatic stress disorder. Shock, denial, withdrawal, confusion, and psychological numbing are common (Browne, 1993). Survivors of partner violence show high levels of depression and suicidal ideation (McGrath, Keita, Strickland, & Russo, 1990). Chronic fatigue, nightmares, and disrupted eating patterns are also common (Goodman, Koss, & Russo, 1993). Assaulted women may become dependent and suggestible, or they might become unrealistically optimistic that everything can be made right (Browne, 1993). The cumulative effects of repeated violence can be psychologically devastating, but the effects of even one violent episode should not be underestimated. Whatever balance might have existed in the relationship is destroyed, and the woman loses the trust and caring she should have been able to depend on.

The children in families experiencing domestic violence can also be seriously affected. First, they are at greater risk of being physically abused by both parents than children in families who are not experiencing partner violence (McCloskey et al., 1995). (Their risk of abuse by fathers is greater than by mothers.) Second, girls in families experiencing domestic violence are at greater risk of sexual abuse by their father, even if they are not physically beaten. In addition to the risk of physical or sexual harm, children of battered women report increased anxiety and lower self-esteem and are likely to have poor school performance and extreme behavior problems (e.g., aggression, conduct disorders) and psychopathology (Fantuzzo et al., 1991; McCloskey et al., 1995; Rosenberg, 1987).

Several factors may explain these problems of children in violent families. The most obvious is that witnessing violence against one's mother is traumatic. Problems are compounded if the violence is also directed at the child. In addition, the mental health of the mother is usually affected by the abuse she has sustained or is experiencing, quite likely reducing her effectiveness as a parent. Both mother and child are in need of intervention.

Implications for Home Visitors

The research on family violence has several implications for home visitors. First, home visitors need to become conscious of their own feelings about spouse abuse and be aware that they will bring their own orientation toward this form of family violence into the home visiting process. Second, it is important to know the signs and symptoms of spouse abuse and how and why women may endure violent relationships. Third, it is helpful to know various approaches to take when working with abused women. Finally, home visitors also need to be aware of safety and legal issues.

Why is it important for home visitors to examine their feelings about spouse abuse? The primary reason is that such examination will prepare them for their own reaction when confronted with the reality or potentiality of spouse abuse and will enable them to moderate their reactions in a way that will be helpful to their clients. Although it may be natural to want to express strong negative feelings toward the perpetrator and steer a course of rescue for the victim, these reactions may not turn out to be helpful to the client. Home visitors who have had the opportunity to discuss domestic violence as part of their training and to share their thoughts and experiences with colleagues and supervisors will be better equipped to handle it.

To assist women in violent households, home visitors must be able to recognize the situation when it is present. It is not likely that a woman will disclose an abusive act unless she has a long-standing, trusting relationship with her home visitor. In light of this, home visitors must be sensitive to signs and clues suggesting violence in the home. The following have been identified as particularly significant: (a) signs of violence such as bruises, cuts, burns, scratches, and blackened eyes; (b) multiple somatic complaints on the part of the victim; (c) children with multiple somatic complaints, behavioral problems, and emotional disturbance; (d) high levels of anxiety, fearfulness, apprehension, and depression; (e) self-destructive behavior, including suicidal ideation and threats, self-mutilation, and chronic self-deprecating remarks; and (f) insomnia and/or violent nightmares (Renz, Munson, Wayland, & Fusaro, 1980). None of these signs will always be linked to spouse abuse but, when present, should alert the home visitor that something is wrong. When a home visitor sees evidence that arouses his or her suspicions, the visitor is obliged to pursue the subject with the client, albeit carefully.

What can a home visitor do when he or she suspects that a woman being visited is being abused? First, a home visitor needs to make it clear that he or she is willing to talk about and deal with the topic. As a part of the trusting relationship that a home visitor and client have established, a client needs to know that the home visitor is aware of the potential for violence in people's lives (not just in this particular situation) and is open to addressing it. This approach is very different from confronting a client with suspicions.

If a home visitor is working with a woman who does not want to talk about the abuse she is experiencing, a visitor initially should voice concern and willingness to listen. A home visitor may judge it appropriate to raise this concern on several occasions. If a client does not respond to this approach, a home visitor must not insist on pursuing the subject, for doing so could alienate a client and destroy a good home visiting relationship. Home visitors have found that most abused women will, in time, want to talk about abusive incidents.

If an abused woman should disclose to a home visitor that she is being harmed, the home visitor should respond with concern and a willingness to listen empathetically. When a client first shares her experience of abuse, or at a later time, the home visitor may bring up several items for further discussion. These include (a) safety, (b) available resources, (c) coping strategies, and (d) possible referral for additional help.

To help a client with safety, it is important to obtain information about the type, severity, frequency, and context of the violent episodes (Renz et al., 1980). For example, is the woman in imminent danger of severe harm? If so, precautions must be taken, if the woman allows, to ensure her and her children's safety. If the violence is predictable, is there any way to avoid it? Is she aware of resources that are available to help her such as crisis hotlines, shelters for battered women and their children, legal assistance, counseling, and financial relief? Discussing with a client these very practical options can be helpful, perhaps life saving, in emergencies.

Providing a client with information about other resources is another way a home visitor can help. Knowledge of the local resources for protection and aid—even if the woman's current decision is not to use them—may expand her perception of alternatives and reduce her sense of entrapment (Browne & Williams, 1989). Often, a battered woman has become isolated physically, emotionally, and socially. The regular presence of a home visitor can help reduce that sense of isolation, but other sources of support should be called on. Perhaps the home visitor can help the client join a support group for battered women.

Research has found that most battered women are unaware that others have similar problems (Gelles, 1987). Learning that others have experienced the same stresses, have had the same feelings, and have dealt with the same realities can be very effective in decreasing a woman's sense of isolation. Through hearing about other women's experiences and sharing her own, a woman may also be better able to think about alternatives to her situation. Learning that they are not alone also tends to help battered women become less self-critical and decreases their sense of being mentally unstable (Duncan, 1982). Battered women are often relieved to discover that their reactions are "normal" for their situations and that others also feel afraid, helpless, angry, guilty, ashamed, and responsible for the violence.

Possibly the most important concept for an abused woman to learn and accept is that she does not deserve to be abused, no matter what circumstances surround the beating. It is critical that the victims do not blame themselves for the brutality they suffer. Popular stereotypes and myths, although beginning to change, have tended to perpetuate the concept that women actually provoke violence and even enjoy it, and thus they are not deserving of assistance (Hofeller, 1982). Battered women often come to believe these ideas themselves, which increases their sense of shame and makes it more difficult to seek help. Home visitors can do much to correct these misconceptions.

A third way to offer help, in addition to helping with safety and knowledge of local resources, is to engage an abused woman in active problem solving on her own behalf. Helping her to say what she really wants, identifying options and resources, and discussing the consequences of the options can help her become aware of the strengths and resources that she does indeed possess. This problem-solving approach is particularly suitable for battered women because people under extreme stress have difficulty thinking through their concerns and have often lost hope. Improving an individual's coping skills and sense of self-efficacy through successful problem solving is an obvious goal for effective home visiting and is especially appropriate when visiting in households where violence is a problem.

A home visitor may suggest several different courses of action for a battered woman to consider, but the visitor needs to refrain from telling the woman what she should do. There are several reasons for this: The woman bears the consequences of whatever action she chooses to take (or not take); the home visitor does not. The woman knows her husband or boyfriend intimately; the home visitor does not. Another reason to refrain from giving direct advice is that only the battered woman knows exactly how she feels. Despite the most sincere and skillful efforts at understanding, a home visitor cannot know his or her client's actual feelings. An additional reason for not making decisions, even for a client willing to allow it, is that this may reinforce a client's feelings of powerlessness and inability to control her own life (Renz et al., 1980).

When visiting families who may be overwhelmed with problems of family violence, it is critical that home visitors not take on the responsibility of this knowledge and its demands for treatment alone nor be overwhelmed themselves by unrealistic expectations about what they can accomplish. Research on posttraumatic stress disorder, the broad diagnostic category that encompasses trauma from partner violence, indicates that the trauma must be recognized and dealt with directly for interventions to be effective (Dutton, 1992). A home visitor can help an abused client by making connections with other clinically trained therapists who can provide the appropriate intervention.

The final topics we want to mention about visiting in violent households are safety and legal issues. If at any time a home visitor feels in danger on a visit, the visitor should leave the situation as quickly as possible. When threats to a home visitor's personal safety are grave enough, home visiting should be terminated until the danger abates. Such a decision should be made in consultation with program staff. Every home visiting program should have clear policies and procedures for handling dangerous situations, and these should be a part of each home visitor's training. Should home visits be stopped, the program should make strenuous efforts to maintain contact with the abused spouse, possibly visiting her in another, safer environment or establishing other methods for communicating. It is especially critical in this situation that home visitors leave the lines of communication open and offer an abused woman continued support.

Just as for child abuse, a home visiting program should know their state laws governing reporting domestic violence because they vary state to state. In a mid-1990s review of all state statutes, 45 states required health practitioners to report injuries due to weapons, crimes, violence, or abuse (Hyman, Schillinger, & Lo, 1995). Generally such a reporting requirement would apply to physicians and nurses who treat the physical injuries resulting from partner violence and not the home visitor who just talks about partner violence with a client. However, two state statutes require "any person" to report family violence, and the laws regarding reporting continue to change. A home visiting program director must be aware of specific laws governing reporting in his or her state and assure that the staff members know the statues and their responsibilities.

In summary, visiting in homes where family violence is a problem can be a challenge for home visitors, yet it can be an effective method for change. Research has shown that support from outside the family influences the patterns of violence; battered women who receive outside support and encouragement are better able to get help and make changes in their family lives (Pahl, 1985). Home visitors can contribute to the support abused clients will need to improve their relationships or leave their abusive mates. Such changes can benefit all individuals in the family.

Substance Abuse

Every home visitor needs to be aware of the possibility of substance abuse among his or her client population. Although some individuals are more at risk for substance abuse than others, home visitors should be aware of the possibility that all clients (any age, male or female, and in all educational and socioeconomic groups) are potential abusers of alcohol and other drugs. In some neighborhoods, illegal drug dealing may be a relatively common situation that can affect home visiting procedures as well as the lives of clients and their families.

Relevant Theory and Research

Alcoholism and other drug addictions are debilitating illnesses that severely affect the addict and his or her family. It is estimated that 1 in 10 American adults has a significant problem with his or her own use of alcohol. Approximately 7% of adults use illegal drugs (U.S. Department of Health and Human Services [U.S. DHHS], 1996). Together, these two substance abuse disorders are the most frequently occurring mental health problem in the United States (Regier et al., 1990). Furthermore, alcohol is involved in nearly half of all traffic deaths as well as a substantial proportion of violent deaths, suicides, drownings, falls, and other fatal accidents (Stinson, Dufour, Steffens, & DeBakey, 1993). Alcohol and illegal drug use create huge health and mental health costs to society; they also cause considerable harm to families.

The signs of alcoholism and other drug addictions range from the obvious, such as acute intoxication, to the subtle, such as confusion. A client who does not remember having set up an appointment may have scheduled it while under the influence of a drug. In addition to anxiety disorders, marital problems, personality disorders, sleep disorders, and psychoses (Hesselbrock, Meyer, & Keener, 1985), depression also frequently accompanies alcoholism (Madden,

1984). An inability to function on the job, financial difficulties, and poor social relationships may indicate a problem with substance abuse. Home visitors have also found that extreme changes in mood from one visit to the next often signal problems with substance abuse (e.g., changes from friendliness and cooperation during one visit to blatant hostility at the next). Problems with the legal system, such as an arrest for drunken driving, may be part of the constellation of symptoms. Family relationships may be unstable and unpredictable.

♦ *Outcomes of Substance Abuse*

The consequences of maternal substance abuse for children can begin before birth. It is widely recognized that heavy alcohol consumption can result in serious birth defects, collectively known as Fetal Alcohol Syndrome (Streissguth, 1997). Children with this disorder are usually born with low birthweight and have mental retardation, facial malformations, or other abnormalities. Even moderate amounts of alcohol consumption are believed to have harmful effects on fetal development. Fetal Alcohol Syndrome is the third leading cause of mental retardation in children (Streissguth & Randels, 1988).

The sparse research that exists on the developmental outcomes of drug-exposed children is difficult to interpret because many of these children are also exposed to other adverse factors, such as poor maternal health, inadequate nutrition, and lack of prenatal care, and undoubtedly many are exposed to multiple types of drugs, including alcohol. However, it does appear that babies born to mothers who abuse cocaine during pregnancy are often premature and low birthweight (National Institute on Drug Abuse, 1999) and are at somewhat greater risk for cognitive delays (Singer et al., 1997). In the late 1980s, when increasing numbers of "crack babies" were delivered, they were often written off as lost causes because of an assumption that they had suffered irreversible damage. This assumption appears to have been an extreme exaggeration because the majority of substance-exposed babies develop fairly well *if* their postnatal caregiving environment is adequate (National Institute on Drug Abuse, 1999). However, new assessment technologies are beginning to find subtle deficits in attentional and mental processing functions that are important for school, so the predicted developmental outcomes should not be considered normal for all drug exposed babies.

Another serious risk is that mothers infected with AIDS can transmit the virus to the developing fetus or newborn. This danger is relevant to substance abuse because two of the groups at high risk for contracting AIDS are intravenous drug users and their sexual partners. Thus, a mother who is injecting herself with cocaine, opiates, or other substances and who shares needles with AIDS-infected users is acutely vulnerable to AIDS. Infected mothers can, in turn, transmit the virus through the placenta to the developing fetus, to the newborn through exposure to infected blood and vaginal fluids during birth, or to the nursing baby through infected breast milk (Peckham & Gibb, 1995). Although not all babies born to mothers who have AIDS are infected, they are clearly at significant risk.

After infancy, children show a variety of effects of growing up in a family with a substance-abusing parent. Children may be anxious or fearful when a parent acts in an unusual manner. They may fear fights and violence between their parents. Children may have difficulty establishing close relationships with other people because they have been disappointed so often because of their parent, and they might feel lonely and helpless to change the situation. Young children need consistency, something lacking in a home with a drug-abusing parent; even basic activities such as mealtime and bedtime are not predictable. Some young children try to cope by becoming the responsible "parent" in the family and may strive hard to achieve in all they do (American Academy of Child and Adolescent Psychiatry, 1999).

The effect that parental substance abuse can have on parenting is also of grave concern. As mentioned earlier in this chapter, a clear link exists between substance abuse and child maltreatment. Parenting skills usually suffer when substances are abused. Behaviors that are at least in part a result of substance abuse include mothers' increased irritability, depression, anxiety, and aggression in addition to a decreased ability to learn from experience (Mello, 1980; Pickens & Heston, 1981). Substance-abusing parents may have poor communication skills, low expressiveness, and trouble with organization and problem solving (Sheridan, 1995). Parents who are seriously involved with substances can become so preoccupied with obtaining and maintaining their drug supply that they neglect their children. When a mother is addicted to any substance, she may become too impaired to be able to care for her children properly. Home visitors have found very young children left alone while their mother went out to obtain or use drugs; they have also found clients acutely intoxicated or comatose while their infants and young children were present and unsupervised.

Substance abuse is often associated with violent behavior in families (Roizen, 1997). This relationship is not surprising because it is well known that substance abuse impairs judgment and self-control. Many home visitors have worked with clients who say, "He hits me and the kids only when he's been drinking and otherwise things are fine." Yet, "only when he's been drinking" can translate into a potentially dangerous and dysfunctional family.

Implications for Home Visitors

The appropriate responses for a home visitor who suspects that his or her client may be abusing a substance are similar to the responses discussed earlier in the sections on child abuse and family violence, including openness to discussing the problem, offering support, and helping the client obtain professional services. A review of recent research on treatment approaches concluded that problematic alcohol or drug use can be modified by the same psychological principles used to modify other problem behaviors and do not require specialized alcohol-drug treatment modalities (Miller & Brown, 1997; Project MATCH Research Group, 1997). Therefore, more than one type of treatment program offered in the community could be of benefit.

Behaviors associated with substance abuse can have many different causes, and a home visitor should not conclude that a client is having problems with substance abuse on the basis of any one of these behaviors. However, if he or she observes such dysfunctional behaviors over a period of time, a home visitor is well advised to investigate the possibility that substance abuse may be involved.

A home visitor who is aware of the risks to infants arising from maternal substance abuse is in a position to share this knowledge with a client who is either considering pregnancy or is already pregnant. The visitor is obliged to inform an unknowing mother about such conditions as Fetal Alcohol Syndrome and AIDS and to provide or help a client obtain counseling and medical care. In almost every community there are programs for the treatment of addiction, usually including public clinics (outpatient and inpatient), offered through community mental health centers, private clinics, and counselors. Self-help groups such as Alcoholics Anonymous and support groups for family members, such as Al-Anon and Al-a-Teen, are found in most communities as well as self-help groups for the abusers of other drugs. These groups are free of cost and confidential. Home visitors must realize, however, that clients often deny that they have a substance abuse problem or are very adept at hiding one. Until they accept that they have a problem, these clients will not be willing to accept help.

Although alcoholism and the abuse of other drugs are comparable in symptomatology and consequences, there is one clear difference between them: Alcohol consumption is legal for individuals above the drinking age, whereas the use of nonprescription drugs is not. The difference for a home visitor is a question about whether to report illegal drug use to the proper authorities.

Unlike child abuse laws, there are no specific laws requiring the reporting of illegal drug use. However, there is an element of moral pressure exerted on members of society to abide by the laws and not to condone those who break them. Our suggestion is that a home visitor first help his or her client secure professional treatment for the drug problem. Also, if a home visitor believes that the children of a client are endangered because of drugs, further action is warranted, specifically notification of child protective services. Exposing children to a dangerous environment is neglectful.

As we discussed in an earlier section on safety issues, home visitors need to be aware of their own vulnerability to danger as well as the vulnerability of their clients. When families are deeply involved in drug addiction or drug dealing, home visitors must assess the potential danger to themselves in continuing to visit in the home. Under no circumstances should home visitors remain in a client's home when drug dealing or illegal drug use is openly occurring. A home visitor must make it clear to the client that he or she cannot condone or participate in illegal activities and that the visitor will have to leave the home if this happens. This position does not mean that a home visitor must leave a home immediately if he or she suspects that a client is under the influence of drugs or when he or she sees drug paraphernalia is scattered about the home. However, if drug dealing is occurring in an adjacent room, the home visitor should leave.

Visiting families heavily involved with substance abuse on a continuing basis can be very stressful. In addition to the support a home visitor needs to visit such families, ongoing assessments should be made of the client's ability to benefit from home visiting services. If a client is unwilling to seek help for substance abuse that seriously impairs his or her ability to function, especially parental functioning, the client may well be unable to benefit from whatever the home visiting program has to offer. Under such circumstances, alternatives may need to be considered. If children are being neglected, arranging for child care or foster home placement may need to occur, along with continued efforts to assist the client.

Adolescent Parents

Because home visiting programs often address the needs of infants and children, it is likely that home visitors will have adolescent mothers in their caseloads. These young parents may present particular challenges to home visitors and require additional knowledge or level of awareness of specific issues in order to visit most effectively.

Relevant Theory and Research

In 1990, more than one million teenagers and young women younger than the age of 20 became pregnant, and approximately 530,000 of these women gave birth (Alan Guttmacher Institute, 1994). The rate of births in 1995 to female adolescents was 56.8 births per 1,000 for 15- to 19-year-olds, and 1.3 per 1,000 for 10- to 14-year-olds (U.S. DHHS, 1995). Compared with other developed countries, the rate of teenage births in the United States is almost twice as high as in the next highest country, Great Britain (Coley & Chase-Lansdale, 1998).

Although the teenage birthrate is now lower than it was a few decades ago, teen pregnancy is a major policy concern because of welfare issues and because teenage parents are poor, single, and have low levels of education. Of teenage parents, 75% are unmarried (95% for Black Americans, 68% for Whites, and 67% for Hispanics). Teenage parents are more likely to be poor (60%), have additional children during the next few years, and spend more time overall on welfare than older parents (Alan Guttmacher Institute, 1994; Ventura, Martin, Curtin, & Matthews, 1997). Alcohol and drug use are more common among adolescent parents as is, obviously, early sexual activity (Udry, Kovenock, & Morris, 1996). Given these statistics, it is evident that home visitors need to understand the social, psychological, economic, and health status of adolescent parents.

The life experiences associated with poverty seem to have a lot to do with teenage pregnancy—alienation at school, lack of opportunities, and models of teenage parenthood in their own family (Coley & Chase-Lansdale, 1998). Poor students with low educational aspirations are more likely to be teenage mothers. In one study, one third of teenage mothers had reading skills below the sixth-grade level, and 30% of teenage mothers had already dropped out of school before they became pregnant (Maynard, 1995). Dropping out of school compromises the potential wage-earning capacities of a young woman just when those capacities acquire new and urgent meaning: a child to support. Although having a baby before the age of 18 significantly reduces the likelihood of graduating from high school (Hotz, McElroy, & Sanders, 1997), it is not impossible to do so. One study found that if young women with infants stay in school, they are just as likely to graduate as their nonparent peers (73% and 77%, respectively) (Upchurch & McCarthy, 1990).

Teenage mothers are less likely to receive prenatal care than are older mothers (Hughes, Johnson, Rosenbaum, Butler, & Simons, 1988). Adolescent mothers have more problems with their pregnancy and delivery and have less healthy babies overall than do older mothers. Fortunately, such differences are becoming less notable in recent years, perhaps due to better health care for adolescents (Coley & Chase-Lansdale, 1998). The poorer birth outcomes for teenage parents may have more to do with their low socioeconomic status and poor nutritional status than their young age per se (McCormick, 1984; Scholl, Hediger, & Belsky, 1994).

The social consequences of adolescent parenthood are also great. Sadler and Catrone (1983) describe adolescent parents as dealing with a dual developmental crisis: adolescence and parenting. They provide a conceptual framework for understanding the processes of both developmental stages and how these are in potential conflict with each other. Adolescence and early parenting are both periods of growth and change with unique developmental tasks and challenges, and the resulting pressure of these two growth periods on adolescent parents is significant.

The characteristic egocentricity of adolescence stands in direct conflict with the requirement that parents recognize their infants as separate from themselves and in need of intensive care and attention. Often, young mothers are not able to differentiate between their own feelings and needs and those of their infants. Consequently, they may project their own thoughts, feelings, and reactions onto their infants, such as preferences for foods or clothing. This lack of perception that their infants' needs are separate and different from their own may have harmful consequences for the infant, although the mother may have no harmful intent. One home visitor whose adolescent client's baby was diagnosed with "failure-to-thrive" found that her client had been trying to feed her 4-month-old those foods she herself most enjoyed: french fries, soft drinks, ice cream, and even pizza!

Another developmental task that may create conflict between adolescence and parenting is that of cognitive development. In Piagetian terms, the adolescent is in the process of acquiring the ability to think abstractly. This acquisition is a gradual process and not speeded up simply because of the arrival of a new baby. Consequently, an adolescent mother may not yet be able to think in the abstract or in future-oriented terms that are necessary to problem solve for her infant's care. A teenage mother may know about developmental milestones but not understand the concepts of individual child development. Thus, she might have unrealistic expectations of the child's abilities and limited ability to plan for the child's future needs, which, in fact, research has shown to be characteristic of adolescent mothers (Brooks-Gunn & Chase-Lansdale, 1995).

A third developmental task of adolescence is the diverting of attention from the nuclear family to others in the social environment (Sadler & Catrone, 1983). Teenagers need to develop social relationships in preparation for establishing and maintaining mature adult relationships in the future. This need to intensify social relationships with peers collides head-on with the infant's need for the mother's attention. Consequently, teenage mothers may feel isolated. In addition, just when adolescents must and do begin to strive in earnest for independence from their families, having an infant to care for will usually increase the adolescent mother's dependence on her own parents for emotional and economic support as well as for direct care for the infant.

♦ *Grandmothers*

Home visitors often interact with both the teenage mother and her mother, the baby's grandmother. A number of studies have looked at the role that grandmothers play in coparenting, housing, and supporting teenage mothers and their children. Through extensive observations and interviews, Wakschlag, Chase-Lansdale, and Brooks-Gunn (1996) found that the extent to which young mothers found autonomy from and communicated with their mothers best predicted positive parenting behaviors. Another study found that shared child rearing worked well when grandmothers helped their daughters and modeled appropriate parenting but did not take total control (Apfel & Seitz, 1991).

Residing with the grandmother may not be as protective as it was once thought to be (Furstenberg, Brooks-Gunn, & Morgan, 1987). In a three-generational study of Black families of 3-year-olds, both mothers' and grandmothers' parenting practices were less supportive and authoritative and more negative and disengaged when young mothers lived with grandmothers (Chase-Lansdale, Brooks-Gunn, & Zamsky, 1994). Similarly, another study found that coresidence among adolescent mothers and grandmothers was associated with greater conflict between mother and grandmother and poorer child functioning (East & Felice, 1996). This research seems to suggest that older teenage mothers may be more effective parents and their children may develop better if they live apart from the grandmother but receive high levels of support from the grandmother.

♦ *Children of Teenage Mothers*

In addition to these social challenges, children of adolescent parents may be more difficult to care for than children of older parents. They may be less healthy in infancy, and as toddlers and preschoolers they may have more cognitive or behavioral problems. Infants born to teenage mothers are significantly more likely to be of low birthweight than are infants born to older mothers (Hughes, et.al., 1988). Low birthweight carries certain risks to an infant, including increased likelihood of developmental delays, serious illness, and hospitalizations. Low birthweight infants place a heavier burden of care on parents than normal-weight infants, who typically do not present such an array of problems (McCormick, 1985).

Studies have also found that adolescent parents, particularly the poorest and youngest ones, generally do not provide cognitive stimulation sufficient for normal development. The effects may not be obvious in infancy, but as they grow up, the children of teenage mothers have more problems. These children are often deficient in cognitive areas and have higher rates of school retention (Moore, Morrison, & Green, 1997). Behavior problems are more likely among the preschool children of teenage mothers, and they are more likely to have delinquency problems as adolescents (Furstenberg et al., 1987).

It is important to note that many of the studies mentioned here were not able to control for many of the other factors that may influence teenage parents and teenage parenting. When studies can control for poverty, for example, by having appropriate comparison groups (e.g., mothers in their early 20s who live in poverty), some of the commonly accepted characteristics of teenage parents seem less related to their age and more to their circumstances (Benasich & Brooks-Gunn, 1996).

Implications for Home Visitors

A home visitor who is aware of research findings on adolescent parents can use it to individualize assistance—whether social-emotional support, information resources, or help with coping and problem solving—to the strengths and needs of the teenage clients. It is helpful to remember that adolescents do not comprise a homogeneous group. They vary widely in levels of maturity, cognitive development, personality characteristics, and environmental setting.

Home visiting is a good avenue for providing social-emotional support to adolescent parents. Colletta and Gregg (1981) found that the level of stress adolescent mothers experienced depended primarily on the amount of support they received, their level of self-esteem, and their coping style. Social support is widely recognized as an important element in reducing stress (Caplan, 1974; Moroney, 1987), and stress has been shown to interfere with mothers' ability to care for their children due to its role in contributing to maternal depression (Belle, 1982). Being supportive to a teenage mother does not necessarily mean that a home visitor should do things or make decisions for the mother. There may be more of a tendency to do this for teenage clients than for older women because a teenager may be the age of a home visitor's own daughter, but as with any client, a teenage client must take responsibility for herself.

A home visitor can provide social-emotional support more readily by being aware of the developmental tasks and needs of adolescents. This knowledge can help enable home visitors to accept, without judgment, behavior and attitudes that they might find unacceptable in adult parents. This does not mean that home visitors should be willing to compromise the health and safety of their adolescent clients' children. Rather, it means that home visitors should acknowledge the developmental context of the adolescent and make allowances for adolescent behavior.

Establishing a positive, trusting, supportive relationship may be somewhat more difficult with a teenage mother. The Child Welfare League of America has published a mentoring manual for adults who work with pregnant and parenting teenagers (Kanfer, Englund, Lennhoff, & Rhodes, 1995). This manual includes many practical suggestions for establishing relationships with teenage clients. Home visitors may need to learn not to take a client's behaviors personally and to be prepared for a teenage client to do something to test the relationship. Communicating with teenagers requires patience and learning to hold a conversation when a client may not be very talkative. Teenagers are good at one-word comments and shoulder shrugs. Home visitors need to allow for periods of silence and not fill the silence with chat. Really listening to a teenage client, even when what he or she is saying seems irrelevant, is a good way to pick up clues as to what he or she thinks or what motivates the client. Spending time together and talking about something other than problems, such as what the teenager likes to do, is beneficial. The manual has many positive suggestions and strategies for visiting with teenagers.

The information provision role of a home visitor may be especially helpful to adolescent parents, but visitors should keep in mind the literacy level of many teenage mothers when they provide written information. Although resources are often available to teenage parents in many communities, they are often fragmented and confusing. Navigating the bewildering network of bureaucratic procedures can be a formidable obstacle for young parents (Moore & Burt, 1982). Helping a client learn how to make use of available services is a significant responsibility for a home visitor and can have many beneficial effects. Clients learn not only where the services are and how to use them but, through the modeling of the home visitor, can learn how to be better advocates for themselves and their children.

Home visitors can also help adolescent parents learn to identify and solve problems in more effective ways. When faced with tough decisions, adolescent girls often see only one either-or choice rather than a series of options (Beyth-Marom & Fischhoff, 1997). As described in Chapter 5, home visitors can use various strategies to help clients learn to set goals, list and investigate a number of options, determine the consequences of available options, and follow through with decisions. This assistance can be especially helpful to teenagers whose maturity of judgment is not yet well developed.

Although we have emphasized in earlier sections the importance of responding to clients' needs when they seem to override program goals, this suggestion deserves particular emphasis when working with adolescent parents. These young people are often experiencing high levels of stress, confusion, frustration, and despair, and home visitors' efforts should first be directed to addressing the parents' needs. In the Parent to Parent Program in Vermont (Halpern & Covey, 1983), in which home visitors met with adolescent parents for the purpose of improving their parenting skills, most visitors found that in the early weeks of the program, the greater part of their effort was focused on the personal problems of the adolescent mother. Over time, the majority of these home visitors found that they could shift their attention more closely to the planned content of the program. Our experience has been similar with most parents, but especially with adolescent parents.

One unintended side effect of any home visiting program, as we have mentioned earlier in this book, is that clients can feel overwhelmed by the expectations of the program and by copious amounts of new information. This situation may be particularly true for adolescents. Home visitors we know have found that concentrating on only one aspect of parenting at a time is often essential when working with teenaged mothers. Prioritizing children's needs may serve as a guideline in helping home visitors determine which issues to address with an adolescent parent. Another strategy is to build on the interests and achievements of the adolescent.

As research has indicated, one of the fundamental tasks of adolescence is the development of independence from the family of origin. This development becomes especially problematic for an adolescent mother who depends on her own family for child care and other support. Because a home visitor is an objective and reliable adult outside the teenager's family, he or she is in a unique position to assist an adolescent with learning her new role as mother and to help her continue to develop those skills needed to increase her own independence.

The confusion over parenting roles in a multigenerational household can present home visitors with several challenges. We have found that home visitors are often unwillingly (and sometimes unwittingly) thrust into the controversy between the adolescent mother and her parents over the issue of who is really responsible for the adolescent's baby. Home visitors in other programs have reported similar difficulties (Olds, 1988a). There are no easy answers to this dilemma, but we do have several suggestions we believe are helpful.

Foremost, the home visitor needs to approach the adolescent parent and her family from a family systems perspective. The imbalance that invariably results when an adolescent parent and her child reside with the adolescent's parents must be openly acknowledged, and all family members need assistance in learning to accept this imbalance and restructuring family roles and boundaries (Nathanson, Baird, & Jemail, 1986). A home visitor must take care not to contribute to family disequilibrium by aligning closely with any one family member against other family members. Supporting all family members honestly will help to alleviate angry and painful feelings and help minimize the possibility that the baby will become the center of a power struggle.

If an infant's grandmother is significantly involved in the child's care, her feelings and contributions need to be acknowledged. However, over the child's lifetime, the mother will most likely assume ultimate responsibility for the child's care, so she needs to learn to be the primary caregiver. This responsibility would involve appropriately providing for the child's daily needs, giving the child emotional support and cognitive encouragement, and taking advantage of community resources that might benefit the child, such as an intervention program or high-quality child care. The strengths that a home visitor helps the adolescent client develop, such as advocating for a child with community agencies, will benefit both child and mother as the mother learns to generalize these skills to other aspects of her life.

Home visiting with adolescent parents can be frustrating and difficult. Yet, as we know from our own and many home visitors' experiences, visiting teenagers can be one of the most rewarding aspects of home visiting, for both the young parents and the home visitor. Keeping in mind some of the unique problems and perspectives of adolescent parents should enable home visitors to find ways to provide them with the help they so keenly need.

Summary

This chapter has presented four distinct topics for consideration: child abuse, spouse abuse, substance abuse, and teenage parenting. Although these topics have been treated separately in this chapter, in reality, home visitors may expect to find elements of all of these influencing some of their clients' lives. For example, the abused children we discussed may grow up to abuse their own children or be the perpetrators or victims of spouse abuse. Substance abuse in a family is frequently associated with child abuse and domestic violence. The stresses of adolescent parenting may well increase the vulnerability of these young parents to abusing their children, being abused by their parents and sexual partners, and turning to alcohol or other drugs for escape. Therefore, home visitors are likely to encounter families who are dealing with more than one of these problems. In addition, the entire family system is affected by the problems we have presented in this chapter because multiple relationships are involved. When faced with such situations, home visitors need to help families sort through and prioritize concerns and see what a family is committed to addressing. In such situations, supporting and strengthening a family as a unit is the ultimate and underlying goal for most home visiting interventions. When circumstances prevent a home visitor from doing so, there are still constructive options for helping individual family members.

8

Ethical and Professional Issues Facing Home Visitors

Although the roles of home visitors vary considerably, concern about human welfare is a common thread in the profession. However, the best ways to promote and support that welfare are not always clear. Because home visitors work in multicultural settings and in a multidisciplinary helping profession, they frequently face differences in values, customs, and beliefs; differences between clients and themselves; and sometimes differences between their thinking and that of their program. These situations are not unique to home visiting but are a part of all the helping professions.

Ethical questions home visitors must address include whether to intervene in a particular situation, how best to do so, and how to balance the needs of different family members. Sometimes home visitors wonder whether to tell the truth in certain situations or when, if ever, they can share information given to them in confidence. Visitors may wonder how they will know when they have helped all they need to and when, perhaps, it is time to stop visiting.

Working as a home visitor on a multidisciplinary team can present ethical issues about the kinds of information to share as well as broader professional issues of communication, decision making, and leadership. The many challenges involved in the day-to-day work of home visitors sometimes result in burnout, an issue of considerable concern to the profession.

In the first half of this chapter, we will focus on several ethical concerns that can emerge in the relationship between a home visitor and a client, and present some guidelines that may help a home visitor weigh his or her obligations when faced with dilemmas. The last half of the chapter will deal with the following two specific professional issues that face the profession of home visiting: burnout and working in multidisciplinary teams.

Home Visitor/Client Issues

Many different ethical questions are likely to arise during the life of a home visitor's relationship with a client. In this section, we describe two types of ethical dilemmas that occur with home visiting. We will then propose a framework for evaluating such situations and explore several specific ethical issues, including honesty, confidentiality, and the fair and equitable allotment of a home visitor's time.

Determining what is in a client's best interest often involves balancing individual needs and family needs. If a mother has agreed to participate in a home visiting program to acquire parenting skills and to learn specific educational activities to use with her child, the mother is clearly the client. But sometimes grandparents, partners, or other household members become involved, either through program intent to provide family-focused intervention or through the interests of family members. Visiting a client who lives with extended family members can lead to home visitors being drawn into conflicts between different family members, such as a disagreement between a parent and a grandparent about how best to raise a child. At these times, deciding what is in a client's best interest may become more difficult because three or four people in the family or the whole family may be considered the client.

A different kind of ethical dilemma is raised when there is a law or policy that seems to conflict with a home visitor's ability to help a family. The decision to report suspected child abuse is a classic example of such a dilemma. Most states require professionals to report cases of suspected abuse to state authorities. However, home visitors may sometimes believe that such reporting would disrupt their relationship with a parent, a relationship that they believe is more helpful to the abusing parent than the services the state agency might be able to deliver.

Regardless of individual family circumstances and no matter how doubtful the outcome of reporting may be, home visitors must follow the law on reporting abuse or neglect. Although the policy and procedure may be clear, that does not alleviate the anxiety or reduce the difficulty faced by a home visitor in deciding to report such suspicions. When has a parent gone over the line from firm discipline to child abuse? When is neglect reportable? Once abuse is reported, how does one continue to be an effective home visitor with the family? No set of "right" answers can be applied to all situations; rather, each situation involves judgments based on knowledge of the individual family's circumstances. The following section presents several guidelines that can be helpful when making these judgments.

A Framework for Assessing Values Conflicts

In his book *Ethical Dilemmas in Social Service*, Frederick Reamer (1990) discusses the place of reason and moral principles in social service. Fundamental to any discussion of ethics are two features of the actions involved, specifically, whether the actions are voluntary and purposive. If the actions are voluntary, they are under a person's control. If they are purposive, they are to achieve basic goods (food, shelter, life) or additive goods (goods beyond the basic, such as education, self-esteem, income). By considering the voluntary nature and purpose of actions involved in human service work, Reamer suggests six guidelines when resolving conflicts between values and duties.

1. *Rules against basic harms to the necessary preconditions of action (such as life, health, food, shelter, mental equilibrium) take precedence over rules against harms, such as lying or revealing confidential information, or threats to additive goods, such as recreation, education, and wealth.*[1] This guideline means that the basic well-being of a person is more important than following rules or acquiring secondary benefits. For example, a person's safety or health is more important than a home visitor's absolute honesty. We know of one home visitor who was faced with a dramatic example of such a conflict. She felt compelled to lie to a threatening father concerning the location of his child and the child's mother, even though the home visitor herself had taken them to a women's shelter and knew where they were. In this case, pro-

tecting the safety of the woman and child took precedence over telling the truth as to their whereabouts. This guideline also justifies a home visitor's decision to report an abusive or neglectful parent to a protective service agency. In such cases, a child's safety takes precedence over protection of the parent's confidentiality.

2. *An individual's right to basic well-being (the necessary preconditions of action) takes precedence over another individual's right to freedom.* A client may freely choose to do something that we might consider self-destructive, unless the exercise of that freedom interferes with someone else's basic well-being. A home visitor may consider it a problem that a client continues to take drugs while on probation, even though the client and home visitor both know that not taking drugs is a condition of the client's parole. A home visitor may counsel the client and may urge him or her to attend a treatment program. The framework of intervention for the drug problem at this point is between the home visitor and the client. However, if the client's behavior begins to harm children in the household, through neglect or by placing them in dangerous situations, the need for additional intervention becomes necessary. The children's basic well-being takes precedence over the parent's freedom of choice to take drugs while placing his or her children in potentially dangerous circumstances. The home visitor needs to follow local and state guidelines for reporting these circumstances. He or she also must evaluate the effectiveness of the help the client is receiving through home visiting and possibly seek alternatives and discuss them with the client. For example, a drug rehabilitation center that allows parents to bring children might be an alternative intervention acceptable to the parent.

3. *An individual's right to freedom takes precedence over his or her own right to basic well-being.* If an informed client voluntarily chooses to take an action that could threaten him or her, the client's freedom to do so takes precedence over his of her basic mental and physical well-being. Determining whether a person is informed about the options is key. A teenager in a court-ordered program for youthful offenders may be free to leave the halfway house treatment program when reaching age 18, although the public school resource visitor wishes the teenager would continue the program in which he or she receives counseling and GED classes rather than return to a non-

supportive home. The visitor can explain all this to the client and may even urge the client to get other advice (e.g., from the program's social worker), but, ultimately, an 18-year-old can make his or her own decision.

What if a client is seriously depressed or developmentally delayed? In those situations, would decisions be informed and voluntary? Sometimes other family members or professionals need to be involved because many home visitors are not mental health professionals and will need to consult with others or make a referral. In other situations, a client may be seriously depressed and suicidal. Even for a trained mental health professional, weighing a client's right to privacy with the risk of suicide is a difficult decision (Begler, 1997). Most home visitors are not trained mental health professionals, so they must act reasonably and quickly if such a situation arises with a client. Immediately consulting a supervisor or contacting a family member can lead to quick and necessary action.

4. *The obligation to obey laws, rules, and regulations to which one [the home visitor] has voluntarily and freely consented ordinarily overrides one's right to engage voluntarily and freely in a manner which conflicts with these laws, rules, and regulations.* This guideline means that home visitors are generally expected to obey the laws of society and the policies of their employer and their profession. For example, home visitors may be expected to follow an agency rule that a supervisor must be consulted before any referral is made to an outside agency on behalf of a client. Although a home visitor may believe that this rule inhibits the ability to work effectively and quickly for a client, he or she voluntarily agreed to the rule when the visitor accepted employment with the agency. The home visitor may work to change the policy but, until that time, the policy must be honored.

5. *Individuals' (clients') rights to well-being may override laws, rules, regulations, and arrangements of voluntary associations in cases of conflict.* Following this guideline, a home visitor is obligated to violate a rule if a client's well-being is in clear jeopardy. In one program, a home visitor arrived for a home visit and observed a child in serious respiratory distress, a situation that was being ignored (or perhaps misunderstood) by the mother. The home visitor immediately took the mother and child to an emergency room for treatment of what turned out to be a severe asthma attack. What if her agency had the

referral rule mentioned in the example above? Should she have had her supervisor's authorization? What if no supervisor could be reached by phone? What if the family had no phone? In this case, a child's right to timely medical care should override the agency's rules. Home visiting programs should provide guidelines for making decisions under such circumstances.

6. *The obligation to prevent basic harms such as starvation, and to promote public goods such as housing, education, and public assistance overrides the right to retain one's property.* Reamer presents this guideline as the justification for society to tax its members to provide for those in need. Among home visitors, one often sees this guideline in action when home visitors use their own money to buy groceries that will feed a family through the weekend or give clothes their own children have outgrown to their client families with younger children. These activities are certainly not necessary to be an effective home visitor and may be discouraged by some programs, but for some clients in some circumstances, we know that home visitors do use their own resources.

Consideration of Reamer's (1990) six guidelines can help home visitors assess their relative obligations toward family members, themselves, and society and be aware of alternate possibilities for action. However, neither this set nor any other set of ethical principles can be followed rigidly in daily practice. Rules cannot cover every kind of choice that a home visitor must make when helping a client. Nevertheless, knowledge of ethical guidelines, thoughtful consideration of each situation, and consultation with other professionals can make difficult judgments easier.

Ethics Training

Many home visitors have some familiarity with the ethical issues that surface in their profession because of their educational or experiential background in other areas or through a home visitor training program. For example, home visitors with training in child development may be familiar with Kohlberg's (1984) conception of six stages of moral development and can relate some of this knowledge to ethical decision making in home visiting. Other home visitors have had no specific instruction or ethical training.

Because of the complexities of ethical issues in home visiting, we believe that a discussion of ethics should be mandatory in home visitor training programs and should be covered periodically during in-service sessions. Expecting home visitors to learn about ethics informally or through experience is not as effective as formal exposure through training. Formally addressing ethical issues in preservice or in-service training provides the support home visitors need in their day-to-day work, and it also underscores the importance of ethics. Even a 3-hour workshop, when focused on ethical decision making using a problem-solving approach, has been shown to significantly improve the quality of students' decision-making processes compared with students in a control group (Gawthrop & Uhlemann, 1992). Several problem-solving approaches to teaching ethics have been summarized by Knauss (1997). In addition, supervision is another forum in which home visitors can discuss ethical issues and their obligations with their supervisor.

A Code of Ethics

Most helping professions have an established code of ethics. Psychologists have published *Ethical Principles of Psychologists* (American Psychological Association, 1992, 1993), counselors have the *Code of Ethics and Standards* (American Counseling Association, 1995), and social workers have the *Code of Ethics* (National Association of Social Workers [NASW], 1996). The National Association for the Education of Young Children (1997) developed a code of ethical conduct for early childhood educators. Because home visiting has no formal professional organization, it has no formalized professional ethical code of its own. We believe that the NASWs' code of ethics provides relevant guidance for ethical conduct in the home visiting profession.

The NASW's code of ethics summarizes the mission and core values of the social work profession: service, social justice, dignity and worth of the person, the importance of human relationships, integrity, and competence. The constellation of core values has an accompanying set of ethical principals that inform social work practice. For example, the value *integrity* is linked with the ethical principle emphasizing the role of trust in the helping relationship and the need for social workers to act honestly and responsibly. The last section of the code includes 155 specific ethical standards to guide social workers' conduct organized by ethical responsibilities to clients, colleagues, employers, the profession, and society. Reamer

(1998) has written a comprehensive review of this code of ethics using hundreds of case situations to illustrate how the code can offer guidance to human service workers as they face a variety of ethical dilemmas. The situations faced by home visitors are very similar to those faced by social workers, and this book can be a good source of examples to use in home visitor training.

A code such as the NASW's code of ethics can offer guidance in the general principles of ethical conduct underlying home visit practice, but it is not a set of rules describing specific behavior in all situations. Although hard decisions still have to be made concerning individual client situations, a code of ethics describes the fundamental values and the overall spirit in which practice decisions can be made.

As the population of the United States has become increasingly diverse, some theorists have questioned the extent to which professional codes impose guidelines that may not be appropriate to the cultural context of minority groups (LaFromboise, Foster, & James, 1996; Pedersen, 1995). For example, most professional codes of ethics strongly support the worth and dignity of the individual, reflecting the traditional American view of individualism, but many people now living in the United States have come from societies that value collectivism and cohesive social groups (Pedersen, 1997).

To work effectively in multicultural settings, two components are important. Home visitors must first recognize that their own values and attitudes have been shaped by their culture and then remain open to other values and attitudes their clients may have learned in a different cultural context (Goodwin, 1997). Although it is difficult to teach the self-awareness needed to be sensitive to others, some studies have shown that keeping journals or reflecting on one's own spirituality and religious beliefs might be helpful (LaFromboise et al., 1996). The second component of multicultural competence is to have knowledge of other cultures and effective strategies of working with individuals of different cultural backgrounds. As noted in Chapter 5, training programs that provide systematic didactic and experiential education can enhance this aspect of home visitors' work (Ridley, Mendoza, Kanitz, Angermeier, & Zenk, 1994).

We now turn to the following four issues of particular ethical concern to home visitors: honesty, confidentiality, professional limits, and terminating services.

Honesty

Some would agree with the philosopher Emmanuel Kant that truth is unconditional: A home visitor should always tell the truth. Others believe that under some circumstances, withholding information or telling a lie might avoid harmful consequences to a client's well-being. Following a rigid always-tell-the-truth rule might be shortsighted and result in harm to a client. We mentioned earlier the situation in which a home visitor lied about the location of a child when an angry, potentially violent father came looking for the child. In the home visitor's judgment, a lie in this situation protected the client's best interest by keeping the mother and her child away from a threatening situation. Although this principle says it is permissible to lie, certainly the circumstances under which lying is justifiable must be carefully considered and relatively extreme. On this issue, caring, competent professionals are certain to have some disagreement. Home visitors need to be aware that they may face dilemmas that call into question their own values and challenge them to make difficult but necessary judgment calls. The old adage, "honesty is always the best policy," does not apply to every interpersonal circumstance.

Confidentiality

Confidentiality is an ethical obligation for a home visitor. It is a duty included in the code of ethics of every helping profession. It may be violated only if an individual's well-being is in jeopardy or in specific types of professional situations described later. Conveying to a client that information a home visitor learns about the client and the client's family will be kept confidential is an essential part of the trust-building process. To be successful in their work, home visitors need to gain their clients' trust. Home visitors often learn intimate personal details from some of their families not only from what they are told but also from what they see and hear while in the home. Indeed, they may learn more than clients intend, making it even more important that the confidential nature of the home visiting relationship be understood.

Each program will have its particular policies and procedures to ensure confidentiality, but several guidelines are applicable to all programs. Home visitors should not discuss clients by name unless they are doing so with their supervisor or in a case conference with team members. They should always make certain that the setting in which they discuss clients is appropriately private, and they should never discuss clients in public places. If home visitors are helping link clients to other community services, they must obtain their clients' permission to do so beforehand. If a client has given permission for a home visitor to share confidential information with specific agencies or individuals, the home visitor should limit the information to what is essential for the specific situation involved.

Especially for written materials, precautions should be established to protect confidential materials from being lost, damaged, or inadvertently combined with nonconfidential materials that may be distributed during a visit. It would be a serious breach of confidentiality to allow confidential written materials about one client to be seen by another client. Special care should be taken to keep clients' files and materials separate, especially because home visitors spend much of their time working out of their cars.

A home visitor is usually part of a larger team of people (e.g., physicians, nurses, school counselors) who are also involved in the delivery of special services to the family. To contribute to the overall program, a home visitor has an obligation to share pertinent family information with these other professionals, but even in these situations, to avoid any undue invasion of the family's privacy, the visitor should carefully consider and balance any information that is disclosed. In these professional situations, many home visitors have concerns about what and how much to share. Some are hesitant to share any information at all. The key word seems to be *pertinent*. If other members of the team know the concerns of the home visitor, they might have useful information to share. They may see the family in other settings (i.e., medical clinics) and could help the home visitor monitor the family's needs. In these situations, sharing pertinent information enhances the client's well-being and is therefore acceptable practice in the team approach to service.

Because home visitors may occasionally have to convey personal family information to others, they should avoid giving a client the impression that absolutely no information will ever be shared with others. For example, families should know that most information will be held in confidence, but that in circumstances involving safety and well-being, a home visitor may disclose information to third parties. If information is routinely shared with a treatment team, then the client should be informed that this is the case. (Many programs include such a statement in their initial participation consent form.) Visitors should discuss this issue with clients in the initial stages of home visiting and make note of the discussion in the client's file (Begler, 1997). Once a visitor has built bonds of trust and respect with clients, the clients will usually be open with their conversations with visitors not because they believe there will be absolute confidentiality, but because they trust the visitor's judgment about sharing information.

Professional Limits

At times, a home visitor may believe that he or she is the only outside helper who has a good relationship with a family. As a result, the visitor may also assume that he or she should take the lead in responding to all family problems, for example, by providing in-depth counseling for a family in a crisis situation. Yet there are prudent and ethical limitations on the practice of all service providers, and home visitors are no exception. Levenstein (1981) called this ethical issue the "skills mismatch" between a home visitor who delivers a program and the services that he or she undertakes to deliver. The likelihood of having to address this professional issue may be greater for some home visitors than for other helpers because a home visitor may be the only service provider the family sees, and some clients may not be willing to seek services from other professionals.

Home visitors must recognize that they cannot be all things to all people. We have identified many situations in which home visiting is a desirable service alternative, but a visitor cannot be expected to respond to all the difficulties and stresses encountered in the families that he or she visits. Home visitors need to recognize family situations that are beyond a visitor's ability and training. A home visitor's response to family needs must be directly related to the visitor's competence.

One of the ways to minimize the problem of skills mismatch is for a home visitor to explain clearly to a client what his or her role will be. The sooner the limits and structure of the home visitor–client relationship are established, the sooner the visitor and client can focus on productive work together (Combs & Avila, 1985). This clarification of role may need to be discussed during the course of the home visiting for the client to clearly understand the visitor's role.

Sometimes the boundaries that define the home visitor–client relationship become blurred. The professional relationship between the two individuals can begin to feel and look like a personal friendship. The positive feelings that a visitor may develop about a client should not be confused with friendship. A balance needs to be struck between genuine professional concern and maintaining appropriate professional boundaries. This recommendation is, of course, easier said than done, but to be most effective, a home visitor must maintain objectivity and not overidentify with a client. This balance helps a visitor better serve a client and may help a client feel comfortable by knowing the boundaries of the relationship.

Clarifying the home visitor–client relationship is especially important in small communities in which a home visitor may have professional interactions with a person he or she knows well. A home visitor and a client may have gone to school together or a client may be the daughter of an acquaintance of the visitor. Maintaining professional limits while acknowledging an ongoing association can cause some conflicts for a visitor and, perhaps, the client. Discussing home visitor-client issues in the foyer after church would not be appropriate, but it is not necessary to avoid all social interactions. It is important in such situations for supervisors to discuss the nature of the dual relationship and use regular supervision sessions to discuss boundaries for appropriate visitor-client interactions.

Terminating Services

Some home visiting programs end after a predetermined amount of time, for example, after an infant has reached the age of 1 year. Other programs end when the goals of the program are achieved, such as when a teen mother has found the resources to help herself obtain a stable living situation, return to school, and provide for her child. In these situations, the ethical obligation of a home visitor is to prepare a client for ending home visiting by talking about it ahead of time, reviewing accomplishments, and helping the client plan for the future. Transitions are so important that one early childhood journal devoted an entire issue to effective transitioning (*Topics in Early Childhood Special Education,* 1990).

Although the program goals have not been met, are there situations when services to a family can or should be terminated? There are frustrating days when home visitors must surely want to "dismiss" some of their clients. They have been stood up for the 10th time, discovered that the client had missed the hard-to-set-up appointment at the hearing clinic, or observed once again the glassy gaze of a young mother who had vowed to stay off drugs. When can or should home visit services be terminated and what are the issues that would justify such a decision?

Usually a consideration to terminate arises because a client is not cooperating with the program's or the home visitor's plan, or at least appears to be uncooperative. In such situations, visitors must investigate the reasons for the client's lack of cooperation. Did the client have any say in the decision making about the type or course of intervention being conducted? If not, perhaps a renegotiation of the terms of the visitor-client relationship is in order and would bring about more cooperation. Clients are rarely motivated to follow a plan that has been imposed on them. Is the client freely participating in the program or was he or she coerced in some way? If participation was court ordered, then what are the conditions for a client who is no longer participating in the home visits? What motivation is there to continue? Does the client have the motivation but not the skills necessary to carry through with the program's objectives? If so, how can the home visitor teach or improve those skills?

After examining such issues, a home visitor may determine that a new course of treatment is required. For example, a program may decide to switch home visitors to see if another helper may be better able to reach a client or family. A home visitor may decide that a client is lacking in the motivation or skills to cooperate with the program in the foreseeable future, but a referral to another type of program may be worthwhile. He or she may decide that termination of services is appropriate. Under no circumstances is a home visitor under obligation to continue revising treatment endlessly to try to achieve cooperation.

Decisions to terminate are also influenced by the very real issue of time distribution. For a program with a waiting list, it is natural to think about enrolling a new family who may benefit from the program if efforts in trying to serve a difficult client were stopped. In such a case, a home visitor and the program director must weigh the needs and resources of both families. Issues to consider include determining which client may benefit more from the services, how large the visitor's caseload is, and/or whether two new families could be served by dropping one uncooperative family who lives far away and requires extensive travel time. Issues such as these become relevant when considering whether to close a case. Making the decision thoughtfully requires the consideration of the consequences for the families' well-being as well as weighing the duties of a limited resource: the home visitor.

Summary

The first part of this chapter has described some of the ethical concerns that a home visitor is likely to face in the course of visiting and helping an individual or a family. These problems are common to all home visitors working in the field, affecting them at the day-to-day practice level as they make specific decisions concerning individuals or families. Recognizing formal ethical guidelines, discussing ethics in training, and providing ethically and culturally sensitive supervision are ways that the profession can foster positive relationships between home visitors and their clients.

Issues Concerning the Profession

Among the professional issues related to home visiting, two particularly important issues stand out: burnout (a concern of home visitors because of the difficulty involved in the kind of work they perform) and working in multidisciplinary teams (a situation inherent in the settings in which home visitors typically work).

Professional Burnout

As a term, *burnout* has only been in the professional literature since 1974, when Freudenberger wrote about the problem in free clinics and other alternative agencies that depended on volunteer help. It was soon apparent that the concept applied to paid, salaried, and self-employed professionals as well.

Edelwich and Brodsky (1980) defined burnout as a "progressive loss of idealism, energy, and purpose experienced by people in the helping professions as a result of the conditions of their work" (p. 14). Burnout can result from many conditions, including low pay, insufficient training, ungrateful clients, heavy caseloads, and political constraints and realities. Another condition is the unpredictability of work with clients, a situation found to be more stressful to social workers than the actual amount of work (Fineman, 1985). Maslach and Leiter (1997) emphasize the cultural and workplace conditions that lead to burnout and note that all professions, not just human services, are now concerned with burnout. The costs of burnout are high—staff turnover, the expense of training a new person, lowering of project staff morale, and loss of continuity of contact and communication with a client.

It would be impossible to prevent burnout among all home visitors because the difficult conditions that inevitably exist in most home visiting programs (i.e., clients in poverty, heavy caseloads, long hours, low salaries) combine to create burnout. However, preparing to resist and successfully overcome burnout can be accomplished by better recognizing or anticipating how, when, and why burnout occurs.

Edelwich and Brodsky (1980) describe a four-stage progression of burnout: (a) idealistic enthusiasm, (b) stagnation, (c) frustration, and (d) apathy. They also suggest possible interventions that can be used at these four points. Unfortunately, the need for interventions with the professional are often not noticed until the last stage, when the symptoms of burnout are most apparent.

At the very beginning of a job, idealistic enthusiasm may actually be a sign of impending burnout. A home visitor may have unrealistic expectations of clients and the progress they might make and in their own personal expectations—for example, how much he or she might accomplish with clients. At this stage, an appropriate intervention is a dose of realism. A supervisor, a trainer, or an experienced colleague can be the voice of reason, making it clear that not all goals can be met and not all clients will welcome their visitor. Home visitors need to tell themselves that being realistic is not the same as backing down, and setting realistic goals is one way to prevent burnout.

The second stage toward potential burnout is stagnation, when the initial burst of enthusiasm ebbs and the home visitor may feel stalled in his or her work with clients. Time away from one's own family may begin to take its toll. The visitor may be sleeping poorly, eating irregularly, or skipping exercise classes or social events. The job is getting done, but the visitor's personal needs are not being met. The home visitor may feel like he or she is handling too many cases and putting in too much overtime.

At this stage of burnout, a supervisor can play an effective role by helping a visitor reflect on the balance of work and personal life and by reinforcing the need to maintain some boundaries between work and home. A supervisor can also help a home visitor look at his or her clients a little differently and perhaps renew the meaning of the work. Focusing or refocusing on the process of home visiting may be one way to recharge the energy of a home visitor. If realistic goals have been forgotten, perhaps goals can be revised with plans put in effect for moving toward those goals. A supervisor can validate how much has been accomplished by home visitors, infusing visitors with a renewed sense of purpose and helping them see that small victories are part of the overall success of their work.

The interventions for burnout mentioned thus far involve a rethinking or cognitive reappraisal on the part of the home visitor, perhaps with the help of a supervisor. Having realistic expectations, focusing on the process, and celebrating the small successes can help a home visitor keep work in perspective and maintain a positive focus. However, reappraisal may not be a sufficient intervention for the next two stages of burnout.

The stagnation phase of burnout is followed by the frustration phase, what Edelwich and Brodsky (1980) call the "core of burnout." Not only is the visitor unhappy about the job but she is no longer doing the job. The quality of service to the clients is reduced. Perhaps physical symptoms appear, such as headaches, backaches, or nervousness. If something does not help the home visitor find satisfaction in the work with clients, the fourth stage of burnout, apathy, will inevitably follow. In this stage, one might see an obvious turning away from others and a sense of detachment and distance from clients and coworkers that is often perceived as boredom and indifference.

Cognitive reappraisal may help with the third and fourth levels of burnout, but additional action is usually needed. Such action could include further education, setting a different routine or schedule, making an on-the-job adjustment such as changing some job activities, or, ultimately, leaving the field. Sometimes attending a workshop can rejuvenate enthusiasm and be a useful tool for learning, but the "workshop high" is only temporary and other changes need to be made in the routines of the work or in the definition of the job to curtail burnout.

Support from colleagues and supervisors is also important in burnout prevention, preferably support opportunities that are built into the program such as regular individualized supervision or peer support groups (Maslach, 1982). In some home visiting programs, visitors themselves organize regular, though informal, after work or lunch get-togethers where they can meet. In one home visiting project, the Infant Health and Development Program (IHDP), annual meetings were conducted for home visitors from eight cities because these workshops were important for in-service training and skills improvement (Gross et. al., 1997). These annual meetings were also of immeasurable value in providing contact with the network of other home visitors, and these informal contacts provided home visitors with knowledge and support from each other. These informal benefits may have been as important and useful as the formal content of the workshops. These experiences emphasized to us the importance of providing such ongoing opportunities to home visiting program staff members. Although regular travel to out-of-state meetings will not be possible in many service programs, other arrangements can be made to bring together home visitors (e.g., state, regional, or agency-wide meetings). In the past decade, we have seen a considerable increase in such meetings across the country.

Working to become a better helper has been suggested as one way of counteracting burnout. When a home visitor improves his or her own skills, the rewards accrue to the home visitor as well as to the client. Even when some of the clients do not seem to make progress, a home visitor should be able to see personal progress and therefore feel some accomplishment in his or her work. Many of the skills mentioned in Chapter 5 (i.e., listening, questioning, problem solving) help a home visitor interact well with clients, but they can also help insulate against burnout. Through conscious action on the part of the home visitor and supervisor to improve and fine-tune these skills, the process of home visiting and self-development can be made a focus. A home visitor can then assess his or her own progress as well as that of the clients and find successes in one's own work even at times when it may be hard to see success in the clients' lives.

The Multidisciplinary Team Approach

Many home visitors will find themselves operating in a team with other professionals who approach child and family problems from differing backgrounds. The advantage of a multidisciplinary team approach is that several individuals are able to work together to communicate, collaborate, and consolidate specialized knowledge to develop and carry out a well-informed plan of action with a client (Bruder, 1996). Many problems, such as child abuse, are so complex that treating them adequately often requires expertise from different people.

Although the advantages of the team model are numerous, there can be disadvantages or frustrations for the team member, often a home visitor, who is in the field and who has the most frequent contact with the family. Frequent contacts may lead a home visitor to feel that he or she is shouldering a disproportionately large share of the work involved with the family, especially if the visitor does not feel supported by the team or if fundamentally does not agree with all aspects of the intervention approach. Some team members may be perceived as having more status or influence than others. In work with teams of physicians, nurses, and social workers, home visitors have reported that more credence is sometimes given to the opinions of those with a medical background regardless of whether the problem is medical, educational, social, or psychological. Even among the different medical members of a team, there is frequently a tendency for the physician to take the lead in decision making regardless of his or her programmatic role. This problem of group hierarchy seems especially prevalent in teams whose members have worked solely in one professional area and who do not have previous multidisciplinary team experience. Some home visitors often feel that they are at the bottom of the professional totem pole and perceive that their opinions are not as valued as those members with higher degrees or higher administrative rank. This situation is potentially nonproductive and divisive.

Research shows that members of effective teams have a clear understanding of the team's goals; are results driven; have members with both content and collaborative competence; work in a climate of openness, trust, and respect; have enough resources to accomplish their job; and, most critically, have a leader with vision and commitment (Larson & LaFasto, 1989). As the leader, the home visit program director must set the tone for the team by promoting an atmosphere of collegiality, respect for each person's contribution, and recognition of the need for varying competencies. If the program director has delegated the role of team leader to another person, then that individual is responsible for creating and supporting the collaborative team culture.

The leader can more easily facilitate team collaboration if all the professionals participating in the team—educators, social workers, nurses, physical therapists—are members of the same unit or same project because there are more opportunities for team members to interact, and more advantages are gained by the project as a result of good teamwork. Sometimes home visitors may participate in community-based teams in which each member represents a different agency and the team leader has limited authority over individual team participants. In such teams, home visitors may have to work a little harder to be heard or to promote collegiality. Teams have many different roles, including selecting cases, sharing information, planning services, and monitoring community-wide needs. In the process of carrying out these activities, a team will be involved in many aspects of problem solving, such as discussing family needs, resources, and possible treatment plans. In all these activities, it is important that each team member be assumed to carry equal weight in the decision making, although each may defer at times to those with the most pertinent knowledge about a particular situation. Equally important, a team should provide emotional support and encouragement to a team member most directly responsible for carrying out the treatment plan. This approach not only boosts staff morale but also provides a client with the best services possible.

A leader can also improve a team's effectiveness by providing frequent opportunities for communication. In team meetings, discussions should be facilitated and all relevant information exchanged. This exchange of information is another area in which some teams have difficulty. A member who does not value the expertise of another team member may be less willing to share all of the relevant information about the family or to give careful consideration to each team member's perspective.

A team member's professional attitude can change after spending some time walking in the other person's shoes. When a home visitor spends a day in a hospital pediatric clinic, or when a pediatrician accompanies a home visitor on a few visits, each may come to a better understanding of the other's position. Experiencing a family or a job from another's point of view is, for some, a totally new discovery that can result in greater understanding of the family.

Sometimes a leadership change as simple as rotating the group facilitator can help improve team communication. Outside consultation, such as hiring a psychologist to conduct sessions on professional communication and values, can help a team recognize the value of information from many sources. Although it specifically focuses on teams dealing with child abuse, *The New Child Protection Team Handbook* (Bross, Krugman, Lenherr, Rosenberg, & Schmitt, 1988) is an excellent source of useful information about types of multidisciplinary teams and information on conducting effective team meetings (Grosz & Denson, 1988).

Summary

In this chapter, we have described the need to assure training and discussion of ethical issues before sending home visitors into the field to participate in relationships that will often raise thorny issues of conscience. The framework for ethical decision making described by Reamer (1990) and the code of ethics of the NASW are useful to us in considering this area, but there are other codes that can also serve this purpose. However, no framework or set of guidelines will always make decision making easy. Visiting people in their homes with the potential of influencing and affecting their lives will inevitably lead to ethical dilemmas. This situation will occur regardless of the main intent of the visiting program (medical, educational, or social support) or characteristics of the clients (teenagers, parents of premature infants, or abusive parents). Responding thoughtfully, acting competently, and referring clients to other services when appropriate are the actions of an accountable home visitor; one who is best able to promote the welfare of the client.

Note

1. The six guidelines are quoted directly from Reamer (1990, pp. 62-65). The examples are our own.

9

Assessment and Documentation in Home Visiting

Record-keeping is probably the least favorite task of home visitors. Although it can seem tedious, the appropriate documentation of home visits is an essential component of most home visiting programs. By keeping records of visits, home visitors can monitor the progress of their clients, and program directors can monitor the progress of their overall services.

Most home visiting programs do not have the resources to conduct comprehensive program evaluations, nor are they required to do so. Almost all program directors, however, will be interested in collecting basic information about their clients and their program, especially if it can done efficiently. In this chapter, we have tried to keep these conditions in mind.

The purpose of this chapter is to review the types of record-keeping often used by home visiting programs, provide a rationale for record-keeping techniques, and elaborate on the benefits of record-keeping through the use of examples. Individuals desiring more information on recent home visiting program evaluations will find that Gomby (1999) provides a good summary of the evaluation designs and measures of several major home visiting studies of children and families conducted during the past decade. For program directors desiring guidelines to evaluate their own services, books by Rossi and Freeman (1989) and Weiss and Jacobs (1988) may be beneficial.

Home visiting programs typically require the following two types of record-keeping: client assessment and program documentation. Client assessments are generally conducted to determine (a) client needs or goals, (b) a program's effectiveness for clients, and (c) client satisfaction with a program. Documentation procedures often used in home visiting programs include (a) recording information about each home visit to ensure their delivery and quality and (b) recording specific content or procedures of the visits to document adherence to a specific protocol. Client assessment and program documentation provide information useful for evaluation purposes, and both types of data are sometimes needed to meet legal, reimbursement, or certification requirements.

In this chapter, we discuss different reasons for assessment of clients and several different strategies for measurement. We will also describe different types of program documentation that are useful in home visiting, including some illustrative forms. The advantages and disadvantages associated with each kind of record-keeping will be discussed, as well as those associated with the process of data collection in general. Several important characteristics of assessments, including their utility, validity, and reliability, will be briefly summarized because these characteristics should be considered in deciding to use a measure. Finally, we will conclude with a discussion of the benefits of using assessment and documentation information as a part of program evaluation, looking at evaluation from the standpoint of the client, visitor, supervisor, program director, and public policy maker.

The overall importance of record-keeping for home visitors is indicated by its inclusion in the National Credentialing Program (1987) competency goals for the Child Development Associate and home visitor: "the competent [home visitor] candidate develops and uses observation skills and evaluation instruments to record relevant information about children and their families in a nonjudgmental manner" (p. 38).

We have divided our discussion of record-keeping into the following three sections, distinguished by the time period during which the procedures are typically used: (a) initial data collection, (b) outcome data collection, and (c) ongoing program documentation. *Initial data collection* is often part of an intake process conducted by a home visiting program. Information about a client is gathered, ranging from descriptive demographic information to client attitudes, problems, and needs. *Outcome data collection* typically takes place at or near the end of a program or periodically during a program (e.g., annually). Information about client attitudes, characteristics, and/or behaviors is gathered to determine the effectiveness of a program. This type of data collection is often associated with home visiting research projects, although many projects whose primary function is service delivery also collect outcome data on their clients. With increased emphasis on performance-based budgeting (also called outcomes-based budgeting) and other government accountability efforts, the need for good outcome data increases. *Ongoing program documentation* is record-keeping done throughout the course of home visiting to describe or summarize the procedures and content of the program delivered to the client or to record client progress. These three types of record-keeping will be further elaborated in this chapter and are summarized in Table 9.1.

Because the time of both visitors and their clients is valuable, any type of data collection used or required by a program should have specific and valid reasons for inclusion in the routine home visiting procedures. Client assessments, whether focused on individuals or families, can be time consuming and sometimes intrusive, and documentation of home visiting can also take a visitor's time away from activities perceived to be more constructive. Thus, the advantages to be gained by the assessment or documentation information should outweigh the potential disadvantages. The following sections discuss in more detail several of the specific reasons for including the various types of record-keeping as a part of the responsibility of home visitors.

Initial Data Collection

Two kinds of initial data collection will be discussed here: gathering basic demographic and descriptive information about clients and about their needs. Both kinds of information are typically part of a program's intake process and may be gathered by a home visitor or by another staff member. If a home visitor does not gather the information directly, he or she should have access to all relevant initial records concerning the client in order to make good decisions with the client about potential services.

TABLE 9.1 Assessment and Documentation Overview

	Client Assessments		
	Collection Initial Data	*Collection Outcome Data*	*Ongoing Program Documentation*
Types	▪ Intake ▪ Demographic ▪ Client needs	▪ Client functioning ▪ Attitudes and behavior ▪ Home environment ▪ Client satisfaction	▪ Home visit procedures ▪ Program content ▪ Referral contacts ▪ Client behavior
When	▪ Early visits	▪ Typically yearly, biannually, or end of program	▪ Daily or weekly
Examples	▪ Interviews ▪ Checklists	▪ Questionnaires ▪ Observations	▪ Home visit reports ▪ Case notes
Goals	▪ Document client needs ▪ Individualize program	▪ Show client progress and program effectiveness	▪ Monitor program delivery and client progress ▪ Replicate successful programs

Demographic and Descriptive Data Collection

If basic demographic information has not already been collected by the program, a home visitor will want to obtain this information in the earliest stages of visiting, probably during the first or second visit. Obtaining such information during the initial intake process is usually easy because people typically expect to answer certain kinds of questions when they enroll in new programs.

Learning about the constellation of household members and their roles helps a home visitor know the supports available to her client and what problems a client or family may be facing. If a parent-child pair is the focus of the home visits, the home visitor should know something about how they spend their days. Is the child in day care? If the mother is a teenager, does she attend school? Who cares for the child when the mother is out? What is her phone number at work and would it be all right to phone her there to schedule visits? Many of these facts are easy to obtain in the course of the first or second visit through friendly conversations with a client. Talking about some of the daily routines of life also helps build rapport between a parent and home visitor. Completion of a basic questionnaire listing some of this information is useful, especially if a home visitor's caseload is extensive. Examples of such questionnaires are included in *The Head Start Home Visitor Handbook.* (Wolfe & Herwig, 1986). Use of any interview form should be done in a conversational manner.

An ecomap is another useful assessment for developing a description of family systems and relationships (Hartman, 1995). Using a large piece of poster paper and colored markers symbolizing different resources, a home visitor and parent graphically "map" all of the systems and important people involved with the family or the child (e.g., family, church, school, peers, health providers). Sometimes this process has the effect of pointing out the many resources already available to a family; other times it makes obvious the issues that may need to be addressed. Specific goals can be added to the ecomap, with notations made of systems or individuals who might help with progress toward those goals. A periodic review and updating of the ecomap can enable the parent and visitor to monitor progress.

Determining Clients' Goals and Needs

Another type of early assessment involved in some home visiting programs is an assessment of the goals or needs of an individual client or family. Whether using an interview or checklist, a good assessment of needs (a) identifies client or family strengths and needs, (b) sets priorities for goals, and (c) begins to plan ways to meet the goals (Wolfe & Herwig, 1986).

Needs assessment is consistent with the first principle of home visiting presented in Chapter 2, which specifies that family support should enhance the ability of families to work toward their own goals. A home visitor should not presume to know the needs of a client. It is too easy for his or her biases and beliefs to be projected onto the client. Identifying needs *for* clients can reinforce their view of themselves as ineffective problem solvers and begins the home visitor–client relationship with a built-in inequity ("I know what's best for you") rather than a sharing and collaborative relationship.

An informative assessment of client needs can be conducted just by listening well during the first few visits and letting a parent verbalize his or her worries, joys, and hopes. Good interviewing skills will help a home visitor elicit parent needs, even during early visits before the visitor and client get to know each other very well.

Another way of conducting a needs assessment is through the use of a checklist of client needs, concerns, skills, and strengths. The checklist can be answered in writing by a client on a rating form, or it can be completed with a visitor reading the items and explaining them, if necessary. The process of completing a checklist may act as a mechanism for family members to state verbally a concern they had been harboring for some time. Completion of a checklist provides an opportunity for the concern to be discussed openly. The *Head Start Home Visitor Handbook* (U.S. Department of Health and Human Services, 1993) includes examples of needs assessments that have been adapted by a number of different Head Start programs. The Head Start Family Needs Assessment can be ordered from the Head Start Bureau.

We describe here two measures to illustrate the kind of assessment data that can be gathered early in the program and that can be of functional use to a home visitor and program planners as well as to a family. The Family Needs Survey (Bailey, 1995; Bailey & Simeonsson, 1988) is an example of an instrument that assesses parents' needs for information about their child; for family, friend, and professional support; for information about resources; and for other needs that may be present in a family of a child with a disability. The first section of the 35-question Needs for Information Scale is displayed in Table 9.2. Although the survey was specifically written for families of children with disabilities, most of it is general enough that it could be used with families with many different issues. It is a relatively direct and nonthreatening approach to assessment of client needs, and one that has immediate implications for the interventionist.

TABLE 9.2 Family Needs Survey (excerpt)

Donald Bailey
Rune Simeonsson
Frank Porter Graham Child Development Center
The University of North Carolina at Chapel Hill

Family name/ID ___________Relationship to child ______________
Date _______________

INSTRUCTIONS: Listed below are some of the needs expressed by parents of special children. Please read each statement and decide if you need help in this area. Then circle the number (1, 2, or 3) that represents your response to the need.

	Definitely do not need help with this	*Not Sure*	*Definitely need help with this*
NEEDS FOR INFORMATION			
1. I need more information about my child's condition or disability.	1	2	3
2. I need more information about how to handle my child's behavior.	1	2	3
3. I need more information about how to teach my child.	1	2	3
4. I need more information on how to play with or talk to my child.	1	2	3
5. I need more information about the services that my child might receive in the future.	1	2	3
6. I need more information on the services that are presently available for my child.	1	2	3
7. I need more information about how children grow and develop.	1	2	3

A home visitor should make a special effort to ask about any areas that are noted to be of concern. After completing the paper-and-pencil part of the needs assessment, further discussion is important for two reasons: First, parents have many individual needs that do not fit these questions (Bailey, 1995); second, home visitors may need to help families prioritize their needs. Although an answer on a survey may indicate a family's awareness of a need, home visitors need to remain sensitive to the fact that a client or family may not necessarily be ready to address a particular need.

The Family Information Preference Inventory (Turnbull & Turnbull, 1986) is a measure that takes into account the ways in which families would like to receive information or help. Similar to the Family Needs Survey, parents are asked to indicate which of several listed topics are of interest to them. They are then asked about the format in which they would like to receive help or information about topics of interest (e.g., written information, parent groups, home visits). The checklist includes an open-ended section to let parents indicate any additional needs they might have. No summary scores are calculated from this particular measure, but the service provider uses answers to individual questions to plan intervention content and procedures. Any home visiting program could adopt the format of this measure by tailoring the list of needs to match those typically experienced by a client population and the list of alternative ways of meeting those needs to the types of services offered by the program.

Informal Interviewing

The use of paper-and-pencil assessments such as the two just described has been called into question (Summers et al., 1990). These kinds of assessments, as well as structured interviews, are often used to gather information needed for required processes (e.g., Individualized Family Service Plans [IFSPs]). However, data from more than 100 parents and professionals involved in IFSPs indicate that they overwhelmingly prefer informal approaches and open-ended conversations as the most family-sensitive way of developing an IFSP. Although validated instruments are often required for objectivity or accountability, a more informal process is clearly preferred by families and should be considered either as a part of the process or for a complete interview.

The preference for informal approaches highlights the need for a home visit program to ensure that the formal assessments that are used provide useful information to a home visitor. Many programs spend extensive time and effort collecting information about topics that may not enlighten a home visitor or help plan the course of the visits. For example, family stress is a frequently assessed characteristic that knowledge of may be of little benefit in the day-to-day practices involved in home visiting; most families in home visiting programs face a variety of stresses. Information on stresses relevant to an individual family's situation will usually come up in informal discussions.

To summarize the major purpose of initial data collection, information obtained from a needs assessment and initial demographic information should help a home visitor individualize a particular home visiting program to best meet a client's needs. To the extent that this information can be gathered in an informal and unstructured way, family preferences will be better met.

Outcome Data Collection

Most home visitors have an impression about the effectiveness of their services in supporting a family or client. They see parents making progress toward self-sufficiency, and they see children learning and playing more appropriately. Home visitors can tell when a client needs extra encouragement to continue making progress toward a goal. These clinical impressions are valuable and often very accurate. However, impressionistic data tend to be imprecise and subjective and may be influenced by home visitor expectations. As a result, many home visiting programs require the collection of systematic outcome data.

From an ethical standpoint, a professional will always want to know whether an intervention provided to a client was successful. Not only is this information part of good practice but accountability is increasingly required as part of program funding or certification. For a home visiting program, outcome questions might address whether the support provided by a home visitor was useful to a client, whether the information delivered was acted on, and whether a family seemed to make any progress toward identified goals. Measuring a program's effectiveness for a client may indicate whether the interventions can be repeated with other similar clients or whether they need to be modified or discontinued.

Many different kinds of outcome assessment have been used in home visit programs. The domains of measurement frequently tapped are the home environment, client or family functioning, a client's physical or mental health, and client satisfaction. If a child is part of a home visit program, outcome measures might include assessments of cognitive, social, or self-help skills; parent knowledge or attitudes about child rearing; and/or parent-child interaction. Because entire books have been written about each of these types of assessment, this section will only briefly mention some of the instruments that have been used frequently by home visiting programs.

Home Environment and Family Functioning

A variety of methods have been used to evaluate the family context, including self-reports, questionnaires, interviews, formal and informal observational procedures, and structured tasks. Reviews of family assessments can be found in Touliatos, Perlmutter, and Straus (1990). Here we describe a few measures that have been used by home visiting programs.

The Home Observation for the Measurement of the Environment (HOME) (Caldwell & Bradley, 1984) is probably the best known measure used to document the physical and social environment of infants and young children. The HOME can be scored after a 30- to 60-minute visit with a parent in the family's residence. It uses a yes-no format for scoring items based on observation by the assessor and through parental report. Higher scores indicate more optimal, stimulating environments for young children. Versions of the HOME exist for infants and toddlers, preschoolers, and school-age children. The HOME is also available in Spanish. Major subscores include the physical organization of the environment, maternal involvement with the child, and play and learning materials (Caldwell, 1998).

The HOME was used as an outcome measure in five of the six major randomized studies of home visiting reported in *The Future of Children* (1999). In two of these studies, the Memphis Nurse Home Visiting program (described in Chapter 3 of this book) and the Virginia Healthy Families America program, the HOME was significantly higher for families who had participated in home visiting when compared with families who had not.

Variants of the HOME have been developed to administer in clinic settings. For example, the Home Screening Questionnaire (HSQ) (Coons, Gay, Fandal, Ker, & Frankenburg, 1981) can be completed by a parent in a waiting-room setting. In a study with a sample of 799 children, Frankenburg and Coons (1986) reported a correlation of .71 between the HSQ and the HOME. They also reported that the HSQ correctly identified 81% of families who would need intensive intervention. Another measure, called the PROCESS (Pediatric Review and Observation of Children's Environmental Support and Stimulation) (Casey, Bradley, Nelson, & Whaley, 1988), has 24 items that are filled out by a parent and 20 items that are rated by someone who has seen the family in a clinic. Correlations between the PROCESS and the HOME are very high (above .80).

The goal of many home visiting programs is to help clients better understand some aspect of family living, such as how to raise children without being abusive or to cope better with a particular problem, such as learning to provide home care for a chronically ill child. Although the HOME is often used to measure family environment, no single measure of family functioning has become a standard of practice. Selection of a measure in this domain depends on the outcomes desired by the program. Client outcome measures include problem solving or coping scales, such as the Wasik Problem Solving Rating Scale (Wasik et al., 1988) and the Folkman-Lazarus Ways of Coping Checklist (Folkman & Lazarus, 1980). These measures help determine the cognitive and behavioral strengths that are deemed important for handling both short- or long-term problems. In these cases, the objective of home visiting is to help a client obtain coping skills sufficient to handle a particular situation.

The Adult-Adolescent Parenting Inventory (AAPI) (Bavolek, 1989), a 32-item self-administered measure of attitudes about child rearing and beliefs about parenting, has been used in some home visiting programs. In the Comprehensive Child Development Program (St. Pierre & Layzer, 1999), the corporal punishment scale of the AAPI was significantly lower at the end of the study for families receiving home visits than for families in the control group. In the Memphis Nurse Home Visit Program, another AAPI scale related to beliefs associated with child abuse was also significantly lower for home visited families than for control families (Kitzman et al., 1997). Because improvement of parenting skills is a goal of many programs, this measure makes sense, is relatively easy to administer, and has been sensitive to interventions in some studies.

Home visiting is usually conducted in a family environment, and the functioning of the family system is often an outcome of interest, even if one specific family member is the identified client. Based on different theories of family functioning, many different measures are available. Several measures of family functioning that are generally easy to score have been developed. Data from various comparison samples are also available on these measures. The Family Adaptability and Cohesion Evaluation Scales (FACES III), a 20-question rating scale measuring family cohesion and adaptability, is useful in measuring perceived and ideal functioning (Olson, Portner, & Lavee, 1985). A family's coping ability is measured by the Family Crisis Oriented Personal Evaluation Scales (the F-COPES) (McCubbin, Olson, & Larsen, 1981). The F-COPES is a 30-item inventory measuring problem solving, support seeking, family mobilization, and other relevant family characteristics.

As mentioned earlier, many home visiting programs include a measure of stress as one kind of family functioning measure. In fact, measures of stress and coping are often included together in an assessment package under the presumption that they are tapping similar client or family constructs (Krauss, 1988). Stress measures include checklists of recent life events, such as the Schedule of Recent Events (Holmes & Rahe, 1967), an older measure that is still frequently used based on its proven relationship to the frequency of illnesses. The Life Experiences Survey (Sarason, Johnson, & Siegel, 1978) yields separate indices of undesirable and desirable life changes that have occurred recently, as well as a rating of the extent to which those changes influenced the individual. Scores are related to measures of anxiety, depression, and lack of coping. The Parenting Stress Index (Abidin, 1983) includes sections measuring the stress involved in the parent-child interaction and whether the family is at risk for dysfunctional parenting.

For a program to choose these particular measures of client and family functioning as outcome assessments there should be some presumption that the home visit intervention could reasonably be expected to have an effect on these complex and sometimes pervasive family problems. Because many of these measures overlap considerably in their concepts of family roles, support, and problem solving, selection of the measures should be guided by the philosophy and techniques of the particular home visiting program.

Parent-Child Interactions

Many home visiting programs are designed for parents and their children, so parent-child interaction is an outcome often measured. The goal of many parent-child home visiting programs is to improve some aspect of the parent's knowledge of his or her child, information on child development, or behavior with his or her child or children. The purpose of a parent-child assessment in these programs would be to measure whether a parent's behavior with the child changed as a result of the home visit intervention. Does the parent respond more often to the child's cues? Is the parent's language with the children less directive and more informative? How and when does the parent try to exercise control over the child?

Attempts have been made to answer these and other questions in the area of parent-child interaction, but currently there is no standard assessment instrument or procedure. A frequently used procedure is the Nursing Child Assessment Satellite Training (NCAST) Teaching Scale (Barnard, 1994), in which the quality of the parent-child interaction is rated by a trained observer as a parent teaches a child a developmentally appropriate task. Home visiting programs that have focused on parent language and teaching styles have sometimes noted significant changes in families by using the NCAST, either over time with treatment families or between treatment and control families, although an equal number of programs have not found significant differences on this measure. (See the review of home visit evaluations in *The Future of Children*, 1999.)

Other programs have developed rating scales for visitors or other staff to describe the general tone of the interaction between mother and child, and/or the pacing, language exchanges, or reinforcement seen during the home visits or clinic sessions. In a program conducted with low-income teen mothers in Washington, D.C., visits occurred in a mobile van that traveled around to parents' homes and apartments. Home visitors were public health nurses who delivered well-baby health care and discussed infant stimulation. They also brought an educational toy on almost every visit, talked with the mother about learning and development, and placed major emphasis on language stimulation. Using a rating scale to judge the frequency with which mothers vocalized to their children, this study showed that intervention mothers vocalized more often than nonintervention mothers. The groups did not differ in the extent to which the mothers permitted their children's exploratory behavior, nor in how they handled unacceptable behavior (Gutelius et.al., 1977).

Other home visiting programs have set up problem-solving situations to see how a mother helps a child with a prescribed or semistructured task. In the Mother-Child Home Program (MCHP), a program of home visits for low-income mothers of 2- to 4-year-old children, a visitor delivered toys and then modeled how to use them, encouraging the mother to participate. At the end of the program, mothers and children were left alone in a room to play with a toy train and a form board. From videotapes of these sessions, 10 categories of behavior were tallied, such as labeling, verbalization of actions, and verbal praise. The mean frequencies of these desirable behaviors were from 33% to 51% higher in the intervention groups (Madden, O'Hara, & Levenstein, 1984).

Howrigan (1988) has written a thorough review of parent-child interaction measures in family-oriented programs, noting several methodological considerations and describing the research on many different kinds of parent-child assessment. In particular, she notes that we must be aware of the wide diversity in parent-child interaction styles and seriously question our assumptions about which styles or behaviors are "better." Slaughter (1988) has recommended that measures should be normed with racially and ethnically diverse populations and that data should be gathered by people of the same race or ethnic group. In addition to considering the issues mentioned by Howrigan and Slaughter, special weight should be given to the match between program goals and what the parent-child assessment actually measures. Given the time and effort usually involved in collecting parent-child interaction assessments, a home visiting program should choose instruments carefully.

Client Satisfaction

The measurement of client satisfaction is important because clients are more likely to follow through with the goals or procedures of programs that they like. If a program is ongoing, a client's self-report can lead to changes that might be made in an undesirable aspect of the program that might help the client become more responsive or involved. Even if program changes were not possible for a current client, the home visitor could use the information to modify his or her approach with the next client, or it could be used by a program director to revise overall program goals or content.

However, satisfaction is a highly individualized and volatile construct that can be difficult to define and measure (Schwartz & Baer, 1991). In addition, as McNaughton (1994) verified in a study of 14 early intervention programs that included parent satisfaction measures, satisfaction with social programs is almost always extremely positive. Parents may report high satisfaction simply because they know of no better alternative or are happy to have some service when compared with no service at all. Nevertheless, parent satisfaction, particularly if used in combination with other activities that solicit parents' views (e.g., focus groups, IFSPs), seems to be an outcome worthy of measurement.

Because each program is different, a client satisfaction measure may need to be tailored for a specific home visiting program. We include a basic client satisfaction question in Table 9.3, an example of a relatively short questionnaire that is very broad in content. Bailey (1987) suggests that satisfaction questionnaires should also include some open-ended questions (e.g., "What did you most like/least like about this program?") because they might elicit novel feedback or areas of dissatisfaction (Perreault & Leichner, 1993). Periodically collecting satisfaction data alerts home visitors to issues that can be addressed before they further affect the quality of services.

Regular Assessment of Client Progress

Most of the examples of outcome assessments mentioned so far in this chapter are given relatively infrequently to clients, perhaps every 6 months or yearly, because they require time and sometimes special expertise to administer. In addition, if the behaviors of interest change slowly, frequent measurement may not indicate change.

Bloom, Fischer, and Orme (1999) list several reasons why it is important to use some kind of regular assessment of client progress. Such assessment enhances intervention planning, focuses on specific goals, allows progress or regression to be noted quickly (even

(Continued p. 240)

TABLE 9.3 The Client Satisfaction Questionnaire

Please help us improve our program by answering some questions about the services you have received at the ______________. We are interested in your honest opinions, whether they are positive or negative. *Please answer all of the questions.* We also welcome your comments and suggestions. Thank you very much, we appreciate your help.

Circle Your Answer

1. How would you rate the quality of service you received?

4	3	2	1
Excellent	Good	Fair	Poor

2. Did you get the kind of service you wanted?

1	2	3	4
No, definitely not	No, not really	Yes, generally	Yes, definitely

*3. To what extent has our program met your needs?

4	3	2	1
Almost all of my needs have been met	Most of my needs have been met	Only a few of my needs have been met	None of my needs have been met

4. If a friend were in need of similar help, would you recommend our program to him/her?

1	2	3	4
No, definitely not	No, I don't think so	Yes, I think so	Yes, definitely

5. How satisfied are you with the amount of help you received?

1	2	3	4
Quite dissatisfied	Indifferent or mildly dissatisfied	Mostly satisfied	Very satisfied

---

TABLE 9.3 (*Continued*)

6. Have the services you received helped you to deal more effectively with your problems?

4	3	2	1
Yes, they helped a great deal	Yes, they helped somewhat	No, they really didn't help	No, they seemed to make things worse

*7. In an overall, general sense, how satisfied are you with the service you received?

4	3	2	1
Very satisfied	Mostly satisfied	Indifferent or mildly dissatisfied	Quite dissatisfied

8. If you were to seek help again, would you come back to our program?

1	2	3	4
No, definitely not	No, I don't think so	Yes, I think so	Yes, definitely

Write Comments Below

*Can be used as a shorter scale

SOURCE: Reprinted with permission from *Evaluation and Program Planning*, E. Larsen, C. Attkisson, W. Hargreaves, and T. Nguyen, Assessment of client patient satisfaction: Development of a general scale.

small changes), serves as a motivator for the client and practitioner, and provides clear evidence about the effectiveness of specific practices or the need for a modification of approach. These authors provide guidelines on how to use single system designs in practice that are useful to any helping professional, including home visitors. (These designs are also called *single subject* or *single-case* designs; we prefer the latter term.) Additional information on single-case designs relevant for home visiting programs can be found in Neuman and McCormick (1995).

Single-case designs involve regular and continuing observation or recording of a client's progress toward specific targets before, during, and after interventions (Hersen & Barlow, 1976). A single-case design might be used when a home visitor and client have discussed and agreed on a specific goal and want to monitor progress toward that goal. Regular recording of progress toward goals can be a very informative practice. For example, if the goal of a specific home visiting program is to assure that a medically fragile newborn receives appropriate medical care, then visits to a follow-up clinic may be an appropriate and measurable behavior. If a home visitor and mother could see that an increasingly higher percentage of appointments were being kept, then this positive change would indicate program success and would be rewarding to both the visitor and the mother. Ultimately, the expected outcome of better child health might also be documented, but because it is a characteristic less reliably and less frequently measured, it should not be the only measure of program success.

Another example of using regular recording is when a home visitor helps a parent learn new strategies to set limits with his or her child, helping the parent learn to record the child's positive and negative behaviors and the parent's responses to those behaviors in the process. To increase prosocial skills and decrease negative behaviors, many parenting programs (e.g., Dishion & Patterson, 1996) have been developed to help parents learn to respond with consequences to a child's appropriate and inappropriate behaviors. Parental recording of day-to-day events helps parents see their progress and the child's progress. In addition, progress toward behavioral goals may be more readily observed by the visitor and parent than progress on the standardized child measures that many programs use.

Children's cognitive and language progress are often measured to document the success of an intervention, for example, the delivery and use of a specific curriculum for children. These assessments include the Bayley Scales of Infant Development, the Stanford-Binet Intelligence Scale, the Wechsler Intelligence Scale for Children—III, the Sequenced Inventory of Communicative Development, and the Peabody Picture Vocabulary Test—III. These tests are widely used in research but must be administered by a qualified person, usually in an office setting rather than in a home. The measures are time-consuming and are not designed to be given frequently. Thus, these measures provide an overall assessment of one type of outcome but are not given regularly enough to measure incremental progress or to indicate when to modify an existing approach with a particular family.

Measuring specific targeted behaviors on a regular basis can also indicate program outcomes and is relatively easy to accomplish. For example, the goal of many programs is to have parents participate in learning activities with their child. As a home visitor introduces each new activity, parents can add it to their list of activities to be used with the child. If parents make a check mark beside an activity each time they play with the child using the activity, then parents and home visitors have a visual record of progress in interacting with the child with different activities.

Most readers will recognize these simple recording procedures as one of the hallmarks of behavioral assessment. In the context of home visiting, behaviors such as keeping clinic appointments and using learning activities with a child can be systematically recorded, just as better child health and improved cognitive development can be measured. The progress measures of behavior are more easily and frequently recorded and provide more immediate and useful information to the home visitor and parents than outcome measures recorded only once at the end of a program. In addition, a parent is able to monitor personal progress, and a home visitor can regularly monitor the effectiveness of his or her approach with each family. A home visiting program director can document the array of different interventions being used and the ongoing progress of individual clients in addition to the overall effectiveness of the program for the clients. The use of single-case evaluations with numbers of clients can lead to new practice ideas that can further the knowledge base of the profession. In summary, a number of advantages can be gained by the use of single-case designs by home visitors in their work with clients.

Ongoing Program Documentation

Obtaining information on program implementation is another basic purpose of some documentation often requested of home visitors. Documentation of program delivery requires procedures that allow a home visitor to describe the frequency, content, and quality of his or her interactions with a client and to describe a client's receipt of or use of any other services that may be offered by a program. As Olds (1998b) says, we "must demonstrate that there was a clear program plan and that the service providers followed it faithfully" (p. 252). However, this demonstration is difficult to do in complex human services programs, so program documentation is the area in which home visit interventions have reported the least amount of information. This situation may be in part attributable to the uniqueness of programs: They deliver many different services in different ways. Programs that emphasize individualization of services face special challenges in documenting their intervention efforts. In addition, although standardized measures are available to document program outcomes such as language or cognitive development, standardized measures are not available to document the process of home visiting.

To document program implementation, some home visit projects or supervisors require detailed case notes about each visit; other programs require little more than a weekly log sheet of contacts. Striking a balance between over- and underdocumentation is important. Reporting too little about what was actually done by a home visitor makes it difficult to know whether an intervention as described was really delivered or which components or techniques may have been successful. On the other hand, reporting extensively on the program delivery (e.g., preparing detailed case notes on every visit or contact) is time consuming for the visitor and the supervisor who may read such notes. Extensive recording may also lead to careless documentation by home visitors who feel overburdened with paperwork. As valuable as thorough documentation may be in some cases, program directors should realize that excessive paperwork is often cited as a reason for burnout in the social services field. Program directors or supervisors must make choices about what kinds of documentation will be required, considering their own program's needs and weighing the advantages and disadvantages.

In the 1980s, our research group at the Frank Porter Graham Child Development Center received private foundation funds to develop, implement, monitor, and document the intervention used in the IHDP (Ramey et al., 1992). The home visit report form used in IHDP is included in the appendix as an example of program documentation. Because the IHDP was a research study, we needed to know that the home visit intervention was actually delivered to the families as intended, to draw conclusions about the effects of the program. Detailed information on the process and content of home visiting also helped us more easily tell others how to replicate the program.

The IHDP Home Visit Report Form was completed by home visitors after each home visit and turned in to the supervisor weekly. Information contained in this form documented the participants in the visit, the location and length of the visit, the main content of the visit (problem-solving and curriculum activities), and the general tone of the visit. (The technical information at the top of the first page—e.g., form number, version—was required for data management procedures.) The last page of this form was available for written notes about events not captured by the multiple-choice questions on the form. This form is a more elaborate version of the home visit report form used in Project CARE in North Carolina (Wasik, Ramey, et al., 1990), which was itself a modification of a home visit report form used by the Parent Educational Program in Florida (Gordon & Guinagh, 1978). As the content and nature of our visiting programs have evolved, so have the forms used to document them.

In the IHDP, home visitors completed the Home Visit Report Form as soon as possible after a visit, often in their cars if the neighborhood was safe, in a nearby coffee shop on a break between visits, or back at the office after the visit. Immediate completion of visit documentation is important for accuracy. The home visitors' supervisors used these same forms as the basis for their supervisory sessions with the visitors, and researchers used them for studying the process of home visiting.

Responses to the questions on the Home Visit Report Form were entered weekly into a computerized database by staff at the sites. Data were summarized monthly for each individual visitor, for each of the eight IHDP sites, and for all participating families in the intervention group. This way, home visitors could check their own progress, and we could monitor the progress of individual sites to see that the program was consistently delivered from site to site as planned. On a bimonthly basis, we were also able to use the data from these forms to summarize each family's participation in the program. We are aware that research programs rely on more documentation than service programs and that most home visiting programs do not have the time for such frequent and careful documentation activities. Nevertheless, this high level of documentation was helpful for many nonresearch purposes—for home visitors, their supervisors, and ourselves. Consequently, we suggest that programs consider the routine use of a home visit report form that, at a minimum, summarizes time, place, participants, participant engagement, and major content themes of the visit.

IHDP home visitors also completed a much shorter (less than one page) Family Contact Form to document the many interactions they had with families other than during home visits, such as telephone calls or conversations with another family member when the mother was not at home or contact with other agencies on behalf of families, such as with social services staff, clinic staff, or food and nutrition programs. In addition to the home visit report information, the Family Contact Form more completely depicted the actual work of a visitor during the course of a week. For example, one visitor spent most of 2 days with a mother making contacts with various social workers and community service agencies to obtain temporary shelter for the mother and her two children. Although these activities were not part of a home visit, it was important support for the mother that was provided because of her participation in IHDP. A review of such activities provides data that program directors and supervisors can use in planning work loads, making decisions on training activities, supervising home visitors, and evaluating their program's relationships with other community agencies.

In IHDP, home visitors reported yearly on the amount of time they spent engaged in various project activities, such as direct interaction with families, attending meetings, travel to and from home visits, and completing paperwork such as the two forms mentioned above. Their estimates of the amount of time spent on record-keeping averaged 15% or about 6 hours per week, slightly more than an hour a day. To some of them that seemed like a long time, but at the end of the program home visitors reported that the required documentation had helped them consolidate their thoughts about families and plan for future visits. When asked to suggest changes in the Home Visit Report Form, few visitors suggested shortening the form. In fact, many even suggested *additional* questions that they felt should have been regularly included. Their reaction suggests that when documentation procedures are relevant to the specific program and useful to the home visitors, record-keeping is not likely to be considered a burden.

Basic Characteristics of Assessment Measures

If a home visiting program chooses to use an assessment measure, several characteristics should be considered, including the utility of the measure, its reliability and validity, the time it takes to administer or collect data, and how directly it measures a person's behavior or feelings. This section is intended as a brief overview of the major factors home visitors or program directors need to consider when choosing assessment instruments. (For more information on these characteristics, see Bloom et al., 1999; Brinkerhoff, Brethower, Hluchyj, & Nowakowski, 1983.)

Usefulness of a Measure

Before administering needless questionnaires to clients, the first consideration should be whether to use one at all. What will be gained by using an assessment measure, and of what value is the particular one under consideration? Does it provide information that will help plan the most appropriate intervention? Does it help ascertain a client's needs or the factors influencing a client? Choosing a measure because it looks interesting or measures a current trendy topic are not valid reasons for assessment. Other questions relate to resources: Who is available to administer the instrument? How much time or money will it take to collect the information? Who will summarize and analyze the information? Sometimes good assessment instruments are given, but the data from them are never used because the data are not helpful to the program. Addressing the questions raised here can help assure the selection of useful instruments for obtaining information.

Reliability

Reliability refers to the consistency and stability of the measure. Reliability indicates whether a measure produces the same results when used with the same person over time, with two different versions of the measure, or by two different administrators of the measure. If information from these conditions is highly similar or consistent, then the measure is said to have high (good) reliability and is therefore more useful.

Reliability is important because it indicates that differences that one might see from one test occasion to another are likely due to behavioral changes, or attitude changes, and not to problems with the measure itself. For example, one goal of a home visiting program for teenage mothers might be to increase the supports available to and used by young mothers. If the support level is rated higher after a year in the program than at the beginning, then the program might conclude that it was having a positive effect. If the reliability of the instrument had not yet been determined, however, the higher ratings could have been due to measurement error.

Validity

The validity of an assessment tool means that the instrument actually measures what it is supposed to measure. A measure purporting to assess mother-child interactions should actually measure mother-child interactions, not mother judgment or attitudes. Several types of validity exist. Some involve statistical procedures, and others involve judgments about the properties of the measure. *Content validity* is a judgment based on whether the items or questions on the measure actually do measure the characteristic or behavior of interest. *Criterion-related validity* refers to whether the measure compares well with other possible measures of the same characteristic or behavior whose validity has already been established. *Construct validity* refers to how well the measure assesses a psychological construct or trait, for example, how the items on a measure relate to a specific theory of human behavior.

When choosing assessments, a home visiting program must consider the validity of the assessment. In the example of a teen mother support program used previously, suppose the program's measure of maternal support was really a measure of *perceived* social support rather than *actual* social support. The measure might well have high reliability and show increases for many mothers during the course of a year of home visiting. However, before concluding that the program helped the mothers find and use more social supports, the validity of the measure should be determined. Otherwise, the wrong conclusions might be drawn.

Home visiting programs serving families from minority cultures need to be especially concerned about construct validity. Measures that have been standardized on White children and parents may not have the same meaning for Black or Hispanic children and parents (Laosa, 1991). Before adopting a measure, a program should find out if the measure has a history of use among families from that culture. It is inappropriate to use majority culture expectations to interpret the scores of minority clients on measures that were developed for the majority culture (Conoley & Bryant, 1995).

Directness

Directness is another characteristic of instruments that should be considered when selecting them for use in a home visiting program. Direct measures of how a person actually behaves or thinks are more useful than indirect measures that require inferences or interpretations (Hersen & Barlow, 1976). Direct measures are usually more predictive of later behaviors than indirect measures. Direct measures are also easier to relate to the specific intervention being considered or delivered. For example, the very purpose of the home visitor may be to assure that a mother keeps clinic appointments for her newborn baby. Assessing clinic attendance is a direct measure of that intervention goal. Asking the mother why clinic visits are made or not made would involve indirect information, that is, the mother's interpretation of why she did or did not keep visits. This information might be useful, but in most cases, a direct measure is better.

In summary, a home visiting program should use valid and reliable instruments that are easy to implement. The measures should supply useful information, as directly as possible, about a client or a potential intervention strategy.

Assessment and Documentation From Different Perspectives

Assessment and documentation have been an essential part of the research knowledge base of home visiting. Many of the instruments and procedures mentioned in this chapter were used in research studies of home visiting; a number of these are summarized in Chapter 3. Most of these studies used a classical experimental design with procedures such as random assignment of families to treatment and control groups or case-control matching, as well as other procedures typical of well-designed research—systematic client assessment and program documentation.

These latter features of a research study are also an integral part of program evaluation. Determining the extent to which a program's goals have been met and providing information for decision making are the major goals of program evaluation. With increasing demands for program accountability from federal, state, and private agencies, more home visiting programs that have been exclusively service delivery projects will be required to gather evaluation data—information that will document service delivery and/or effectiveness. In this sense, they will become more research oriented, too.

Lest home visitors worry that additional requirements for evaluation will be burdensome, we should say that we believe that home visitors, in fact, are engaged daily in a type of research with each of their clients. Whether he or she consciously labels it as research, an effective home visitor regularly follows the following research procedures: making a preliminary assessment of the situation (called *baseline data collection* in research), stating goals with a client (operationalizing the variables), noting progress or regression based on the visitor's observation of the client (recording data), and summarizing the situation for his or her supervisor (data analysis and discussion). To the extent that a home visitor is already incorporating research strategies into her daily work, participating in an evaluation or research process will not be much different from the visitor's current practice.

Whatever measures or recording procedures are used in a home visiting program, they should have benefits for the client, home visitor, supervisor, program administrator, and public policy maker. In the remainder this chapter, we will look at the advantages of evaluation from these different points of view.

From the Client's Perspective

The ultimate beneficiary of the evaluation process should be the client. In return for the time spent completing forms, answering (sometimes very personal) questions, or being observed or videotaped, the client should expect to receive better services because the program staff should be better informed. If self-monitoring is part of the assessment procedures, a client may also increase in self-awareness and may learn a skill (self-monitoring) useful in handling other situations. Information obtained from assessments or regular documentation may also provide a client with more objective information about progress made during the program. He or she may, for example, be able to see a son or daughter with disabilities master a list of basic self-care skills. Information of this type should ensure better decision making by a client about the course of intervention.

From the Home Visitor's Perspective

From a home visitor's point of view, assessment measures should help him or her be more aware of a client's needs and goals, of alternative strategies to use to help a client, and of progress made toward the selected goals. With good assessment or monitoring data, a home visitor's decision making with a client will be based on objective data as well as subjective feelings about the situation. Tracking of a client's movement toward independence and subsequent reinforcement of such progress will be made easier for a home visitor. In short, assessment benefits a home visitor by making him or her a better helper and a more knowledgeable professional.

Record-keeping may also increase a home visitor's awareness or consciousness of personal and professional growth and development. This potential benefit of assessment and documentation would be more likely if some of the results of the record-keeping were summarized on a regular basis and presented to a home visitor, and if such feedback were interpreted with the help of a supervisor. For programs with extensive data collection, staff members may need to be specifically assigned this task. In most programs, home visitors will need to summarize their own data. It is helpful for home visitors to have training in how to use an evaluation of client progress in case planning for clients.

From the Supervisor's Perspective

From the point of view of a supervisor of home visitors, assessment information can help in the advisement of home visitors, evaluation of client progress, and decision making about intervention procedures. A supervisor can review the visit documentation and assessment information about a client with a home visitor as part of supervision, thereby becoming aware of a visitor's skills and areas needing development. A supervisor and visitor can both monitor client progress via review of the ongoing documentation. A supervisor can use the data in discussions with home visitors to help make appropriate decisions concerning their interactions with clients. A variety of experiences with and knowledge of assessments will allow a supervisor to more effectively guide home visiting staff members in the selection, use, and interpretation of measures.

To a supervisor, having any relevant substantive information is preferable to having none or to having only the home visitor's clinical impression. Thus, although a supervisor is challenged by the breadth of assessments used by his or her staff, the use of relevant and valid measures by home visitors enables a supervisor to gain valuable information to enhance his or her advisement of a home visitor. He or she can ask about decisions made with clients that might have been influenced by a home visitor's personal preference rather than by empirical information. He or she can help a visitor use assessments to compare two sources of information rather than just relying on the primary reporter (e.g., comparing the father's and mother's responses to a needs assessment).

As mentioned in Chapter 4, we also believe that a supervisor should periodically obtain direct information about a home visitor and client by accompanying the home visitor into the home. These clinical observations can be supplemented with information from formal assessments. Of course, all supervision includes clinical judgment, just as home visitors' work with clients relies a great deal on clinical judgment. However, with the home visitor and the supervisor combining their clinical judgments and information gathered from assessments of clients, services to a client most likely will be enhanced (Gambrill & Stein, 1983).

From the Program Director's Perspective

From the point of view of a home visiting program director, program evaluation is becoming an increasingly expected activity, and client assessments and program documentation are integral to this process. The pressure to evaluate service programs increased in the 1960s when the federal government began requiring written program evaluation plans as conditions for receipt of funds for such programs (Linder, 1983). However, as the demands for evaluation of service programs have increased, the demands have not been accompanied by clear statements regarding the purposes for conducting evaluations (Hupp & Kaiser, 1986). In this chapter, we have described at least three valid reasons for conducting evaluations of home visiting programs: (a) to determine whether the activities of the program were delivered, (b) to determine whether the program met clients' needs, and (c) to provide feedback to staff members so that they might improve the services they deliver. An administrator who can show routinely collected information related to each of these topics is in a good position to maintain the support of the agency that is funding the program. Information obtained from assessments and documentation can be used to assure that the services provided by the program are of high quality. Information gathered can provide the mechanism for changing procedures or caseloads when progress is not being made, either in individual cases or overall.

For the administrator considering evaluation, seven questions identified by Wolery and Bailey (1984) provide excellent guidance (see Table 9.4). The strategies that are associated with each question are necessary to develop a comprehensive evaluation plan. Some of these strategies deal with monitoring the program, and others deal with monitoring the clients; some strategies call for ongoing evaluation, whereas others are used only at initial or outcome phases.

TABLE 9.4 Questions and Strategies in Evaluation of Early Intervention (Wolery & Bailey, 1984)

Questions	*Strategies*
1. Can the program demonstrate that the methods, materials, and overall service delivery represent the best educational practice?	Describe program and philosophy. Develop rationale for program components. Document best practices. Offer professional validation.
2. Can the program demonstrate that the methods espoused in the overall philosophy are implemented accurately and consistently?	Generate record of services. Generate record of implementation of services. Provide evidence of replicability.
3. Can the program demonstrate that it attempts to verify empirically the effectiveness of interventions or other individual program components for which the best educational practice has yet to be verified?	Analyze individual components of intervention program.
4. Can the program demonstrate that it carefully monitors client progress and is sensitive to points at which changes in services need to be made?	Collect and monitor data to document provision of services and to facilitate decision-making.
5. Can the program demonstrate that a system is in place for determining the relative adequacy of client progress and service delivery?	Compare child progress with reference group. Calculate gain relative to time in intervention. Interpret gain relative to criteria. Interpret gain relative to expectation.
6. Can the program demonstrate that it is moving toward the accomplishment of program goals and objectives?	Specify program objectives in measurable terms. Generate questions about achievement of program objectives. Identify data sources; collect data. Prepare report.

TABLE 9.4 *Continued*

Questions	*Strategies*
7. Can the program demonstrate that the goals, methods, materials, and overall service delivery system are in accordance with the needs and values of the community and clients it serves?	Review needs assessment. Subjectively evaluate program activities and child and family progress.

SOURCE: Bailey & Simeonsson (1988). Reprinted with permission from the authors.

Question 2, for example, relates to a program's ability to demonstrate that the planned intervention was delivered. The program documentation methods discussed in this chapter would be part of the strategy to address this question. Likewise, assessing client attitudes or behaviors would be part of the strategy necessary to address Question 4.

In addition to the resources referenced above, three additional resources would be helpful for program directors who are interested in evaluating their program. *Working Effectively* (Feek, 1988) is a short but well-organized and nontechnical guide to evaluation, which describes ways evaluation can become part of the normal work of an organization. *Evaluating Family Programs* (Weiss & Jacobs, 1988) is an excellent resource book containing several chapters on ways of assessing families, parents, and children, and approximately 100 different measures (with information on the development of the measure and sources of information about the measure provided in an appendix). The United Way has published a very helpful and reader-friendly manual with many good examples for human service program managers who want to undertake a program evaluation (United Way of America, 1996).

From the Policy Maker's Perspective

Home visiting programs exist within the context of local, state, and national debates about how best to support families. Ultimately, effective use of evaluation in home visiting programs should provide information with which to inform public policy makers as to the need for home visiting, the best approaches to use, and the likely effectiveness of different types of home visiting programs (Gomby et al., 1999). It will be up to program directors and researchers studying home visiting to choose measures wisely, collect data appropriately, interpret results cautiously, and not overclaim effectiveness. In this way, policy makers can make informed decisions based on a sound body of information.

Public policy makers are also often influenced by the cost of a method or program. Although there are difficulties involved in using a cost-benefit or cost-effectiveness analysis of home visiting, White (1988) describes how such approaches should be viewed by program directors and policy makers to make the results of the analysis useful. Barnett and Escobar (1990) provide detailed costs of eight home visiting programs, illustrating the wide range of average per-child costs that result from program differences in staffing expertise, duration of services, frequency of visits, and other variables. MacRae (1989) describes examples of national programs that initially survived based on legal and moral arguments (Medicare and P.L. 94-142) but that began to be evaluated from a cost-effectiveness standpoint as time went on and as costs escalated. A parallel could be drawn for policies on home visiting. More data are needed to support cost-effectiveness arguments, and home visiting advocates should be prepared to provide such data (Zigler & Black, 1989).

Summary

This chapter has stressed the importance and the purposes of different types of client assessment and program documentation that could be used in a home visiting program. Initial assessments should provide information about a client's needs and strengths, and outcome assessments should help the client and home visitor determine progress. Regular recording of specific behaviors targeted by a home visiting program may help determine progress more immediately and validly. Ongoing program documentation is important for accountability and replication. Some types of assessment are time consuming and intrusive and may be met with resistance by clients and home visitors. However, information from well-chosen instruments can be obtained with cooperation from staff members and clients and can benefit the client, home visitor, and program. Ultimately, assessment data can add empirical support to the base of already existing philosophical support for home visiting programs, and program documentation data can guide the development of new programs that follow the best approaches. Together, both types of data should enhance the willingness of public policy makers to fund effective programs for clients and families.

10

Future Directions in Home Visiting

We have written *Home Visiting* because we believe that visiting with people in their homes is one of the most humane and family-centered approaches to service delivery in our society. Home visiting is uniquely supportive of family life, bringing services to families, providing services in a familiar setting, and reducing obstacles to service. It is linked with the community and able to facilitate both coordinated and culturally responsive services. As Minuchin and colleagues (1998) have stated, through home visiting, "the aura of authority that characterizes an official setting is muted and the reality of the family's life environment is acknowledged" (p. 204).

In this chapter, we reflect on some of the major considerations for home visiting in the next decade. We believe change, accountability, staff preparation, prevention, and partnerships are all part of the future, and we believe that the ways in which home visitors serve families will undoubtedly continue to evolve. In the future, some of our current practices may no longer be seen as best practices. We also believe that research on home visiting must continue. Although home visiting has a long history and many advocates, it has not had a strong empirical knowledge base. Having conducted evaluations of four intervention programs involving home visiting, we know personally, and all too well, the challenges involved in conducting useful and scientifically credible evaluations of home visiting. But we also know how essential research and evaluation are to program quality.

To organize our thinking about the future of home visiting practice and evaluations, we used a model that identifies the major components of home visiting programs placed within a broader ecological model (Wasik, Lam, & Kane, 1994) (see Figure 10.1). This model provides a framework for analyzing important background characteristics, program processes, outcome variables, and the relationships between these variables. This model can also help policy makers, program directors, evaluators, and home visitors attend to factors that can influence a particular program component at any point in time and can help promote policies and decisions that take into account existing relationships between important program variables. We have observed that researchers in the field are conducting studies with an increased sophistication, recognizing the potential interactions between program goals, family characteristics, and the qualifications of those who provide the services. This trend should continue because we need information on a variety of family, program, and community variables to understand better the effects of interventions on all members of the family.

The relationships between background, program, and outcome variables are complex and occur in circular and recursive ways. For example, changing family needs can result in changes in program procedures. Staffing patterns can result in more limited services, and limited outcomes can prompt change in intervention procedures or raise questions about the characteristics of families who benefit the most.

Characteristics of Children, Families, and Communities

Children and Families

Child characteristics are often the driving force behind many home visiting programs. Services are offered to families at the time of a child's birth or to a family with a low birthweight infant, a child with disabilities, or a delinquent youth. Providing services to cate-

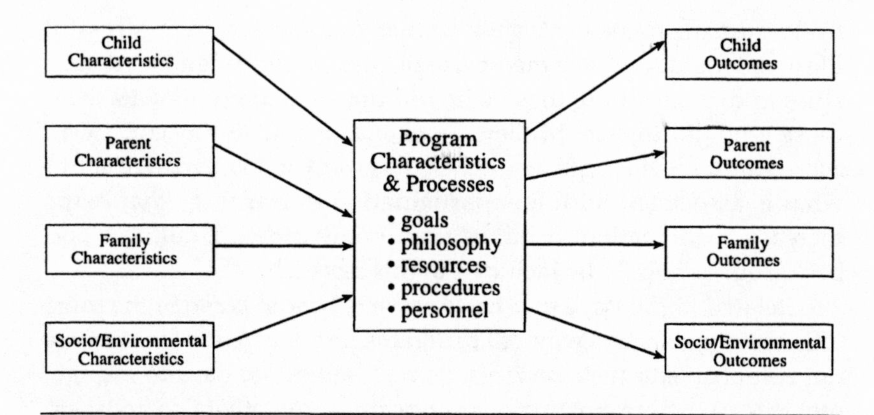

Figure 10.1. A Model Illustrating Major Relationships Among Different Program Processes and Factors That Influence These Processes

gories of families, however, can result in numerous home visiting programs in a single community, often providing very similar services. We need to rethink how we provide family services. Surely a more comprehensive, integrated system (even if it were not universal) would result in better and more economical care.

Parental characteristics influence outcomes, and we need to know more about which families are most likely to benefit most from home visiting or which family needs can be best met through home visiting services. Given that universal home visiting is not likely in this country in the near future, gaining more knowledge about who benefits is essential to guide policy and practice. Focusing on the most needy may not be the wisest policy if they are not able to benefit from home visiting. For example, maternal care via home visiting offered to pregnant women who have no other children appears to have more positive outcomes than the same services offered to pregnant women who have other children, a finding that emphasizes the importance of timing in the delivery of services.

Programs recruit parents or families, engage them in a collaborative process, and help maintain their participation. We know little about the time typically required for these activities, about the relationship between program efforts and success, and between family characteristics and these program processes. An analysis of client characteristics associated with not keeping appointments for public health nursing home visits showed that younger age, more stressful life events, and receipt of medical assistance were all significant variables in distinguishing those who did not keep appointments from those who did (Josten, Mullett, Savik, Campbell, & Vincent, 1995). More studies of this type would help us go beyond knowledge about what is associated with low participation to learning what helps increase participation. Families from many different cultures and backgrounds should be included in this research.

Related to the issue of who to serve is how to serve in the most efficient and effective way. All programs find that some families are not responsive to their services. Some families are hard to engage, others leave before meeting their own goals, and others do not seem to make any progress. Sometimes serious emotional difficulties can make it impossible to help families change. Furthermore, clients' poor motivation and low level of commitment interfere with program services and influence outcomes.

Considerably more effort needs to be expended to study family characteristics as they relate to family needs, family acceptance of services, and family responsiveness to intervention procedures. Because many variables can influence family functioning—social, emotional, cognitive, physical, and educational—program developers need new tools or new methods to enable them to factor in the unique attributes of each family as the program tailors its services to that family. Recognition of the diversity of families, even within specific demographic or ethnic groups, is crucial to the provision of effective home visiting. Because we will never have unlimited services, we need to understand and use information related to differences for individual families.

Communities

In Chapter 2, we discussed home visiting within the framework of ecological theory. Within this theory, we see home visiting as uniquely community based. Good home visiting services are inextricably linked with the life of their respective communities.

Community characteristics are often incorporated into program deliberations, such as the decision to hire visitors who are sensitive to the needs of and knowledgeable about those who live in the community. Other community issues also need to be considered in the development of programs, especially the coordination among family agencies. In the same way that the family is considered a system, with each member influencing the total family's functioning, the different components of a community influence its overall effectiveness. How different agencies and groups plan and act together toward mutually agreed on goals can significantly influence the quality of life for all members of the community. An encouraging trend is that many home visiting programs are already closely coordinated with other community organizations, such as school systems and medical agencies.

Home visiting programs can participate in local efforts to resolve situations adversely affecting many people in the community. Severely inadequate job opportunities or child care facilities, for example, could contribute to child neglect, family stress, family economic hardship, and the social and cognitive development of large numbers of children. Home visitors are often in an advantageous position to observe family issues that could be addressed on a community level rather than individually. Such knowledge needs to find a way into our community agencies in a manner that can facilitate change. Home visiting programs need not nor can they divert large resources to the solution of community concerns. However, by acting in collaboration with other agencies, home visiting programs can focus attention on problematic community situations and participate in finding resolutions.

We are aware that this broader role moves beyond serving the needs of individual clients to focusing on changes that might more appropriately and effectively meet the needs of a community of clients. The collective experience of home visitors in any one program can be a considerable asset for initiating potential changes that may have widespread positive effects. This advocacy role was associated with home visitors at the beginning of the 20th century, and we recognize it again as an important service as we enter the new millennium. Families need multiple resources to function well. Each person has personal resources for coping with the events in their lives. Other resources in the community, referred to as *social capital*, are also essential for individual well-being (Brooks-Gunn, 1995).

Program Characteristics and Processes

Program characteristics and processes include goals, philosophies, resources, procedures, and personnel. Program goals are usually set in response to needs perceived in the community. These goals, in turn, influence the resources that will be used. At times the available resources can influence the goals themselves; if resources are expensive, goals may have to be modified. When more financial support is available than a program anticipated, it may expand its mission by providing additional services or by adding to the number of clients served.

Program goals are related to program philosophy. Many of these more specific beliefs have their basis in theories and guidelines about good practices. Although it may seem too obvious to state, a home visiting program should have a written and well-understood statement of goals and a set of guiding principles. The goal statement and the overarching principles that guide the program should be clear enough for a lay person to understand. The theory that links program services to desired outcomes for children and parents should be included. The goals and principles can be posted on the lobby bulletin board, discussed with potential employees, and included as the first section of the staff manual. The statement of principles should not be a list of "how to" practices but a document that makes clear the program's beliefs (such as a belief in family-focused rather than individualized services), and the connection between what they do and what they want to achieve with parents and children. A shared vision among personnel is important for productive relationships. A program that makes explicit its beliefs and principles of practice can help its home visitors focus on their most important tasks and emphasize optimal ways of interacting with families.

Program resources include personnel, financial status, and community collaborators. Each of these resources has a major effect on the potential accomplishments of a given program. In the home visiting field, we are in the initial phases of studying these variables, and there are many questions to be asked. Although the goals of the programs may be the same, do well-funded programs that pay visitors high salaries have different outcomes from programs that rely on volunteers? Should one spread resources to reach the maximum number of families, or should one work more intensely with the most needy families? Although Richmond (1899) raised this issue of resource allocation more than a century ago, we still have little empirical support to guide practice, and the issue continues to be debated.

Program resources also directly influence program procedures. We strongly recommend that research be conducted on the process of home visiting because so little empirical support or documentation is available. Process variables range from identifying quantitative issues such as the frequency of home visiting and its duration to an analysis of the content of the visit, the roles played by a visitor, and the nature of the home visiting curriculum. One example of a process variable is how frequently home visits are offered. A program that visits families once every 2 weeks or once a month can provide services to many more families than a program that provides weekly visits. In doing so, a program may sacrifice stronger program effects that could occur as a result of more frequent visits (e.g., Powell & Grantham-McGregor, 1989).

Advances in technology may also influence the future of home visiting. Intervention programs in rural areas are already providing parent education materials using a diskette or CD-ROM, with personal contacts via phone and only occasionally in person. With the increasing use of personal computers, the World Wide Web, chat rooms, and other technological advances, it seems likely that, at least for some families, some services provided by home visiting may change form. Costs will need to decrease even further to make some of these new ways of interacting viable for families in poverty, but we should begin capitalizing on these advances now.

Issues related to personnel will continue to be critical for the field of home visiting. In Chapter 4, we discussed the major characteristics, skills, and educational background of home visitors desired by program directors. This topic needs continued practical and research attention because, in reality, our experience in hiring home visitors is that we always have too few applicants. With few candidates having all of the desired qualifications, which criteria should be weighted most heavily? Programs face these decisions every day, and most directors would welcome new information in this area.

The changing demographics of families in America in the direction of more diverse culture and ethnicity calls for changes in home visiting. Those who provide services should, but currently do not, reflect the diversity of people who are served. Consequently, we need to strengthen recruitment in multiple ethnic and cultural groups, provide training in other languages, and assure cultural competence in service delivery.

Considerable agreement exists about the optimal interpersonal characteristics of home visitors: good interpersonal and communication skills, empathy, warmth, judgment, and maturity. In the home visiting field, these characteristics have not received much research attention either in relation to program outcomes or to other home visitor credentials, although interest in empirically examining the role of these home visitor skills and characteristics is increasing (De la Cuesta, 1994; Jessee, Cecil, & Jessee, 1991).

The availability of appropriate and high-quality training is one of the most critical issues facing home visiting. Several conditions have contributed to this critical need for training. Over time, the expectations of home visiting services have increased. However, even in many professional training programs, the knowledge and skills needed by home visitors are not sufficiently covered. The continuing interest in employing community or lay visitors (who by definition do not have prior professional training and supervision) has prompted the need for more training. Lay visitors are providing services in homes characterized by multiple problems, including drug abuse, spouse or child abuse, marital discord, and other family difficulties. The need for training is great.

The current availability of training can be grouped under the following four categories: (a) in-service training provided by individual programs or coordinated community efforts; (b) individualized competency training under the national competency program for Child Development Associate; (c) training in professional education credentialing programs such as social work, counseling, nursing, and other health related areas; and (d) national training efforts such as Head Start, Parents as Teachers, and Healthy Families America. Given the widespread interest in home visiting services and the likelihood of increases in the use of home visiting, it is essential to consider the preservice and in-service training needs of home visitors in a more systematic and thorough manner.

We recommend that educational institutions engage in partnerships with communities to make these opportunities available. We also recommend that there be more community-based training efforts, coordinating needs across different service agencies. There is a strong common knowledge base of home visiting procedures relevant across professional fields. Training across professional areas can be an efficient community effort as well as a way to increase understanding and collaboration.

With the current expansion of home visiting programs, coordinating and consolidating training activities in communities becomes more important. Such efforts serve as a bridge for interaction between different home visiting programs as well as provide home visitors with a broader and more in-depth training than they may have been able to obtain otherwise. Coordinated training may be particularly appropriate for ongoing professional development activities. A coordinated process would help assure the opportunity for sharing information between home visitors and for newly developed programs to have their visitors learn from experienced home visitors. It is important to note, however, that programs with different philosophical orientations may have difficulty combining training activities, and efforts would have to be made to avoid confusing home visitors by presenting differing philosophical orientations.

Several efforts need to be initiated in the immediate future. First, formal educational agencies at the community college, 4-year college, and graduate educational levels need to rethink the programs being provided for students who may be future home visitors. Educators need to seriously consider whether we are adequately preparing these students for family support services in the home. Such an analysis would most likely lead to an enrichment of the content and experiences that are provided to students to prepare them for future positions.

In Chapter 4, we stressed our belief in the critical role supervision plays in the practice of home visiting, noting the necessity for support, education, and evaluation of home visitors. We doubt that home visiting programs can provide quality services without providing adequate supervision for those whose work takes them into homes on a continuing basis. To address the increasing need for supervisors, we recommend that professional training programs begin to prepare individuals to assume supervisory roles. Such preparation could be a part of graduate programs in social work, psychology, nursing, or education. Reiterating a point we made earlier: Home visiting is a front-line, stressful, and at times, lonely position, and thus it calls for more supervision than many other jobs.

In 1990, we wrote that the field had limited written, audio, or video materials for the training of home visitors, and those that did exist were not readily known by or accessible to others. Because of the considerable effort it takes to develop materials, we recommended that programs review the published materials of others before taking on curriculum development activities. We also suggested that additional work on summaries and catalogues of materials were needed so that programs could build on the work of each other rather than repeating similar efforts. Taking our own recommendations seriously, we prepared two such guides: one for written materials and one for audiovisual materials (Wasik, Shaeffer, et al., 1996; Wasik, Thompson, et al., 1996). These guides are a good starting point for obtaining information on materials currently used by other home visitors. Materials continue to be developed within programs for the use of other trainers and visitors, representing a refreshing advance in the field (e.g., Cohen et al., 1996; Shaeffer et al., 1999).

Outcome Variables

The importance of evaluating program outcomes has been noted for many years. As early as 1967, Suchman wrote that "all social institutions or subsystems, whether medical, educational, religious, economic, or political, are required to justify society's continued support" (p. 2). The emphasis in government at both the federal and state levels for accountability will drive more research and evaluation at the national and local levels. As part of this work, we recommend more intensive research on program processes and procedures and the relationship between program variables and program outcomes. We support collaborative research studies between different programs at the local, state, and national levels to broaden the generalization of research findings.

Among the most pressing questions facing those who conduct research and evaluation efforts is the appropriate selection of outcome variables. Questions on outcomes should be considered for children, adults, and even the community. Decisions must be made about how restrictive or broad outcome assessments need to be. Issues must be resolved regarding the desirability of data on some outcomes versus the limited resources with which to obtain the information, or there will be too few data points to be able to draw conclusions from the data.

Evaluation has a role in every service program. Program evaluation information can be gathered from staff members and clients to obtain input on their perceptions of program procedures and effects. Outside consultants can provide an unbiased judgment of a program's procedures and outcomes. Through evaluation, a program can determine if its own goals and objectives are being met and, if not, modify objectives or procedures or increase or redirect resources.

Evaluation efforts can add to our empirical database through systematic research studies. Even with limited resources, programs can use designs such as the single-case design to study clients' behaviors and home visitors' activities over time to determine if the procedures being implemented are effective for a given client (Neuman & McCormick, 1995). By contrast, random assignment or quasi-experimental research designs typically require significant financial and personnel resources beyond the scope of most service programs. Nevertheless, it is important to recognize that research and service not only can be combined but must be combined if we are to expand the empirical foundation for home visiting.

General Conclusions

In the first edition of *Home Visiting* in 1990, a time when only a small number of research studies served as the empirical base, we recommended that the decade of the 1990s include an extensive series of studies designed to address many issues in the practice of home visiting. The 1993 and 1999 *Future of Children* issues devoted to home visiting provided strong evidence of the research interest in home visiting for young children and their families, especially families living in poverty. The results from these studies, some of which are summarized in Chapter 3, form a much stronger empirical foundation for the field than we had only a decade ago. The methodological issues and outcomes of these studies have, however, raised many significant questions related to research in the field. As a result, our strong call 10 years ago for more research and evaluation is just as serious and necessary today as it was then. In the face of increasing emphasis on accountability, research and evaluation may be even more critical.

A few research issues for the future cut across the three broad areas of background, program processes, and outcomes considered so far in this chapter. Although there are several noteworthy instruments (some are identified in Chapters 3, 4, 5, and 9), the availability of research instruments to measure process and products has generally lagged behind the needs in the field. Because accurate measurement is essential for the advancement of any science, we recommend that additional attention be devoted to the development of measures that are sensitive to the goals of home visiting services, specifically measures of program procedures, program outcomes, and transactions between family, community, and programs.

We also recommend that future measurement efforts incorporate the unique opportunities for assessment that are afforded by home visits. Traditionally, many assessment procedures were developed because a client could be observed in his or her natural environment. Home visiting makes possible naturalistic assessment procedures. Both observation and interviewing procedures should be studied for their utility in providing information on the process of home visiting as well as the outcomes.

We need to conduct research on the relationship between the sociocultural characteristics of the home visitor and process and outcome variables. We know that some families prefer visitors to share the same ethnic characteristics, and this is clearly an important preference to consider. But does this assure a higher quality service? How do home visitor qualifications interact with a family's preference for a visitor from a similar background? We need to increase our knowledge in this area so that we can make better matches between families and visitors.

We believe prevention needs to be stressed. There will never be enough funding to address all the needs that might be addressed through home visiting or even through all service modalities. Although prevention never seems as popular as interventions designed to address some existing human concern such as illness, poverty, literacy, or delinquency, prevention efforts will be necessary for us to witness significant long-term societal changes. Home visiting is an important preventive service.

We recommend continued emphasis on partnerships between home visiting programs and other family services. Home visiting has special advantages, but it is often not sufficient, especially for families affected by poverty, low educational levels, depression, alcoholism, drug abuse, or marital difficulties (Halpern, 1993; Weiss, 1993). Home visitors may need to work in teams, work in collaboration with other resources, refer families to services, or even bring home visiting to an end if other types of help better meet family needs.

We also suggest that it is timely to consider the formation of a national association on home visiting, one that would appeal to individuals across professions and to home visitors and other professional staff in these programs, including trainers, supervisors, and directors. Such an association could serve a number of functions that are not well served presently, especially the coordination of information on training materials and the promotion of collaborative research and training. A national home visiting association could keep home visitors informed of the different programs around the country, current legislation influencing the practice of home visiting, different approaches to home visiting, and the results of research studies. It could be a resource for ongoing professional training. Several national organizations exist that serve as a resource for specific models. As important as these are, we believe an organization addressing issues across models and professions could serve to advance the field.

Summary

As we enter the new millennium, new ways of thinking about home visiting will be needed. The model presented in this chapter showing the interrelations of program components serves as a guide for considering future needs. As many programs evolve toward a broader scope for intervention, program resources must be rethought. We must also begin to evaluate more intensely what can be accomplished through home visiting and what cannot, and plan programs accordingly.

One of the most significant changes during the past decade that will influence changes in the next decade has been the shift in many intervention programs from an individual focus to a family focus. This shift cannot be taken lightly. Providing family services is considerably more complex than providing an educational curriculum for a young child. It demands changes in the credentials and training of home visitors and calls for increasing supports for their professional training and supervision.

For the future, we believe home visiting, long recognized as an important process for helping families, will continue to be a prevalent service in health, education, mental health, and social services; reach more families; serve broader needs; and become a more acceptable and possibly an expected service. We need to be prepared by beginning now to increase the empirical foundation of home visiting, conduct research and evaluation on significant program questions, and assure the availability of well-qualified individuals to serve in this most humane way of reaching out to help families.

Appendix: Home Visit Report Forms Used in the Infant Health and Development Program

Child Name: ______________________ Date: ____/____/____ Visitor Name: ______________________

HOME VISIT REPORT
Identification Information

Form # M 0 1
Form Date 3/9/86 Version: 0 5
Site Name (1st 3 letters) ___ ___ ___
Site # ___

IHDP # ___ ___ ___ ___
Visitor # ___ ___ ___
Week of (Sunday's date) ___ ___ ___ ___ ___ ___ (m m d d y y)
Visit Date (if completed) ___ ___ ___ ___ ___ ___ (m m d d y y)
Time of Day (to nearest hour) ___ ___ (h h) am pm

Part I. General Procedure of the Visit

Y N O **1. Was a visit made this week? (O = A visit was not planned this week)**

___ ___ **2. How many times this week did you or the caregiver call or send a message or did you stop by the home in order to schedule this or future visits? (If this visit was scheduled at the previous visit, enter 0)**

(a)___ ___ (b)___ ___ **3. If a visit was *not* made, the reason was: (Record 1 or 2 responses)**
1) Visitor unable to reach the caregiver to schedule a visit (ex: unable to locate family)
2) Caregiver was not home at the scheduled time, refused, left the home when you arrived, or did not answer the door
3) Caregiver canceled the visit
4) Parent was ill or out of town
5) Child was ill
6) Child was hospitalized
7) Home visitor was unable to visit (ex: scheduling or transportation problems, out of town, illness, bad weather)
8) Vacation or holiday
9) Parent attended group meeting or other IHDP function in lieu of *home* visit (only if child < 1 yr.)
10) Other: ______________________

Additional comments about **scheduling:**

IF A VISIT WAS *NOT* MADE THIS WEEK, STOP HERE AND SEND THE ABOVE INFORMATION TO FPG.
IF A VISIT WAS MADE, CONTINUE.

___ **4. The visit occurred in:**
1) Parent's home 2) Relative or friend's home 3) Daycare center 4) Hospital or clinic 5) Other: ________
6) Parent-Teacher-Home Visitor Conference

___ **5. The visit lasted:**
1) less than 15 minutes 2) 16–30 minutes 3) 31–45 minutes 4) 46–60 minutes 5) more than 1 hour

___ **6. During most of the visit the child was:**
1) awake and involved 2) awake but not involved 3) asleep 4) absent from home

___ **7. During the visit, other children living in the household were:**
1) awake and involved 2) awake but not involved 3) absent or asleep 4) no other children

(a)___ (b)___ **8. The home visit was mainly with: (Record 1 or 2 responses)**
1) mother 2) father 3) grandmother 4) grandfather 5) sitter 6) another adult: ________________

___ **9. During the visit, the relationship between the parent (or main person being visited) and the home visitor could be characterized as:**
1) a cooperative, trusting partnership; parent shared concerns about child and self; reciprocal interaction
2) a working, functional partnership mainly focused on and limited to the curriculum
3) an uncertain partnership; issues of trust and cooperation in implementing the program
4) cannot tell

___ **10. During the visit, other caregiving adult(s):**
0) were not present
1) contributed positively to the visit
2) did not affect the visit either positively or negatively
3) adversely affected the visit

___ **11. Who accompanied the home visitor on this visit?**
0) No one
1) Education director
2) Another home visitor
3) Other: ____________
4) Daycare teacher

11a. What was the major reason for other person accompanying the visitor?

Additional comments about **general procedure** of visit:

Child Name: ______________________ Date: ____/____/____ Visitor Name: ______________________

IHDP # ___ ___ ___ ___ Version 5 Visit Date (if completed) ___ ___ ___ ___ ___ ___ (m m d d y y)

Part II. Problem Solving

___ **12.** If *Problem Solving* was part of the **last visit**, was there evidence of parent follow through?
(Enter 0 if Problem Solving was not part of the last visit.)
1) Parent successfully took action
2) Parent took action, but not successful yet
3) Parent understood and thought about the problem
4) Parent did not understand or use the ideas or procedures
5) Parent did not want to use problem solving
6) No opportunity to evaluate

Additional comments about **previous Problem Solving** activities:

13. If problems were discussed on **this visit**, what were the **major** areas of concern? (Record 1, 2 or 3 responses)

(a) ___ ___
(b) ___ ___
(c) ___ ___

Child functioning
11) Child health
12) Diet and feeding
13) Developmental progress
14) Problem behaviors
15) Other: ______________

Family functioning
21) Parent or family worries due to special needs of LBW infant
22) Family inter-relationships
23) Parent health or emotional problems (anxiety, depression)
24) Health or emotional needs of other family members
25) Other: ______________

Environmental needs/community services
31) Housing or food
32) Financial
33) Employment
34) Transportation
35) Legal matters
36) Medical equipment for infant
37) Finding childcare/daycare
38) Other: ______________

Administrative
41) Scheduling a visit
42) Helping with forms
43) Introduction to Problem Solving
44) IHDP Child Development Center
45) Other: ______________

Additional comments about these or other concerns:

14. If *Problem Solving* was part of **this visit**, complete the following:

___ **14a.** Problem Solving was part of this visit because:
(Enter 0 if Problem Solving was not part of this visit and proceed to Question 15.)
1) visitor had planned to cover problem-solving today
2) visitor saw a need and introduced the topic appropriately
3) parent began a discussion of problems or problem-solving

___ ___ **14b.** What was the main topic of the Problem Solving discussion?
(Use codes from Question 13 above.)

14c. Which, if any, of these stages of Problem Solving were discussed?

Y N 1) Problem identification
Y N 2) Goal selection
Y N 3) Generation of alternatives
Y N 4) Consideration of consequences
Y N 5) Decision making
Y N 6) Implementation
Y N 7) Evaluation

___ **14d.** The parent's reaction to this Problem-Solving discussion was:
1) positive (asked questions, attentive, participated)
2) neutral (listened, but showed little response)
3) negative (inattentive, did not want to participate)

Additional comments about **Problem Solving** discussion:

Child Name: ______________________ Date: ____/____/____ Visitor Name: ______________________

IHDP # ___ ___ ___ ___ Version 5 Visit Date (if completed) ___ ___ ___ ___ ___ ___ (m m d d y y)

Part III. Partners for Learning

Remember to ask about and see the activities of the last 4 visits.

15. List the activities or toys that were reviewed on this visit.

1) ___ ___ ___ 3) ___ ___ ___ 5) ___ ___ ___ 7) ___ ___ ___
2) ___ ___ ___ 4) ___ ___ ___ 6) ___ ___ ___ 8) ___ ___ ___

16. If this visit introduced a new **Partners** activity or toy, complete the following:

16a. The name and code of this week's activity(ies) or toy was (were):
(Enter 000 for Act. 1 if no activities were introduced and proceed to Question 17.)

Act. 1 ___ ___ ___ 1. ______________________
Act. 2 ___ ___ ___ 2. ______________________
Act. 3 ___ ___ ___ 3. ______________________

(Remember to record these activities and today's date on the Cumulative Record.)

16b. The parent's reaction to the activity(ies) or toy was:

Act. 1 ___ 1) highly interested (asked questions, attentive, participated)
Act. 2 ___ 2) interested (listened, but showed little response)
Act. 3 ___ 3) not interested (inattentive, critical of activity, would not participate)

16c. After the demonstration or explanation (if no demonstration), the parent:

Act. 1 ___ 1) wanted to try activity and was able to do it
2) wanted to try activity but needed some help
Act. 2 ___ 3) was hesitant but tried the activity after encouragement from visitor
4) showed little interest in trying the activity but finally did with encouragement
Act. 3 ___ 5) did not try the activity (or child asleep)
6) the activity is not the type that could be tried at the time

16d. How did the child respond to the parent or home visitor's demonstration of the activity or toy?

Act. 1 ___ 0) activity not demonstrated
Act. 2 ___ 1) alert and participated with success
Act. 3 ___ 2) alert and participated, but not yet successful
3) somewhat attentive, responded partially
4) fussy and/or would not participate
5) activity did not require child's participation
6) child not present or child asleep

17. Which of the following *Adult Skills* were emphasized in this visit?

Y N 1) prepare
Y N 2) attend
Y N 3) prompt
Y N 4) model
Y N 5) support
Y N 6) rescue
Y N 7) build

Y N 18. Did the parent contribute any original or creative ideas to the Partners activities or suggest a new activity?
If so, describe:

Additional comments about this week's **Partners** activity(ies):

Part IV. Summary Evaluation of Visit

___ 19. The general tone of the visitor-caregiver interaction was:
1) positive, supportive, receptive, reciprocal
2) cooperative, but not enthusiastic
3) uncertain, unenthusiastic
4) strained

___ 20. The general tone of the caregiver-child interaction was:
1) positive, supportive, concerned, and reciprocal
2) more supportive than nonsupportive
3) more nonsupportive than supportive
4) nonsupportive
5) not observed

___ 21. The caregiver's *positive* feedback to her child was:
1) frequent 2) occasional 3) seldom or never 4) not observed

___ 22. The caregiver responded to the child's vocalizations (other than crying):
1) frequently 2) occasionally 3) seldom or never 4) child rarely vocalized 5) not observed

Y N 23. Since the last home visit, have there been any family changes or family events that might help or hinder the caregiver in the delivery of the intervention program?
If yes, describe:

Y N 24. Were any supplemental materials used on this visit? If so, what were they?

Y N 25. Did this visit involve more than one IHDP family? If so, attach a joint visit form.

Child Name: ______________________ Date of Contact: ___/___/___ Visitor Name: ______________________

Record of Family Contact

Form Number	M 0 2	(1-3)
Form Date 10/15/86	Version: 0 3	(4-5)
Site Name (1st 3 letters)	___ ___ ___	(6-8)
Site #	___	(9)
IHDP #	___ ___ ___ ___	(10-13)
Visitor #	___ ___ ___	(14-16)

1. a. Date of contact: (mm/dd/yy) ______/______/______ (17-22)
   b. Time of Contact: (to nearest hour) ___ ___ A P (23–25)

2. Who initiated the contact? ___ (26)
   1) You
   2) Mother
   3) Father
   4) Grandparent
   5) Foster parent
   6) Community agency: __________
   7) Other: __________________

3. Who received the contact? ___ (27)
   1) You
   2) Mother
   3) Father
   4) Grandparent
   5) Foster parent
   6) Community agency: __________
   7) Other: __________________

4 Type of contact: ___ (28)
   1) Phone call
   2) Clinic visit
   3) Contact in home
   4) In person contact not in home
   5) Daycare center contact
   6) Community agency: __________
   7) Other: __________________

5. How long was the contact? (approximately, in minutes) ___ ___ (29-30)

6. Code the major reason for this contact in columns 28-29: ___ ___ (31-32)

   If secondary topics were covered, code in columns 30-31, 32-33: ___ ___ (33-34)
   ___ ___ (35-36)

Child functioning
11) Child health
12) Diet and feeding
13) Developmental progress
14) Problem behaviors
15) Other: __________________

Family functioning
21) Parent or family worries due to special needs of LBW infant
22) Family inter-relationships
23) Parent health or emotional problems (anxiety, depression)
24) Health or emotional needs of other family members
25) Other __________________

Environmental needs/community services
31) Housing or food
32) Financial
33) Employment
34) Transportation
35) Legal matters
36) Medical equipment for infant
37) Other __________________

Administrative
41) Scheduling a future visit
42) Getting information for IHDP purposes
43) Helping with forms
44) Other: __________________
45) IHDP Child Development Center

7. Written summary or comments about the contact:

References

Abidin, R. R. (1983). *Parenting stress index.* Charlottesville, VA: Institute of Clinical Psychology, University of Virginia Press.

Addams, J. (1935). *Forty years at Hull House.* New York: MacMillan.

Adelman, A. M., Fredman, L., & Knight, A. L. (1994). House call practices: A comparison by specialty. *Journal of Family Practice, 39*(1), 39-44.

Alan Guttmacher Institute. (1994). *Sex and America's teenagers.* New York: Author.

Alexander, J. F., Barton, C., Schiavo, R. S., & Parsons, B. V. (1976). Systems-behavioral intervention with families of delinquents: Therapist characteristics, family behavior, and outcome. *Journal of Consulting and Clinical Psychology, 44,* 656-664.

American Academy of Child and Adolescent Psychiatry. (1999). *1999 violence fact sheet.* Washington, DC: Author.

American Counseling Association. (1995). *Code of ethics and standards of practice.* Alexandria, VA: Author.

American Psychological Association. (1992). Ethical principles of psychologists and code of conduct. *American Psychologist, 47,* 1597-1611.

American Psychological Association. (1993). Guidelines for providers of psychological services to ethnic linguistic and culturally diverse populations. *American Psychologist, 48,* 45-48.

American Psychological Association. (1996). *APA presidential task force on violence and the family report.* Washington, DC: Author.

Ammerman, R. T. (1990). Etiological models of child maltreatment: A behavioral perspective. *Behavior Modification, 14,* 230-254.

Apfel, N. H., & Seitz, V. (1991). Four models of adolescent mother-grandmother relationships in Black inner-city families. *Family Relations, 40,* 421-429.

Azar, S. T., Robinson, D. R., Hekimian, E., & Twentyman, M. T. (1984). Unrealistic expectations and problem solving ability in maltreating and comparison mothers. *Journal of Consulting and Clinical Psychology, 52*(4), 687-691.

Bailey, D. B. (1987). Collaborative goal-setting with families: Resolving differences in values and priorities for services. *Topics in Early Childhood Special Education, 7*(2), 59-71.

Bailey, D. B. (1988). Considerations in developing family goals. In D. B. Bailey & R. J. Simeonsson (Eds.), *Family assessment in early intervention* (pp. 229-249). Columbus, OH: Merrill.

Bailey, D. B. (1995). Development and evaluation of an instrument to assess family needs: Clinical, research, and training implications. In L. Borges, J. B. Fernandex, A. Violante, M. J. Baldaia, Z. Veiga, & V. Micaelo (Eds.), *Families in early intervention: From philosophy to action* (pp. 41-72). Portugal: Ediliber, Lda.

Bailey, D. B., & Simeonsson, R. J. (1988). *Family assessment in early intervention*. Columbus, OH: Merrill.

Baker, A. J., Piotrkowski, C. S., & Brooks-Gunn, J. B. (1999). Home instruction program for preschool youngsters. *The Future of Children, 9*(1), 116-133.

Baladerian, N. J. (1991). *Abuse causes disabilities*. Available from the Disability Abuse and Personal Rights Project, P.O. Box T, Culver City, CA 90230.

Baldwin, L. A., & Chen, S. C. (1989). The effectiveness of public health nursing services to prenatal clients: An integrated review. *Public Health Nursing, 6*, 80-87.

Bandura, A. (1977). *Social learning theory*. Englewood Cliffs, NJ: Prentice Hall.

Barnard, K. (1994). *Nursing Child Assessment Satellite Training Program. NCAST caregiver/parent interaction teaching manual*. Seattle: NCAST Publications, University of Washington Press.

Barnett, S., & Escobar, C. M. (1990). Economic costs and benefits of early intervention. In S. J. Meisels & J. P. Shonkoff (Eds.), *Handboo.: of early childhood intervention* (pp. 560-582). New York: Cambridge University Press.

Barrera, M. E., Doucet, D. A., & Ketching, K. J. (1990). Early home intervention and socio-emotional development of preterm infants. *Infant Mental Health Journal, 11*(2), 142-157.

Bateson, G., Jackson, D. D., Haley, J., & Weakland, J. H. (1956). Toward a theory of schizophrenia. *Behavior Science, 1*, 2521-2564.

Bavolek, S. (1989). *Handbook for the AAPI: Adult-Adolescent Parenting Inventory*. Eau Claire, WI: Family Development Resources.

Beck, D. F., & Jones, M. A. (1973). *Progress on family problems: A nationwide study of clients' and counselors' views on family agency services*. New York: Family Service Association of America.

Begler, A. L. (1997). Legal issues in professional practice with families. In D. T. Marsh & R. D. Magee (Eds.), *Ethical and legal issues in professional practice with families* (pp. 27-49). New York: John Wiley.

Behrens, M. I. (1967). Brief home visits by clinic therapist in the treatment of lower-class patients. *American Journal of Psychiatry, 124*, 371-375.

Bell, R. Q. (1971). Stimulus control of parent or caregiver behavior by offspring. *Developmental Psychology, 4*, 63-72.

Belle, D. (Ed.). (1982). *Lives in stress: Women and depression*. Beverly Hills, CA: Sage.

Belsky, J. (1993). Etiology of child maltreatment: An ecological integration. *American Psychologist, 114*, 413-431.

Benasich, A. A., & Brooks-Gunn, J. (1996). Enhancing maternal knowledge and child-rearing concepts: Results from an early intervention program. *Child Development, 67*, 1186-1205.

Berg, C. L., & Helgeson, D. (1984). That first home visit. *Journal of Community Health Nursing, 1*(3), 207-215.

Berkeley Planning Associates. (1982). *The exploration of client characteristics, services and outcomes* (Contract No. 105-78-1108). Washington, DC: Department of Health, Education and Welfare.

Besharov, D. J., & Laumann-Billings, L. (1996). Child abuse reporting. In I. Garfinkel, J. Hochschild, & S. McLanahan (Eds.), *Social policies for children* (pp. 257-273). Washington, DC: Brookings Institute.

Beyth-Marom, R., & Fischhoff, B. (1997). Adolescents' decisions about risks: A cognitive perspective. In J. Schulenberg, J. Maggs, & K. Hurrelman (Eds.), *Health risks* and developmental transaction during adolescence (pp. 110-135). New York: Cambridge University Press.

Bijou, S. (1984). Parent training: Actualizing the critical conditions of early childhood development. In R. F. Dangel & R. A. Polster (Eds.), *Parent training: Foundations of research and practice* (pp. 15-26). New York: Guilford.

Blechman, E. A. (1974). The family contact game: A tool to teach interpersonal problem solving. *Family Coordinator, 23,* 269-281.

Blechman, E. A. (1980). Family problem-solving training. *American Journal of Family Therapy, 8,* 8-22.

Bloom, M., Fischer, J., & Orme, J. G. (1999). *Evaluating practice: Guidelines for the accountable professional.* Needham Heights, MA: Allyn & Bacon.

Bluma, S. M., Shearer, M. S., Frohman, A. H., & Hilliard, J. M. (1976). *Portage guide to early education: Manual.* Portage, WI: Cooperative Education Service Agency.

Bordin, E. S. (1979). The generalizability of the psychoanalytic concept of the working alliance. *Psychotherapy: Theory, Research and Practice, 16,* 252-260.

Borduin, C. M., Mann, B. J., Cone, L. T., Henggeler, S. W., Fucci, B. R., Blaske, D. M., & Williams, R. A. (1995). Multisystemic treatment of serious juvenile offenders: Long-term prevention of criminality and violence. *Journal of Consulting and Clinical Psychology, 63,* 569-578.

Bowen, M. (1966). The use of family theory in clinical practice. *Comprehensive Psychiatry, 7,* 345-374.

Bowlby, J. (1952). *Maternal care and mental health.* Geneva, Switzerland: World Health Organization.

Bowlby, J. (1984). Violence in the family as a disorder of the attachment and caregiving systems. *American Journal of Psychoanalysis, 44*(1), 9-27.

Boyd, R. D., & Herwig, J. (1980). *Serving handicapped children in home-based Head Start.* Portage, WI: The Portage Project.

Brammer, L. M., & Shostrom, E. L. (1982). *Therapeutic psychology: Fundamentals of counseling and psychotherapy* (4th ed.). Englewood Cliffs, NJ: Prentice Hall.

Bremner, R. H. (1971). *Children and youth in America: A documentary history. Vol. II: 1886-1932.* Cambridge, MA: Harvard University Press.

Brinkerhoff, R. O., Brethower, D. M., Hluchyj, T., & Nowakowski, J. R. (1983). *Program evaluation: A practitioner's guide for trainers and educators.* Boston: Kluwer-Nijhoff.

Bronfenbrenner, U. (1974). *Is early intervention effective? A report on longitudinal evaluation of preschool programs* (Vol. 2). Washington, DC: Office of Child Development, Department of Health, Education, and Welfare.

Bronfenbrenner, U. (1979). *The ecology of human development.* Cambridge, MA: Harvard University Press.

Bronfenbrenner, U. (1987). Family support: The quiet revolution. In S. L. Kagan, D. Powell, B. Weissbourd, & E. Zigler (Eds.), *America's family support programs* (pp. xi-xvii). New Haven, CT: Yale University Press.

Bronfenbrenner, U. (1989). Ecological systems theory. *Annals of Child Development, 6,* 185-246.

Bronfenbrenner, U. (1995). The bioecological model from a life course perspective: Reflections of a participant observer. In P. Moen, G. H. Elder, Jr., & K. Luscher (Eds.), *Examining lives in context: Perspectives on the ecology of human development* (pp. 599-618). Washington, DC: American Psychological Association.

Brooks-Gunn, J., (1995). Children in families in communities: Risk and intervention in the Bronfenbrenner tradition. In P. Moen, G. H. Elder, Jr., & K. Lüscher (Eds.), *Examining lives in context* (pp. 467-519). Washington, DC: American Psychological Association.

Brooks-Gunn, J., & Chase-Lansdale, P. L. (1995). Adolescent parenthood. In M. H. Bornstein (Ed.), *Handbook of parenting: Vol. 3. Status and social conditions of parenting* (pp. 113-149). Hillsdale, NJ: Lawrence Erlbaum.

Brooks-Gunn, J., McCarton, C., Casey, P., McCormick, M., Bauer, C., Bernbaum, J., Tyson, J., Swanson, M., Bennett, F. C., Scott, D., Tonascia, J., & Meinert, C. (1994). Early intervention in low birth-weight premature infants. *Journal of the American Medical Association, 272*, 1257-1262.

Bross, D. C., Krugman, R. D., Lenherr, M. R., Rosenberg, D. A., & Schmitt, B. D. (Eds.). (1988). *The new child protection team handbook.* New York: Garland.

Brown, B. (1962). Home visiting by psychiatrists. *Archives of General Psychiatry, 7*, 98-107.

Browne, A. (1993). Violence against women by male partners: Prevalence, outcomes, and policy implications. *American Psychologist, 48*, 1077-1087.

Browne, A., & Williams, K. R. (1989). Exploring the effect of resource availability and the likelihood of female-perpetrated homicides. *Law & Society Review, 23*, 75-94.

Bruder, M. B. (1996). Interdisciplinary collaboration in service delivery. In R. A. McWilliam (Ed.), *Rethinking pull-out services in early intervention* (pp. 27-48). Baltimore, MD: Paul H. Brookes.

Brunk, M., Henggeler, S. W., & Whelan, J. P. (1987). A comparison of multisystemic therapy and parent training in the brief treatment of child abuse and neglect. *Journal of Consulting and Clinical Psychology, 55*, 311-318.

Bryant, D. (1991, April). *Documenting abuse and neglect in the Infant Health and Development Program.* Paper presented at the Society for Research in Child Development, Seattle, WA.

Bryant, D., & Maxwell, K. (1997). The effectiveness of early intervention for disadvantaged children. In M. Guralnick (Ed.), *The effectiveness of early intervention* (pp. 23-46). Baltimore, MD: Paul H. Brookes.

Buhler-Wilkerson, K. (1985). Public health nursing: In sickness or in health. *American Journal of Public Health, 75*, 1155-1167.

Byrd, M. E. (1997). A typology of the potential outcomes of maternal-child home visits: A literature analysis. *Public Health Nursing, 4*(1), 3-11.

Cabot, R. C. (1919). *Social work.* Boston: Houghton Mifflin.

Caldwell, B. (1998). At HOME—1963-1998. *Zero to Three, 19*(1), 7-17.

Caldwell, B., & Bradley, R. (1984). *Home observation for measurement of the environment* [Manual]. (Available from the University of Arkansas, Center for Research on Teaching and Learning, 2801 South University Ave., Little Rock, AR 72204)

Cameron, R. J. (1984). Portage in the U.K.: 1984. *Journal of Community Education, 3*(3), 24-33.

Campion, E. W. (1997). Can house calls survive? *New England Journal of Medicine, 337*(25), 1840-1841.

Caplan, G. (1974). *Support systems and community mental health.* New York: Behavioral Publications.

Carkhuff, R. R. (1984). *Helping and human relations (Vol. 2).* Amherst, MA: Human Resource Development.

Carkhuff, R. R., & Truax, C. B. (1965). Lay mental health counseling. *Journal of Consulting Psychology, 29*, 426-431.

Carse, J., Panton, N., & Watt, A. (1958). A district mental health service: The Worthing Experiment. *Lancet, 275*, 39-41.

Casey, P., Bradley, R., Nelson, J., & Whaley, S. (1988). The clinical assessment of a child's social and physical environment during the health visit. *Developmental & Behavioral Pediatrics, 9*, 333-338.

Cauthen, D. B. (1981). The house call in current medical practice. *Journal of Family Practice*, 13, 209-213.

Chalmers, K. (1994). Difficult work: Health visitors' work with clients in the community. *International Journal of Nursing Studies, 31,* 168-182.

Chamberlain, P., & Patterson, G. R. (1995). Discipline and child compliance in parenting. In M. H. Bornstein (Ed.), *Handbook of parenting, Vol. 4: Applied and practical parenting* (pp. 205-225). Hillsdale, NJ: Lawrence Erlbaum.

Charity Organization Society of the City of New York. (1883). *Hand-book for friendly visitors among the poor.* New York: G. P. Putnam.

Chase-Lansdale, P. L., Brooks-Gunn, J., & Zamsky, E. S. (1994). Young African-American multigenerational families in poverty: Quality of mothering and grandmothering. *Child Development, 65,* 373-393.

Christensen, L. L. (1995). Therapists' perspectives on home-based family therapy. *American Journal of Family Therapy,* 23(4), 306-314.

Cohen, L. R., Shaeffer, L. G., Gordon, A. N., & Baird, T. L. (1996). *Child development, health, and safety: Educational materials for home visitors and parents.* Gaithersburg, MD: Aspen.

Cole, R., Kitzman, H., Olds, D., & Sidora, K. (1998). Family context as a moderator of program effects in prenatal and early childhood home visitation. *Journal of Community Psychology, 26*(1), 37-48.

Coley, R. L., & Chase-Lansdale, P. L. (1998). Adolescent pregnancy and parenthood, recent evidence and future directions. *American Psychologist, 53,* 152-166.

Colletta, N. D., & Gregg, C. H. (1981). Adolescent mothers' vulnerability to stress. *Journal of Nervous and Mental Disease, 169*(1), 50-54.

Combs, A. W., & Avila, D. L. (1985). *Helping relationships.* Boston: Allyn & Bacon.

Combs-Orme, T., Reis, J., & Ward, L. D. (1985). Effectiveness of home visits by public health nurses in maternal and child health: An empirical review. *Public Health Reports, 100*(5), 490-499.

Conoley, J. C., & Bryant, L. E. (1995). Multicultural family assessment. In J. C. Conoley & E. B. Werth (Eds.), *Family assessment* (pp. 103-130). Lincoln, NE: Buros Institute of Mental Measurements.

Coons, C. E., Gay, E. D., Fandal, A. W., Ker, C., & Frankenburg, W. K. (1981). *The Home Screening Questionnaire reference manual.* Denver: University of Colorado Health Science Center.

Corey, M. S., & Corey, G. (1998). *Becoming a helper* (3rd ed.). Pacific Grove, CA: Brooks/Cole.

Cormier, L. S., Cormier, W. H., & Weisser, R. J., Jr. (1984). *Interviewing and helping skills for health professionals.* Monterey, CA: Wadsworth.

Cormier, L. S., & Cormier, W. H. (1991). *Interviewing strategies for helpers.* Pacific Grove, CA: Brooks/Cole.

Coulton, C. J., Korbin, J. E., Su, M., & Chow, J. (1995). Community level factors and child maltreatment rates. *Child Development, 66,* 1262-1276.

Council for Early Childhood Professional Recognition. (1998). *The Child Development Associate National Credentialing Program: Making a difference in the early care and education of young children.* Washington, DC: Author.

Cox, M. J., & Paley, B. (1997). Families as systems. *Annual Review of Psychology, 48,* 243-267.

Curtis, J. H., & Miller, M. E. (1976). An argument for the use of paraprofessional counselors in premarital and marital counseling. *Family Coordinator, 25,* 47-50.

Daly, M., & Wilson, M. (1988). Evolutionary social psychology and family homicide. *Science, 242,* 519-524.

Daro, D. A., & Harding, K. A. (1999). Healthy Families America: Using research to enhance practice. *The Future of Children, 9*(1), 152-176.

Dawson, P. (1980). Home visiting in Europe. In R. W. Chamberlin (Ed.), *Conference exploring the use of home visitors to improve the delivery of preventive services to mothers with young children* (pp. 272-274). Washington, DC: American Academy of Pediatrics.

Day, J. C. (1996). *Population projections of the United States by age, sex, race, and Hispanic origin: 1995 to 2050* (U.S. Bureau of the Census, Current Population Reports P25-1130). Washington, DC: Government Printing Office.

De la Cuesta, C. (1994). Relationships in health visiting: Enabling and mediating. *International Journal of Nursing, 31*, 451-459.

Deal, L. W. (1994). The effectiveness of community health nursing interventions: A literature review. *Public Health Nursing, 11*, 315-323.

Dewey, J. (1915). *Schools of tomorrow.* New York: Dutton.

Dishion, T. J., & Patterson, S. G. (1996). *Preventive parenting with love, encouragement, and limits.* Eugene, OR: Castalia.

Dodge, K. A., Bates, J. E., & Pettit, G. S. (1990). Mechanisms in the cycle of violence. *Science, 250*, 1678-1683.

Donahue, M. P. (1985). *Nursing—An illustrated history: The finest art.* St. Louis, MO: C.V. Mosby.

Dowie, R. (1983). National trends in domicilary consultations. *British Medical Journal, 286*, 819-822.

Ducheny, K., Crandell, D., Alletzhauser, H. L., & Schneider, T. R. (1997). Graduate student professional development. *Professional Psychology: Research and Practice, 28*, 87-91.

Duggan, A. K., McFarlane, E. C., Windham, A. M., Rohde, C. A., Salkever, D. S., Fuddy, L., Rosenberg, L. A., Buchbinder, S. B., & Sia, C. C. (1999). Evaluation of Hawaii's Healthy Start Program. *The Future of Children, 9*(1), 66-90.

Duncan, D. C. (1982). Cognitive perceptions of battered women. (Doctoral dissertation, University of Southern California). *Dissertation Abstracts International, 43*, 01B.

Dunst, C. J., & Trivette, C. M. (1987). Enabling and empowering families: Conceptual and intervention issues. *School Psychology Review, 16*(4), 443-456.

Durlak, J. (1979). Comparative effectiveness of professional and paraprofessional helpers. *Psychological Bulletin, 86*, 80-92.

Dutton, D. G. (1992). Theoretical and empirical perspectives on the etiology and prevention of wife assault. In R. D. Peters, R. J. McMahon, & V. L. Quinsey (Eds.), *Aggression and violence throughout the lifespan* (pp. 192-221). Newbury Park, CA: Sage.

D'Zurilla, T. J. (1986). *Problem-solving therapy: A social competence approach to clinical intervention.* New York: Springer.

D'Zurilla, T. J. (1988). Problem-solving therapies. In K. D. Dobson (Ed.), *Handbook of cognitive-behavioral therapies* (pp. 85-135). New York: Guilford.

D'Zurilla, T. J., & Goldfried, M. R. (1971). Problem solving and behavior modification. *Journal of Abnormal Psychology, 78*, 107-126.

D'Zurilla, T. J., & Nezu, A. (1982). Social problem solving in adults. In P. C. Kendall (Ed.), *Advances in cognitive-behavioral research and therapy* (Vol. 1, pp. 201-274). New York: Academic Press.

East, P. L., & Felice, M. E. (1996). *Adolescent pregnancy and parenting: Findings from a racially diverse sample.* Hillsdale, NJ: Lawrence Erlbaum.

Edelwich, J., & Brodsky, A. (1980). *Burn-out.* New York: Human Sciences Press.

Egan, G. (1975). *The skilled helper: A model for systematic helping and interpersonal relating*. Belmont, CA: Wadsworth.

Egan, G. (1982). *The skilled helper: Model, skills, and methods for effective helping* (2nd ed.). Monterey, CA: Brooks/Cole.

Egan, G. (1998). *The skilled helper: A problem-management approach to helping* (6th ed.). Pacific Grove, CA: Brooks/Cole.

Ekstein, R. (1972). Supervision of psychotherapy: Is it teaching? Is it administration? Or is it therapy? In D. E. Hendrickson & F. H. Krause (Eds.), *Counseling and psychotherapy: Training and supervision* (pp. 144-152). Columbus, OH: Merrill.

Embry, L. H. (1984). What to do? Matching clients. In R. F. Dangel & R. A. Polster (Eds.), *Parent training: Foundations of research and practice* (pp. 443-473). New York: Guilford.

Emery, R. E., & Laumann-Billings, L. (1998). An overview of the nature, causes, and consequences of abusive family relationships. *American Psychologist, 53*, 121-135.

Evans, J. (1978). The High/Scope Parent-to-Parent Model. In S. Maybanks & M. Bryce (Eds.), *Home-based services for children and families: Policy, practice, and research* (pp. 115-124). Springfield, IL: Charles C Thomas.

Fantuzzo, J. W., DePaola, L. M., Lambert, L., Martino, L., Anderson, G., & Sutonn, S. (1991). Effects of interparental violence on the psychological adjustment and competencies of young children. *Journal of Consulting and Clinical Psychology, 59*, 258-265.

Farran, D. C. (2000). Another decade of intervention for children who are low income or disabled: What do we know now? In J. P. Shonkoff & S. J. Meisels (Eds.), *Handbook of early childhood intervention* (2nd ed., pp. 510-548). New York: Cambridge University Press.

Federal Bureau of Investigation. (1997). *Crime in the United States—1996, Uniform crime reports: 1*. Washington, DC: Author.

Feek, W. (1988). *Working effectively: A guide to evaluation techniques*. London: Bedford Square Press.

Fenichel, E. (Ed.). (1992). *Learning through supervision and mentorship to support the development of infants, toddlers and their families: A source book*. Washington, DC: Zero to Three/National Center for Clinical Infant Programs.

Fiedler, D., Briar, K. H., & Pierce, M. (1984). Services for battered women. *Journal of Sociology and Social Welfare, 11*(3), 540-557.

Field, T. M., Widmayer, S., Greenberg, R., & Stoller, S. (1982). Effects of parent training on teenage mothers and their daughters. *Pediatrics, 69*, 703-707.

Field, T. M., Widmayer, S. M., Stringer, S., & Ignatoff, E. (1980). Teenage lower-class, Black mothers and their preterm infants: An intervention and developmental follow-up. *Child Development, 51*, 426-436.

Fineman, S. (1985). *Social work stress and intervention*. Brookfield, VT: Gower.

Fink, A. E., Wilson, E. E., & Conover, M. B. (1963). *The field of social work*. New York: Holt, Rinehart & Winston.

Finkelhor, D., Hotaling, G. T., & Yllo, K. (1988). *Stopping family violence*. Newbury Park, CA: Sage.

Folkman, S., & Lazarus, R. S. (1980). An analysis of coping in a middle-aged community sample. *Journal of Health and Social Behavior, 21*, 219-239.

Fortune, A. E. (1987). Grief only? Client and social worker reactions to termination. *Clinical Social Work Journal, 15*(2), 159-171.

Foster, S. L., & Robin, R. L. (1998). Parent-adolescent conflict and relationship discord. In E. J. Mash & R. L. Barkley (Eds.), *Treatment of childhood disorders* (2nd ed., pp. 601-646). New York: Guilford.

Fraley, Y. L. (1983). The Family Support Center: Early intervention for high-risk parents and children. *Children Today, 12*(1), 13-17.

Frankenburg, W. K., & Coons, C. E. (1986). Home Screening Questionnaire: Its validity in assessing home environment. *Journal of Pediatrics, 108*, 624-626.

Frey, D., Oman, K., & Wagner, W. R. (1997). Delivering mental health services to the home. In M. G. Winiarski (Ed.), *HIV mental health for the 21st century* (pp. 224-240). New York: New York University Press.

Friedman, R. M. (1986). Major issues in mental health services for children. *Administration in Mental Health, 14*, 6-13.

Furstenberg, F. F., Jr., Brooks-Gunn, J., & Morgan, S. P. (1987). *Adolescent mothers in later life*. New York: Cambridge University Press.

The Future of Children. (1999). Home visiting: Recent program evaluations [Special issue].

Gambrill, E. D. (1997). *Social work practice: A critical thinker's guide*. New York: Oxford University Press.

Gambrill, E. D., & Stein, T. J. (1978). *Supervision in child welfare: A training manual*. Berkeley: University of California Press.

Gambrill, E. D., & Stein, T. J. (1983). *Supervision: A decision-making approach*. Beverly Hills, CA: Sage.

Garbarino, J. (1987). Family support and the prevention of child maltreatment. In S. L. Kagan, D. R. Powell, B. Weissbourd, & E. F. Zigler (Eds.), *America's family support programs* (pp. 99-114). New Haven, CT: Yale University Press.

Garbarino, J. (1995). Growing up in a socially toxic environment: Life for children and families in the 1990s. In G. B. Melton (Ed.), *Nebraska Symposium on Motivation: Vol. 42. The individual, the family, and the social good: Personal fulfillment in times of change* (pp. 1-20). Lincoln: University of Nebraska Press.

Garbarino, J., & Kostelny, K. (1992). Child maltreatment as a community problem. *Child Abuse and Neglect, 16*, 455-467.

Gawthrop, J. C., & Uhlemann, M. R. (1992). Effects of the problem-solving approach in ethics training. *Professional Psychology: Research and Practice, 18*, 353-359.

Gelfand, D. M., Teti, D. M., Seiner, S. A., & Jameson, P. B. (1996). Helping mothers fight depression: Evaluation of a home-based intervention program for depressed mothers and their infants. *Journal of Clinical Child Psychology, 25*(40), 406-422.

Gelles, R. J. (1987). *Family violence* (2nd ed.). Beverly Hills, CA: Sage.

Glendinning, C. (1986). *A single door: Social work with the families of disabled children*. London: Allen & Unwin.

Goldfried, M. R., & Davison, G. C. (1976). *Clinical behavior therapy*. New York: Holt, Rinehart & Winston.

Goldstein, H. (1978). The effective use of volunteers in home-based care. In S. Maybanks & M. Bryce (Eds.), *Home-based services for children and families: Policy, practice, and research* (pp. 237-247). Springfield, IL: Charles C Thomas.

Gomby, D. S. (1999). Understanding evaluations of home visitation programs. *The Future of Children, 9*(1), 27-43.

Gomby, D. S., Culross, P. L., & Behrman, R. E. (1999). Home visiting: Recent program evaluations—Analysis and recommendations. *The Future of Children, 9*(1), 4-26.

Goodman, L. A., Koss, M. P., & Russo, N. F. (1993). Violence against women: Physical and mental health effects. *Applied and Preventive Psychology, 2*, 79-89.

Goodwin, B. J. (1997). Multicultural competence in family practice. In D. T. Marsh & R. D. Magee (Eds.), *Ethical and legal issues in professional practice with families* (pp. 75-93). New York: John Wiley.

Gordon, I. J., & Guinagh, B. J. (1978). A home learning center approach to early stimulation. *JSAS Catalog of Selected Documents in Psychology, 8(6, No. 1634).*

Graham, M., Powell, A., Stabile, I., & Chiricos, C. (1998). *Partners for a healthy baby, a home visiting curriculum for new families: Baby's first six months.* Tallahassee: Florida State University Center for Prevention and Early Intervention Policy.

Gray, S. W., & Klaus, R. A. (1970). The Early Training Project: A seventh year report. *Child Development, 41,* 909-924.

Gray, S. W., & Ruttle, K. (1980). The Family-Oriented Home Visiting Program: A longitudinal study. *Genetic Psychology Monographs, 102,* 299-316.

Gray, S. W., & Wandersman, L. P. (1980). The methodology of home-based intervention studies: Problems and promising strategies. *Child Development, 51,* 993-1009.

Greenson, R. R. (1967). *The technique and practice of psychoanalysis.* New York: International Universities Press.

Gross, R. T., Spiker, D., & Haynes, C. (Eds.). (1997). *Helping low birth weight, premature babies: The Infant Health and Development Program.* Stanford, CA: Stanford University Press.

Grosz, C. A., & Denson, D. B. (1988). Conducting effective team meetings. In D. C. Bross, R. D. Krugman, M. R. Lenherr, D. A. Rosenberg, & B. D. Schmitt (Eds.), *The new child protection team handbook* (pp. 287-298). New York: Garland.

Gutelius, M. F., Kirsch, A. D., MacDonald, S., Brooks, M. R., & McErlean, T. (1977). Controlled study of child health supervision: Behavioral results. *Pediatrics, 60,* 294-304.

Hackney, H., & Cormier, L. S. (1979). *Counseling strategies and objectives* (2nd ed.). Englewood Cliffs, NJ: Prentice Hall.

Haley, J. (1976). *Problem solving therapy.* New York: Harper & Row.

Haley, J. (1987). *Problem solving therapy* (2nd ed.). San Francisco: Jossey-Bass.

Halpern, R. (1993). The societal context of home visiting and related services for families in poverty. *The Future of Children, 3*(3), 158-171.

Halpern, R., & Covey, L. (1983). Community support for adolescent parents and their children: The parent-to-parent program in Vermont. *Journal of Primary Prevention, 3*(3), 160-173.

Halpern, R., & Larner, M. (1988). The design of family support programs in high-risk communities: Lessons from the Child Survival/Fair Start initiative. In D. R. Powell (Ed.), *Parent education as early childhood intervention: Emerging directions in theory, research, and practice* (pp. 181-207). Norwood, NJ: Ablex.

Hancock, B. L., & Pelton, L. (1989). Home visits: History and functions. *Social Casework, 70,* 21-27.

Hannon, P., & Jackson, A. (1987). Educational home visiting and the teaching of reading. *Educational Research, 29*(3), 183-191.

Hardy-Brown, K., Miller, B., Dean, J., Carrasco, C., & Thompson, S. (1987). Home based intervention: Catalyst and challenge to the therapeutic relationship. *Zero to Three, 8*(1), 8-12.

Hartman, A., (1995). Diagrammatic assessment of family relationships. *Families in Society, 76*(2), 111-122.

Hattie, J. A., Sharpley, C. F., & Rogers, H. J. (1984). Comparative effectiveness of professional and paraprofessional helpers. *Psychological Bulletin, 95,* 534-541.

Heins, H. C., Nance, N. W., & Ferguson, J. E. (1987). Social support in improving perinatal outcome: The Resource Mothers Program. *Pregnancy and Social Support, 70,* 263-266.

Henggeler, S. W., & Borduin, C. M. (1995). Multisystemic treatment of serious juvenile offenders and their families. In I. M. Schwartz & P. AuClaire (Eds.), *Home-*

based services for troubled children (pp. 113-130). Lincoln: University of Nebraska Press.

Henggeler, S. W., Rodick, J. D., Borduin, C. M., Hanson, C. L., Watson, S. M., & Urey, J. R. (1986). Multisystemic treatment of juvenile offenders: Effects on adolescent behavior and family interactions. *Developmental Psychology, 22,* 132-141.

Henggeler, S. W., Schoenwald, S. K., Borduin, C. M., Rowland, M. D., & Cunningham, P. B. (1998). *Multisystemic treatment of antisocial behavior in children and adolescents.* New York: Guilford.

Hersen, M., & Barlow, D. H. (1976). *Single case experimental designs.* New York: Pergamon.

Hesselbrock, M. N., Meyer, R. E., & Keener, J. J. (1985). Archives of general psychiatry. *Psychopathology in Hospitalized Alcoholics, 42*(11), 1050-1055.

Heyman, R., O'Leary, D., & Jouriles, E. (1995). Alcohol and aggressive personality styles: Potentiators of serious physical aggression against wives? *Journal of Family Psychology, 9,* 44-57.

Heywood, J. S. (1959). *Children in care: The development of the service for the deprived child.* London: Routledge & Kegan Paul.

Hiatt, S. W., Sampson, D., & Baird, D. (1997). Paraprofessional home visitation: Conceptual and pragmatic considerations. *Journal of Community Psychology, 25,* 77-93.

Hilberman, E. (1980). Overview: The "wife-beater's wife" reconsidered. *American Journal of Psychiatry, 137,* 1336-1347.

Ho, M. K. (1987). *Family therapy with ethnic minorities.* Newbury Park, CA: Sage.

Ho, M. K. (1997). *Family therapy with ethnic minorities* (2nd ed.). Thousand Oaks, CA: Sage.

Hobbs, N., Perrin, J. M., & Ireys, H. T. (1985). *Chronically-ill children and their families.* San Francisco: Jossey-Bass.

Hofeller, K. H. (1982). *Social, psychological and situational factors in wife abuse.* Palo Alto, CA: R & E Research Associates.

Holbrook, T. (1983). Going among them: The evolution of the home visit. *Journal of Sociology and Social Welfare, 10*(1), 112-135.

Hollis, F., & Wood, M. E. (1981). *Casework: A psychosocial therapy* (3rd ed.). New York: Random House.

Holloway, E. (1995). *Clinical supervision: A systems approach.* Thousand Oaks, CA: Sage.

Holmes, T. H., & Rahe, R. H. (1967). The Social Readjustment Rating Scale. *Journal of Psychosomatic Research, 11,* 213-218.

Hotaling, G. T., & Sugarman, D. (1986). An analysis of risk markers in husband to wife violence: The current state of knowledge. *Violence and Victims, 1*(2), 101-124.

Hotz, V. J., McElroy, S. W., & Sanders, S. G. (1997). The costs and consequences of teenage childbearing for mothers. In R. A. Maynard (Ed.), *Kids having kids: Economic costs and social consequences of teen pregnancy* (pp. 55-94). Washington, DC: Urban Institute Press.

Howrigan, G. A. (1988). Evaluating parent-child interaction outcomes of family support and education programs. In H. B. Weiss & F. H. Jacobs (Eds.), *Evaluating family programs* (pp. 95-130). Hawthorne, NY: Aldine de Gruyter.

Hughes, D., Johnson, K., Rosenbaum, S., Butler, E., & Simons, J. (1988). *The health of America's children: Maternal and child health data book.* Washington, DC: Children's Defense Fund.

Hupp, S. C., & Kaiser, A. P. (1986). Evaluating education programs for severely handicapped preschoolers. In L. Bickman & D. L. Weatherford (Eds.), *Evaluating early intervention programs for severely handicapped children and their families* (pp. 233-261). Austin, TX: Pro-Ed.

Hutchins, V. L., & McPherson, M. (1991). National agenda for children with special health needs: Social policy for the 1990s through the 21st century. *American Psychologist, 46,* 141-143.

Hyman, A., Schillinger, D., & Lo, B. (1995). Laws mandating reporting of domestic violence—do they promote patient well-being? *Journal of the American Medical Association, 273*(22), 1781-1787.

Infant Health and Development Program (IHDP). (1990). Enhancing the outcomes of low-birth-weight, premature infants: A multisite, randomized trial. *Journal of the American Medical Association, 263,* 3035-3042.

Intagliata, J., & Doyle, N. (1984). Enhancing social support for parents of developmentally disabled children: Training in interpersonal problem solving skills. *Mental Retardation,* 22(1), 4-11.

International Medical Services for Health for the National Committee to Prevent Infant Mortality. (1994a). *Resource mothers handbook.* Sterling, VA: International Medical Services' MotherNet America Program.

International Medical Services for Health for the National Commission to Prevent Infant Mortality. (1994b). *Resource mothers curriculum sourcebook.* Sterling, VA: International Medical Services' MotherNet America Program.

Jackson, A. M. (1984). Child neglect: An overview. In National Center on Child Abuse and Neglect (Ed.), *Perspectives on child maltreatment in the mid-1980's* (pp. 15-17; DHHS Publication No. OHDS 84-30338). Washington, DC: Government Printing Office.

Jackson, D. D. (1957). The question of family homeostasis. *Psychiatric Quarterly Supplement, 31,* 79-90.

Jacobson, N., & Gottman, J. (1998). *When men batter women: New insights into ending abusive relationships.* New York: Simon & Schuster.

Jahoda, M. (1958). *Current concepts of positive mental health.* New York: Basic Books.

James, W. (1899). *Talk to teachers.* New York: Holt.

Jenkins, S. (1981). *The ethnic dilemma in social services.* New York: Free Press.

Jenkins, S. (1987). Ethnicity and family support. In S. L. Kagan, D. R. Powell, B. Weissbourd, & E. F. Zigler (Eds.), *America's family support programs* (pp. 282-294). New Haven, CT: Yale University Press.

Jessee, P. O., Cecil, C., & Jessee, J. E. (1991). Pediatric family home visitors: Effectiveness in problem solving. *Children's Health Care, 20*(3), 179-184.

Johnson, B. H., McGonigel, M. J., & Kaufmann, R. K. (Eds.). (1989). *Guidelines and recommended practices and the individualized service plan. National Early Childhood Technical Assistance System.* Washington, DC: Association for the Care of Children's Health.

Josten, L. E., Mullett, S. E., Savik, K., Campbell, R., & Vincent, P. (1995). Client characteristics associated with not keeping appointments for public health nursing home visits. *Public Health Nursing, 12,* 305-311.

Kadushin, A. (1976). *Supervision in social work.* New York: Columbia University Press.

Kagan, S. L., Powell, D. R., Weissbourd, B., & Zigler, E. F. (Eds.). (1987). *America's family support programs.* New Haven, CT: Yale University Press.

Kagitcibasi, C. (1996). *Family and human development across cultures: A view from the other side.* Hillsdale, NJ: Lawrence Erlbaum.

Kahle, A. L., & Kelley, M. L (1994). Children's homework problems: A comparison of goal setting and parent training. *Behavior Therapy, 25,* 275-290.

Kamerman, S. B., & Kahn, A. J. (1993). Home health visiting in Europe. *The Future of Children, 3*(3), 39-52.

Kana, R., Barnard, K., Hammond, M., Oshio, S., Spencer, C., Thibodeau, B., & Williams, J. (1995). Preterm infant follow-up project: A multi-site field experiment of hospital and home intervention programs for mothers and preterm infants. *Public Health Nursing, 12,* 171-180.

Kanfer, F. H., Englund, S., Lennhoff, C., & Rhodes, J. (1995). *A mentor manual for adults who work with pregnant and parenting teens.* Washington, DC: Child Welfare League of America.

Kates, N., Webb, S., & LePage, P. (1991). Therapy begins at home: The psychiatric house call. *Canadian Journal of Psychiatry, 36,* 673-676.

Kelley, M. L. (1990). *School-home notes: Promoting children's classroom services.* New York: Guilford.

Kelley, M. L., Embry, L. H., & Baer, D. M. (1979). Skills for child management and family support. *Behavior Modification, 3,* 383-396.

Kempe, C. (1976). Approaches to preventing child abuse: The health visitor concept. *American Journal of Diseases in Children, 130,* 941-947.

Kerr, M. E., & Bowen, M. (1988). *Family evaluation: An approach based on Bowen theory.* New York: Norton.

Kinney, J., & Dittmar, K. (1995). Homebuilders: Helping families help themselves. In I. M. Schwartz & P. AuClaire (Eds.), *Home-based services for troubled children* (pp. 29-52). Lincoln: University of Nebraska Press.

Kinney, J., Haapala, D., & Booth, C. (1991). *Keeping families together: The Homebuilders model.* Hawthorne, NY: Aldine de Gruyter.

Kitzman, H., Olds, D. L., Henderson, C. R., Jr., Hanks, C., Cole, R., Tatelbaum, R., McConnochie, K. M., Sidora, K., Luckey, D. W., Shaver, D., Engelhardt, I., James, D., & Barnard, K. (1997). Effect of prenatal and infancy home visitation by nurses on pregnancy outcomes, childhood injuries, and repeated childbearing: A randomized controlled trial. *Journal of the American Medical Association, 278,* 644-652.

Knauss, L. K. (1997). Professional training in ethics. In D. T. Marsh & R. D. Magee (Eds.), *Ethical and legal issues in professional practice with families* (pp. 289-311). New York: John Wiley.

Knitzer, J. (1982). *Unclaimed children: The failure of public responsibility to children and adolescents in need of mental health services.* Washington, DC: Children's Defense Fund.

Kohlberg, L. (1984). *Essays in moral development: Vol.2: The psychology of moral development.* San Francisco: Harper & Row.

Koop, C. E. (1987). *Surgeon general's report: Children with special health care needs.* Washington, DC: U. S. Department of Health and Human Services.

Krauss, M. W. (1988). Measures of stress and coping in families. In H. B. Weiss & F. H. Jacobs (Eds.), *Evaluating family programs* (pp. 177-194). Hawthorne, NY: Aldine de Gruyter.

LaFromboise, T. D., Foster, S., & James, A. (1996). Ethics in multicultural counseling. In P. Pedersen, J. Draguns, W. Lonner, & J. Trimble (Eds.), *Counseling across cultures* (4th ed., pp. 47-72). Thousand Oaks, CA: Sage.

Langholm, M. (1961). *Family and child welfare in Norway.* Oslo, Norway: Norwegian Joint Committee on International Social Policy.

Laosa, L. M. (1991). The cultural context of construct validity and the ethics of generalizability. *Early Childhood Research Quarterly, 6,* 313-321.

Larner, M., & Halpern, R. (1987). Lay home visiting programs: Strengths, tensions, and challenges. *Zero to Three, 8*(1), 1-7.

Larson, C. E., & LaFasto, F. M. J. (1989). *Team work: What must go right/what can go wrong.* Newbury Park, CA: Sage.

Layzer, J. I., Goodson, B. D., & DeLange, C. (1986). Children in shelters. *Response, 9,* 2-5.

Leahy, K. M., Cobb, M. M., & Jones, M. C. (1982). *Community health nursing* (4th ed.). St. Louis, MO: McGraw-Hill.

Lee, C. C. (Ed.). (1997). *Multicultural issues in counseling* (2nd ed.). Alexandria, VA: American Counseling Association.

Levenstein, P. (1981). Ethical considerations in home-based programs. In M. Bryce & J. C. Lloyd (Eds.), *Treating families in the home: An alternative to placement* (pp. 222-236). Springfield, IL: Charles C Thomas.

Levenstein, P. (1988). *Messages from home: The mother-child home program and the prevention of social disadvantage.* Columbus: Ohio State University Press.

Levine, M., & Levine, A. (1970). *A social history of the helping services: Clinic, court, school, and community.* New York: Appleton-Century-Crofts.

Liaw, F., Meisels, S., & Brooks-Gunn, J. (1995). The effects of experience of early intervention on low birth weight, premature children: The Infant Health and Development Program. *Early Childhood Research Quarterly, 10,* 405-431.

Linder, T. (1983). *Early childhood special education: Program development and administration.* Baltimore, MD: Paul H. Brookes.

Lombard, A. (1981). *Success begins at home.* Lexington, MA: Lexington Books.

Long, L., Paradise, L. V., & Long, T. J. (1981). *Questioning: Skills for the helping process.* Monterey, CA: Brooks/Cole.

Love, J. M., Nauta, M. J., Coelen, C. G., Hewett, K., & Ruopp, R. R. (1976). *National Home Start evaluation: Final report, findings, and implications.* Ypsilanti, MI: High/Scope Educational Research Foundation.

Lung, C. T., & Daro, D. (1996). *Current trends in child abuse reporting and fatalities: The results of the 1995 annual 50-state survey.* Chicago: National Committee to Prevent Child Abuse.

Lutzker, J. R. (1984). Project 12 Ways: Treating child abuse and neglect from an ecobehavioral perspective. In R. F. Dangel & R. A. Polster (Eds.), *Parenting training: Foundation of research and practice* (pp. 260-297). New York: Guilford.

Lutzker, J. R., Bigelow, K. M., Doctor, R. M., Gershater, R. M., & Greene, B. F. (1998). An ecobehavioral model for the prevention and treatment of child abuse and neglect. In J. R. Lutzker (Ed.), *Handbook of child abuse research and treatment* (pp. 239-266). New York: Plenum.

Lutzker, J. R., Bigelow, K. M., Doctor, R. M., & Kessler, M. L. (1998). Safety, health care, and bonding within an ecobehavioral approach to treating and preventing child abuse and neglect. *Journal of Family Violence, 13,* 163-185.

Lutzker, J. R., Frame, R. E., & Rice, J. M. (1982). Project 12 Ways: An ecobehavioral approach to the treatment and prevention of child abuse and neglect. *Education and Treatment of Children, 5,* 141-155.

Lutzker, J. R., & Rice, J. M. (1984). Project 12 Ways: Measuring outcome of a large in-home service for treatment and prevention of child abuse and neglect. *Child Abuse and Neglect, 8*(4), 519-524.

Lutzker, J. R., & Rice, J. M. (1987). Using recidivism data to evaluate Project 12 Ways: An ecobehavioral approach to the treatment and prevention of child abuse and neglect. *Journal of Family Violence, 2,* 282-290.

Lutzker, J. R., Wesch, D., & Rice, J. M. (1984). A review of Project 12 Ways: An ecobehavioral approach to the treatment and prevention of child abuse and neglect. *Advances in Behaviour Research and Therapy, 6*(1), 63-73.

MacRae, D. (1989). The use of outcome measures in implementing policies for handicapped children. In J. J. Gallagher, P. L. Trohanis, & R. M. Clifford (Eds.), *Policy implementation and PL 99-457* (pp. 183-198). Baltimore, MD: Paul H. Brookes.

Madden, J., O'Hara, J., & Levenstein, P. (1984). Home again: Effects of the Mother-Child Home Program on mother and child. *Child Development, 55,* 636-647.

Madden, J. S. (1984). *A guide to alcohol and drug dependence.* Bristol, UK: John Wright.

Mash, E. J., & Barkley, R. A. (Eds.). (1998). *Treatment of childhood disorders* (2nd ed.). New York: Guilford.

Maslach, C. (1982). *Burnout: The cost of caring.* Englewood Cliffs, NJ: Prentice Hall.

Maslach, C., & Leiter, M. P. (1997). *The truth about burnout: How organizations cause personal stress and what to do about it.* San Francisco: Jossey-Bass.

Maynard, R. (1995). Teenage childbearing and welfare reform: Lessons from a decade of demonstration and evaluation research. *Children and Youth Services Review, 17,* 309-332.

McCarton, C., Brooks-Gunn, J., Wallace, I., Bauer, C., Bennett, F., Bernbaum, J., Broyles, S., Casey, P., McCormick, M., Scott, D., Tyson, J., Tonascia, J., & Meinert, C. (1997). Results at age 8 years of early intervention for low-birth weight premature infants. *Journal of the American Medical Association, 277,* 126-132.

McCloskey, L. A., Figuerdo, A. J., & Koss, M. P. (1995). The effects of systemic family violence on children's mental health. *Child Development, 66,* 1239-1261.

McCormick, M. (1984). High-risk young mothers: Infant mortality and morbidity in four areas in the United States, 1973-1978. *American Journal of Public Health, 74*(1), 18-23.

McCormick, M. (1985). The contribution of low birth weight to infant mortality and childhood morbidity. *The New England Journal of Medicine, 312,* 82-90.

McCubbin, H. I., Olson, D., & Larsen, A. (1981). Family Crisis Oriented Personal Scales (F-COPES). In H. I. McCubbin, A. I. Thompson, & M. A. McCubbin (1996). *Family assessment: Resiliency, coping and adaptation—Inventories for research and practice* (pp. 455-507). Madison: University of Wisconsin System.

McGimsey, J. F., Greene, B. F., & Lutzker, J. R. (1995). Competence in aspects of behavioral treatment and consultation: Implications for service delivery and graduate training. *Journal of Applied Behavior Analysis, 28,* 301-315.

McGonigel, M. J., Kaufman, R. K., & Johnson, B. H. (1991). *Guidelines and recommended practices for the Individualized Family Service Plan* (2nd ed.). Washington, DC: Association for the Care of Children's Health.

McGrath, E., Keita, G. P., Strickland, B. R., & Russo, N. F. (Eds.). (1990). *Women and depression: Risk factors and treatment issues.* Washington, DC: American Psychological Association.

McNaughton, D. (1994). Measuring parent satisfaction with early childhood intervention programs: Current practice, problems, and future perspectives. *Topics in Early Childhood Special Education, 14*(1), 26-48.

Mello, N. K. (1980). Some behavioral and biological aspects of alcohol problems in women. In O. J. Kalant (Ed.), *Alcohol and drug problems in women* (pp. 263-298). New York: Plenum.

Melton, G. B., Goodman, G. S., Kalichman, S. C., Levine, M., Saywitz, K., & Koocher, G. P. (1995). Empirical research on child maltreatment and the law. *Journal of Clinical Child Psychology, 24*(Suppl.), 47-77.

Meyer, G. S., & Gibbons, R. V. (1997). House calls to the elderly—A vanishing practice among physicians. *New England Journal of Medicine, 337,* 1815-1820.

Miles, M. S. (1986). Counseling strategies. In S. H. Johnson (Ed.), *Nursing assessment and strategies for the family at risk: High risk parenting* (2nd ed., pp. 343-360). Philadelphia: J. B. Lippincott.

Miller, C. A. (1987). *Maternal health and infant survival.* Washington, DC: National Center for Clinical Infant Programs.

Miller, W. R., & Brown, S. A. (1997). Why psychologists should treat alcohol and drug problems. *American Psychologist, 52,* 1269-1279.

Minuchin, P. (1985). Families and individual development: Provocations from the field of family therapy. *Child Development, 56*, 289-302.

Minuchin, P., Colapinto, J., & Minuchin, S. (1998). *Working with families of the poor.* New York: Guilford.

Minuchin, S. (1974). *Families and family therapy.* Cambridge, MA: Harvard University Press.

Monteiro, L. A. (1985). Florence Nightingale on public health nursing. *American Journal of Public Health, 75*, 181-186.

Moore, K. A., & Burt, M. R. (1982). *Private crisis, public cost: Policy perspectives on teenage childbearing.* Washington, DC: Urban Institute Press.

Moore, K. A., Morrison, D. R., & Greene, A. D. (1997). Effects on the children born to adolescent mothers. In R. A. Maynard (Ed.), *Kids having kids: Economic costs and social consequences of teen pregnancy* (pp. 145-180). Washington, DC: Urban Institute Press.

Moroney, R. (1987). *Social support systems: Families and social policy.* In S. L. Kagan, D. Powell, B. Weissbourd, & E. Ziegler (Eds.), *America's family support programs* (pp. 21-37). New Haven, CT: Yale University Press.

Moynihan, D. P. (1986). *Family and nation.* New York: Harcourt Brace.

Mulvey, L. A. (1988, February). *Training.* Paper presented at the Family Support in the Home: Policy, Practice, and Research conference, Honolulu, HI.

Nathanson, M., Baird, A., & Jemail, J. (1986). Family functioning and the adolescent mother: A systems approach. *Adolescence, 21*, 827-841.

National Association for the Education of Young Children. (1997). *Code of ethical conduct and statement of commitment.* Washington, DC: Author.

National Association of Social Workers. (1996). *NASW code of ethics.* Washington, DC: Author.

National Credentialing Program. (1987). *Home Visitor, Child Development Associate Assessment System and Competency Standards.* Washington, DC: Author. (Available from the Council for Early Childhood Professional Recognition, 1718 Connecticut Avenue, N.W., Suite 500, Washington, D.C. 20009)

National Institute on Drug Abuse. (1999). *NIDA research report—Cocaine abuse and addition* (NIH Publication No. 99-4342) [Online]. Available: www.nida.nih.gov/researchreports/cocaine

National Research Council. (1993). *Understanding child abuse and neglect.* Washington, DC: National Academy Press.

Neuman, S., & McCormick, S. (1995). *Single-subject experimental research: Applications for literacy.* Newark, DE: Internal Reading Association.

Nezu, A. M. (1987). A problem-solving formulation of depression: A literature review and proposal of a pluralistic model. *Clinical Psychology Review, 7*, 121-144.

Nightingale, F. (1894). *Health teaching in towns and villages, rural hygiene.* London: Spottiswoode.

Nuckolls, K., Cassel, J., & Kaplan, B. (1972). Psychosocial aspects, life crisis, and prognosis of pregnancy. *American Journal of Epidemiology, 95*, 431-441.

Okum, B. F., Fried, J., & Okum, M. L. (1999). *Understanding diversity: A learning-as-practice primer.* Pacific Grove, CA: Brooks/Cole.

Olds, D. L. (1988a). The Prenatal/Early Infancy Project. In R. H. Price, E. L. Cohen, R. P. Lorion, & J. Ramos-McKay (Eds.), *14 ounces of prevention: A casebook for practitioners* (pp. 9-23). Washington, DC: American Psychological Association.

Olds, D. L. (1988b). Common design and methodological problems encountered in evaluating family support services: Illustrations from the Prenatal/Early Infancy Project. In H. Weiss & F. Jacobs (Eds.), *Evaluating family programs* (pp. 239-265). Hawthorne, NY: Aldine de Gruyter.

Olds, D. L., Henderson, C. R., Chamberlin, R., & Tatelbaum, R. (1986). Preventing child abuse and neglect: A randomized trial of nurse home visitation. *Pediatrics, 78,* 65-78.

Olds, D. L., Henderson, C. R., Kitzman, H. J., Eckenrode, J. J., Cole, R. E., & Tatelbaum, R. C. (1999). Prenatal and infant home visitation by nurses: Recent findings. *The Future of Children, 9,* 44-65.

Olds, D. L., Henderson, C. R., Jr., Tatelbaum, R., & Chamberlin, R. (1985). Improving the delivery of prenatal care and outcomes of pregnancy: A randomized trial of nurse home visitation. *Pediatrics, 77,* 16-28.

Olds, D. L., & Kitzman, H. (1990). Can home visitation improve the health of women and children in environmental risk? *Pediatrics, 86*(1), 108-116.

Olds, D. L., & Kitzman, H. (1993). Review of research on home visiting for pregnant women and parents of young children. *The Future of Children, 3,* 53-92.

Olson, D. H., Portner, J., & Lavee, Y. (1985). FACES III. In D. H. Olson, H. I. McCubbin, H. Barnes, A. Larsen, M. Muxen, & M. Wilson (Eds.), *Family inventories* (pp. 1-13). St. Paul: University of Minnesota Press.

O'Sullivan, M. C. (1982). *The Sisters of Bon Secours in the United States: 1881-1981.* York, PA: Maple Press.

Pahl, J. (1985). Implications for policy and practice. In J. Pahl (Ed.), *Private violence and public policy* (pp. 181-192). Boston: Routledge. *Parents as Teachers.* Appendix B. (1999). *The Future of Children, 9*(1), 179-189. Routledge & Kegan Paul.

Parents as Teachers, Appendix B. (1999). *The Future of Children, 9*(1), 179-189.

Patterson, G. R., Weiss, R. L., & Hops, H. (1976). Training of marital skills: Some problems and concepts. In H. Leitenbery (Ed.), *Handbook of operant techniques* (pp. 493-523). Englewood Cliffs, NJ: Prentice Hall.

Pawl, J. H. (1994-1995). On supervision. *Zero to Three, 15*(3), 21-29.

Peckham, C., & Gibb, D. (1995). Mother-to-child transmission of human immunodeficiency virus Type 1 from mother to infant: A prospective cohort study in Kigali, Rwanda. *New England Journal of Medicine, 33,* 298-302.

Pedersen, P. B. (1981). The cultural inclusiveness of counseling. In P. B. Pedersen, J. G. Draguns, W. J. Lonner, & J. E. Trimble (Eds.), *Counseling across cultures* (pp. 22-58). Honolulu: The University Press of Hawaii.

Pedersen, P. B. (1995). Culture-centered ethical guidelines for counselors. In J. G. Ponterotto, J. M. Casas, L. A. Suzuki, & C. M. Alexander (Eds.), *Handbook of multicultural counseling* (pp. 34-49). Thousand Oaks, CA: Sage.

Pedersen, P. B. (1997). The cultural context of the American Counseling Association Code of Ethics. *Journal of Counseling and Development, 76,* 23-28.

Perreault, M., & Leichner, P. (1993). Patient satisfaction with outpatient psychiatric services: Quantitative and qualitative assessments. *Evaluation and Program Planning, 16,* 109-118.

Pfannenstiel, J. C., & Seltzer, D. A. (1985). *Evaluation report: New Parents as Teachers* Project. Jefferson City: Missouri Department of Elementary and Secondary Education.

Phillips, E. L., Wolf, M. M., Fixsen, D. L., & Bailey, J. S. (1970). The Achievement Place Model: A community-based, family-style, behavior modification program for pre-delinquents. In J. L. Khanna (Ed.), *New treatment approaches to juvenile delinquency* (pp. 34-86). Springfield, IL: Charles C Thomas.

Pianta, R. B., Egeland, B., & Erickson, M. F. (1989). The antecedents of maltreatment: Results of the Mother-Child Interaction Research Project. In D. Cicchetti & V. Carlson (Eds.), *Child maltreatment: Theory and research on the causes and consequences of child abuse and neglect* (pp. 203-253). New York: Cambridge University Press.

Pickens, R. W., & Heston, L. L. (1981). Personality factors in human drug self-administration. In T. Thompson & C. E. Johansen (Eds.), *Behavioral pharmacology of human drug dependence* (pp. 45-74). Rockville, MD: National Institute on Drug Abuse.

Powell, C., & Grantham-McGregor, S. (1989). Home visiting of varying frequency and child development. *Pediatrics, 84,* 157-164.

Project MATCH Research Group. (1997). Matching alcoholism treatments to client heterogeneity: Project MATCH posttreatment drinking outcomes. *Journal of Studies on Alcohol, 58,* 7-29.

Ramey, C. T., Bryant, D. M., Sparling, J. J., & Wasik, B. H. (1984). A biosocial systems perspective on environmental interventions for low birth weight infants. *Clinical Obstetrics and Gynecology, 27*(3), 672-692.

Ramey, C. T., Bryant, D. M., Sparling, J. J., & Wasik, B. H. (1985). Project CARE: A comparison of two early intervention strategies to prevent retarded development. *Topics in Early Childhood Special Education, 5*(2), 12-25.

Ramey, C. T., Bryant, D. M., Wasik, B. H., Sparling, J. J., Fendt, K. H., & LaVange, L. M. (1992). Infant Health and Development Program for low birth weight, premature infants: Program elements, family participation, and child intelligence. *Pediatrics, 3,* 454-465.

Ramey, C. T., & Campbell, F. A. (1984). Preventive education for high-risk children: Cognitive consequences of the Carolina Abecedarian Project. *American Journal of Mental Deficiency, 88,* 515-523.

Ramey, C. T., & Campbell, F. A. (1987). The Carolina Abecedarian Project: An educational experiment concerning human malleability. In J. J. Gallagher & C. T. Ramey (Eds.), *The malleability of children.* Baltimore, MD: Paul H. Brookes.

Rauh, V. A., Achenbach, T. M., Nurcombe, B., Howell, C. T., & Teti, D. M. (1988). Minimizing adverse effects of low birthweight: Four-year results of an early intervention program. *Child Development, 59,* 544-553.

Raven, J. (1980). *Parents, teachers and children—A study of an educational home-visiting scheme.* Kent, UK: Hodder and Stoughton for SCRE.

Reamer, F. G. (1990). *Ethical dilemmas in social service* (2nd ed.). New York: Columbia University Press.

Reamer, F. G. (1998). *Ethical standards in social work.* Washington DC: National Association of Social Workers Press.

Rees, S. J. (1983). Families' perceptions of services for handicapped children. *International Journal of Rehabilitation Research, 6*(4), 475-476.

Regier, D. A., Farmer, M. E., Rae, D. S., Locke, B. Z., Keith, S. J., Judd, L. L., & Goodwin, F. K. (1990). Comorbidity of mental disorders with alcohol and other drug abuse. *Journal of the American Medical Association, 264,* 2511-2518.

Reiman, A. J., McNair, V., McGee, N., & Hines, H. (1988). Linking staff development and teacher induction. *Journal of Staff Development, 9,* 52-58.

Renz, C., Munson, K., Wayland, K., & Fusaro, B. (1980). *Training manual for battered women advocates.* Durham, NC: Orange/Durham Coalition for Battered Women.

Resnick, M. B., Eyler, F. E., Nelson, M. D., Eitzman, D. V., & Buccizrelli, R. L. (1987). Developmental intervention for low birthweight infants: Improved early developmental outcome. *Pediatrics, 80,* 68-74.

Richmond, M. E. (1899). *Friendly visiting among the poor.* New York: MacMillan.

Richmond, M. E. (1917). *Social diagnosis.* New York: Russell Sage.

Ridley, C. R., Mendoza, D. W., Kanitz, B. E., Angermeier, L., & Zenk, R. (1994). Cultural sensitivity in multicultural counseling: A perceptual schema model. *Journal of Counseling Psychology, 41,* 125-136.

Roberts, D. E., & Heinrich, J. (1985). Public health nursing comes of age. *American Journal of Public Health, 75,* 1162-1172.

Roberts, R. N. (1988). Welcoming our baby: An early intervention program for Hawaiian families. *Children Today, 17*, 6-10.

Roberts, R. N., Akers, A. L., & Behl, D. D. (1996). Family-level service coordination within home visiting programs. *Topics in Early Childhood Special Education, 16*(3), 279-301.

Roberts, R. N., & Evans, J. E. (1994). Cultural competency in maternal and child health community-based programs. In J. C. McQueen (Ed.), *Perspectives in maternal and child health*. San Francisco: Jossey-Bass.

Roberts, R. N., & Evans, J. E. (1997). Cultural competency. In H. M. Wallace, R. F. Biehl, J. C. MacQueen, & J. A. Blackman (Eds.), *Mosby's resource guide to children with disabilities and chronic illness* (pp. 117-124). St. Louis, MO: Mosby.

Robin, A. L. (1979). Problem-solving communication training: A behavior approach to the treatment of parent-adolescent conflict. *The American Journal of Family Therapy, 7*, 69-82.

Robin, A. L. (1981). A controlled evaluation of problem-solving communication training with parent-adolescent conflict. *Behavior Therapy, 12*, 593-609.

Robin, A. L., & Foster, S. L. (1989). *Negotiating parent-adolescent conflict: A behavioral-family systems approach*. New York: Guilford.

Rogers, C. (1951). *Client-centered therapy*. Boston: Houghton Mifflin.

Rogers, C. (1957). The necessary and sufficient conditions of therapeutic personality change. *Journal of Consulting Psychology, 21*, 95-103.

Roizen, J. (1997). Epidemiological issues in alcohol-related violence. In M. Galanter (Ed.), *Recent developments in alcoholism, 13* (pp. 7-40). New York: Plenum.

Rosenberg, M. (1987). Children of battered women: The effects of witnessing violence on their social problem-solving abilities. *Behavior Therapist, 4*, 85-89.

Rosenfield, S., Sarber, R. E., Bueno, G., & Greene, B. F. (1983). Maintaining accountability for an ecobehavioral treatment of one aspect of child neglect: Personal cleanliness. *Education and Treatment of Children, 6*(2), 153-164.

Ross, G. S. (1984). Home intervention for premature infants of low income families. *American Journal of Orthopsychiatry, 5*, 263-270.

Rossi, P. H., & Freeman, H. E. (1989). *Evaluation: A systematic approach* (4th ed.). New York: Russell Sage.

Roy, M. (Ed.). (1977). *Battered women: A psychosociological study of domestic violence*. New York: Van Nostrand Reinhold.

Russell, D.E.H. (1982). *Rape in marriage*. New York: Macmillan.

Rutter, M. (1987). Psychosocial resilience and protective mechanisms. *American Journal of Orthopyschiatry, 57*, 316-336.

Rutter, M., Champion, L., Quinton, D., Maughan, B., & Pickles, A. (1995). Understanding individual differences in environmental-risk exposure. In P. Moen, G. H. Elder, Jr., & K. Luscher (Eds.), *Examining lives in context* (pp. 61-93). Washington, DC: American Psychological Association.

Sadler, L. S., & Catrone, C. (1983). The adolescent parent: A dual developmental crisis. *Journal of Adolescent Health Care, 4*(2), 100-105.

Sameroff, A. (1994). Developmental systems and family functioning. In R. D. Parke & S. G. Kellam (Eds.), *Exploring family relationships with other social contexts* (pp. 199-214). Hillsdale, NJ: Lawrence Erlbaum.

Sarason, I. G., Johnson, J. H., & Siegel, J. M. (1978). Assessing the impact of life changes: Development of the life experiences survey. *Journal of Consulting and Clinical Psychology, 46*, 932-946.

Sassetti, M. R. (1993). Domestic violence. *Primary Care, 20*, 289-305.

Satir, V. (1983). *Conjoint family therapy*. Palo Alto, CA: Science and Behavior Books.

Satir, V., Banmen, J., Gerber, J., & Gomori, M. (1991). *The Satir model: Family therapy and beyond*. Palo Alto, CA: Science and Behavior Books.

Scarr, S., & McCartney, K. (1988). Far from home: An experimental evaluation of the Mother-Child Home Program in Bermuda. *Child Development, 59*, 531-543.

Schaefer, E. S., & Aaronson, M. (1977). Infant education project: Implementation and implications of the home-tutoring program. In R. K. Parker (Ed.), *The preschool in action* (2nd ed.). Boston: Allyn & Bacon.

Schectman, F. (1986). Time and the practice of psychotherapy. *Psychotherapy, 23*(4), 521-525.

Scholl, T. O., Hediger, M. L., & Belsky, D. H. (1994). Prenatal care and maternal health during adolescent pregnancy: A review and meta-analysis. *Journal of Adolescent Health, 15*, 444-456.

Schwartz, I. S., & Baer, D. (1991). Social validity assessment: Is current practice state-of-the-art? *Journal of Applied Behavior Analysis, 24*, 189-204.

Sedlak, A. J., & Broadhurst, D. D. (1996). *Third National Incidence Study on child abuse and neglect*. Washington, DC: U.S. Department of Health and Human Services.

Shaeffer, L. G., Tobe, L. L., Barrios, L. C., Shrem, D. K., Hopkins, K. N., & Letourneau, R. J. (1999). *Child development, health, and safety training manual*. Chapel Hill: University of North Carolina Injury Prevention Research Center.

Shearer, D. E. (1998, November). *Developing together: Portage as CBR (Community Based Rehabilitation)*. Paper presented at the 7th International Portage Conference, Hiroshima, Japan.

Shearer, M. S., & Shearer, D. E. (1972). The Portage Project: A model for early childhood education. *Exceptional Children, 39*(3), 210-217.

Sheridan, M. J. (1995). A proposed intergenerational model of substance abuse, family functioning, and abuse/neglect. *Child Abuse & Neglect, 19*, 519-530.

Shure, M. B., & Spivack, G. (1972). Means-ends thinking, adjustment and social class along elementary school-aged children. *Journal of Consulting and Clinical Psychology, 38*, 348-353.

Shure, M. B., & Spivack, G. (1978). *Problem-solving techniques in childrearing*. San Francisco: Jossey-Bass.

Shyne, A. W., LeMat, A., & Kogan, L. S. (1963). Evaluating public health nursing service to the maternity patient and her family. *Nursing Outlook, 11*(1), 56-58.

Sia, C. J., & Breakey, G. F. (1985). The role of the medical home in child abuse prevention and positive child development. *Hawaii Medical Journal, 44*(7), 242-243.

Singer, L., Arendt, R., Farkas, K., Minnes, S., Huang, J., & Yamashita, T. (1997). Relationship of prenatal cocaine exposure and maternal postpartum psychological distress to child development outcome. *Developmental Psychopathology, 9*, 473-489.

Slaughter, D. T. (1988). Programs for racially and ethnically diverse American families: Some critical issues. In H. B. Weiss & F. H. Jacobs (Eds.), *Evaluating family programs* (pp. 461-476). New York: Aldine de Gruyter.

Slaughter-Defoe, D. T. (1993). Home visiting with families in poverty: Introducing the concept of culture. *The Future of Children, 3*(3), 172-183.

Smith, G. (Ed.). (1975). *Educational priority: Vol. 4. The West Riding Project*. London: HMSO.

Snyder, D. K., & Scheer, N. S. (1981). Predicting disposition following brief residence at a shelter for battered women. *American Journal of Community Psychology, 9*, 559-566.

Sparling, J., & Lewis, I. (1984). *Learning games for threes and fours: A guide to adult and child play*. New York: Walker.

Sparling, J., Lewis, I., Neuwirth, S., & Ramey, C. (1995). *Early partners*. Lewisville, NC: Kaplan.

Sparling, J., Lewis, I., Ramey, C. T., Wasik, B. H., Bryant, D. M., & LaVange, L. M. (1991). Partners: A curriculum to help premature, low birthweight infants get off to a good start. *Topics in Early Childhood Special Education, 11*, 36-55.

Spivack, G., & Shure, M. B. (1974). *Social adjustment of young children*. San Francisco: Jossey-Bass.

Srebalus, D. J., & Brown, D. (in press). *Becoming a skilled helper*. Boston: Allyn & Bacon.

St. Pierre, R. G., & Layzer, J. I. (1999). Using home visits for multiple purposes: The Comprehensive Child Development Program. *The Future of Children, 9*(1), 134-151.

Stabile, I., Graham, M., Chu, K. L., Hakes, A. Dahlem, B., & King, F. J. (2000). *A randomized trial of nurse and paraprofessional home visiting during pregnancy*. Tallahassee: Florida State University Center for Prevention and Early Intervention Policy.

Stark, E., & Flitcraft, A. (1988). Women and children at risk: A feminist perspective on child abuse. *International Journal of Health Services, 18*(1), 97-118.

Steele, B. F. (1980). Psychodynamic factors in child abuse. In C. H. Kempe & R. E. Helfer (Eds.), *The battered child* (3rd ed., pp. 49-85). Chicago: University of Chicago Press.

Steinkuller, J. S. (1992). Home visits by pediatric residents: A valuable educational tool. *American Journal of Disorders of Children, 146*, 1064-1967.

Stephens, D. (1979). In-home family support services: An ecological systems approach. In S. Maybanks & M. Bryce (Eds.), *Home-based services for children and families* (pp. 283-295). Springfield, IL: Charles C Thomas.

Stinson, F. S., Dufour, M. C., Steffens, R. A., & DeBakey, S. (1993). Alcohol-related mortality in the United States, 1979-1989. *Alcohol Health & Research World, 17*, 251-260.

Straus, M. A., & Gelles, R. J. (1990). *Physical violence in American families: Risk factors and adaptions to violence in 8,145 families*. New Brunswick, NJ: Transaction Books.

Straus, M. A., Gelles, R., & Steinmetz, S. (1980). *Behind closed doors: Violence in the American family*. Garden City, NY: Doubleday.

Streissguth, A. (1997). *Fetal Alcohol Syndrome: A guide for families and communities*. Baltimore, MD: Paul H. Brookes.

Streissguth, A., & Randels, S. (1988). Long term effects of fetal alcohol syndrome. In G. C. Robinson & R. W. Armstrong (Eds.), *Alcohol and child/family health* (pp. 131-151). Vancouver, Canada: University of British Columbia Press.

Strube, M. J. (1988). The decision to leave an abusive relationship. In G. T. Hotaling, D. Finkelhor, J. T. Kirkpatrick, & M. A. Straus (Eds.), *Coping with family violence: Research and policy perspectives* (pp. 93-106). Newbury Park, CA: Sage.

Suchman, E. A. (1967). *Evaluative research*. New York: Russell Sage.

Sue, D. W., & Sue, D. (1999). *Counseling the culturally different*. New York: John Wiley.

Sullivan, A. M., & Cohen, N. L. (1990). The home visit and the chronically mentally ill. In N. L. Cohen (Ed.), *Psychiatry takes to the street* (pp. 42-60). New York: Guilford.

Summers, J. A., Dell'Oliver, C., Turnbull, A. P., Benson, H. A., Santelli, G., Campbell, M., & Siegel-Causey, E. (1990). Examining the Individualized Family Service Plan process: What are family and practitioner preferences? *Topics in Early Childhood Special Education, 10*(1), 78-99.

Super, C. M., Herrera, M. G., & Mora, J. O. (1990). Long-term effects of food supplementation and psycho-social intervention on the physical growth of Columbian infants at risk of malnutrition. *Child Development, 61*, 29-49.

Tertinger, D. A., Greene, B. F., & Lutzker, J. R. (1984). Home safety: development and validation of one component of an ecobehavioral treatment program for abused and neglected children. *Journal of Applied Behavior Analysis, 17,* 159-174.

Thompson, K. S., & Fox, A. R. (1994). Why don't psychiatrists do their homework? *Community Mental Health Journal, 30*(3), 303-305.

Thompson, R. A. (1995). *Preventing child maltreatment through social support: A critical analysis.* Thousand Oaks, CA: Sage.

Topics in Early Childhood Special Education. (1990). Transitions [Special issue].

Touliatos, J., Perlmutter, B. F., & Straus, M. A. (Eds.). (1990). *Handbook on family measurement techniques.* Newbury Park, CA: Sage.

Trainor, C. M. (Ed.). (1983). *The dilemma of child neglect: Identification and treatment.* Denver, CO: The American Humane Association.

Truax, C., & Carkhuff, R. (1967). *Toward effective counseling and psychotherapy.* Hawthorne, NY: Aldine de Gruyer.

Turnbull, A. P., & Turnbull, H. R. (1986). *Families, professionals, and exceptionality: A special partnership.* Columbus, OH: Merrill.

U.S. Advisory Board on Child Abuse and Neglect. (1991). *Creating caring communities: Blueprint for an effective federal policy on child abuse and neglect.* Washington, DC: Government Printing Office.

U.S. Department of Health and Human Services (U.S. DHHS). (1993). *Head Start home visitor handbook.* Hyattsville, MD: Author.

U.S. Department of Health and Human Services. (1995). *Report to Congress on out-of-wedlock childbearing.* Hyattsville, MD: Author.

U.S. Department of Health and Human Services. (1996). *Smoking cessation.* Atlanta, GA: Centers for Disease Control and Prevention, Public Health Service, Agency for Health Care Policy and Research.

Udry, J. R., Kovenock, J., & Morris, N. M. (1996). Early predictors of nonmarital first pregnancy and abortion. *Family Planning Perspectives, 28,* 113-116.

Umbarger, C. (1972). The paraprofessional and family therapy. *Family Process, 11,* 147-162.

United Way of America. (1996). *Measuring program outcomes: A practical approach.* Alexandria, VA: Author.

Upchurch, D. M., & McCarthy, J. (1990). The timing of first birth and high school completion. *American Sociological Review, 55,* 224-234.

Ventura, S. J., Martin, J. A., Curtin, S. C., & Matthews, T. J. (1997). *Report of final natality statistics, 1995. Monthly Vital Statistics Report, 45*(11, Suppl. 2). Hyattsville, MD: National Center for Health Statistics.

Villar, J., Farnot, U., Barrose, F., Victora, C., Langer, A., & Belizan, J. (1992). A randomized trial of psychosocial support during high-risk pregnancies. *New England Journal of Medicine, 327,* 1266-1271.

Wagner, M., & Wagner, M. (1976). *The Danish National Child Care System.* Boulder, CO: Westview.

Wagner, M. M., & Clayton, S. L. (1999). The Parents as Teachers Program: Results from two demonstrations. *The Future of Children, 9*(1), 91-115.

Wahler, R. G. (1980). The insular mother: Her problems in parent-child treatment. *Journal of Applied Behavior Analysis, 13,* 207-219.

Wahler, R. G., & Dumas, J. E. (1984). Changing the observational coding styles of insular and noninsular mothers: A step toward maintenance of parent training effects. In R. F. Dangel & R. A. Polster (Eds.), *Parent training* (pp. 379-416). New York: Guilford.

Wakschlag, L. S., Chase-Lansdale, P. L., & Brooks-Gunn, J. (1996). Not just "ghosts in the nursery:" Contemporaneous intergenerational relationships and parenting in young African-American families. *Child Development, 67*, 2131-2147.

Walker, L. (1983). Victimology and the psychological perspectives of battered women. *Victimology, 8*(1-2), 82-104.

Walker, L. E. (1979). *The battered woman.* New York: Harper & Row.

Walker, L. E. (1984). *The battered woman syndrome.* New York: Springer.

Walker, L. E. (1999). Psychology and domestic violence around the world. *American Psychologist, 54*, 21-29.

Walton, E., Fraser, M. W., Lewis, R. E., Pecora, P. J., & Walton, W. K. (1993). In-home family-focused reunification: An experimental study. *Child Welfare League of American, 72*(5), 473-487.

Wasik, B. H. (1984). *Coping with parenting through effective problem solving.* Unpublished manuscript, Frank Porter Graham Child Development Center, University of North Carolina.

Wasik, B. H., Bryant, D. M., Kent, M. E., Powell, J. W., Vatz, C., & Ecklund, K. (1988, August). *Reliability and validity of two social problem solving instruments.* Paper presented at the annual meeting of the American Psychological Association, Atlanta, GA.

Wasik, B. H., Bryant, D. M., & Lyons, C. M. (1990). *Home visiting: Procedures for helping families.* Newbury Park, CA: Sage.

Wasik, B. H., Bryant, D. M., Lyons, C., Sparling, J. J., & Ramey, C. T. (1997). Home visiting. In R. T. Gross, D. Spiker, & C. W. Haynes (Eds.), *Helping low birth weight, premature babies: The Infant Health and Development Program* (pp. 27-41). Stanford, CA: Stanford University Press.

Wasik, B. H., Bryant, D. M., Sparling, J. J., & Ramey, C. T. (1997). Maternal problem solving. In R. T. Gross, D. Spiker, & C. Haynes (Eds.), *Helping low birth weight, premature babies: The Infant Health and Development Program* (pp. 276-289). Palo Alto, CA: Stanford University Press.

Wasik, B. H., & Fishbein, J. E. (1982). Problem solving: A model for supervision in professional psychology. *Professional Psychology, 13*, 559-564.

Wasik, B. H., Lam, W. K., & Kane, H. (1994). *The 1993 Community Integrated Service System Projects: A report of the initial plans and implementation efforts.* University of North Carolina, Chapel Hill, NC. (ERIC Document Reproduction Service No. ED 413 049)

Wasik, B. H., & Lyons, C. (1984). *A handbook on home visiting.* Unpublished manuscript, Frank Porter Graham Child Development Center, University of North Carolina.

Wasik, B. H., Ramey, C. T., Bryant, D. M., & Sparling, J. J. (1990). A longitudinal study of two early intervention strategies: Project CARE. *Child Development, 61*, 1682-1696.

Wasik, B. H., Roberts, R., & Lam, W. K. (1994, October). *The myths and reality of family-centered, community-based, coordinated, culturally-competent, systems of care.* Paper presented at the Maternal and Child Health Bureau Research Priorities conference, Washington, DC.

Wasik, B. H., & Roberts, R. N. (1994a). Survey of home visiting programs for abused and neglected children and their families. *Child Abuse & Neglect, 18*(3), 271-283.

Wasik, B. H., & Roberts, R. N. (1994b). Home visitor characteristics, training, and supervision: Results of a national survey. *Family Relations, 43*, 336-341.

Wasik, B. H., Shaeffer, L., Pohlman, C., & Baird, T. (1996). *A guide to written training materials for home visitors.* Chapel Hill: The Center for Home Visiting, University of North Carolina at Chapel Hill.

Wasik, B. H., & Sparling, J. J. (1998). *Home visit assessment instrument*. Chapel Hill: The Center for Home Visiting, University of North Carolina at Chapel Hill.

Wasik, B. H., Thompson, E. A., Shaeffer, L., & Herrmann, S. (1996). *A guide to audio visual training materials for home visitors*. Chapel Hill: The Center for Home Visiting, University of North Carolina at Chapel Hill.

Watson-Perczel, M., Lutzker, J. R., Greene, B. F., & McGimpsey, B. J. (1988). Assessment and modification of cleanliness among families adjudicated for child neglect. *Behavior Modification, 12*, 57-81.

Weikart, D. P., Bond, J. T., & McNeil, J. T. (1978). The Ypsilanti Preschool Project: Preschool years and longitudinal results. *Monographs of the High/Scope Educational Research Foundation, 3*.

Weiss, H. B. (1989). State family support and educational programs: Lessons from the pioneers. *American Journal of Orthopsychiatry, 59*, 32-48.

Weiss, H. B. (1993). Home visits: Necessary but not sufficient. *The Future of Children, 3*, 113-128.

Weiss, H. B., & Halpern, R. (1990). *Community-based family support and education support: Something old or something new?* New York: National Center for Children in Poverty.

Weiss, H. B., & Jacobs, F. H. (Eds.). (1988). *Evaluating family programs*. New York: Aldine de Gruyter.

Weissbourd, B. (1983). The family support movement: Greater than the sum of its parts. *Zero to Three, 4*(1), 8-10.

Weissbourd, B. (1987). Design, staffing, and funding of family support programs. In S. L. Kagan, D. R. Powell, B. Weissbourd, & E. F. Zigler (Eds.), *America's family support programs* (pp. 245-268). New Haven, CT: Yale University Press.

Wells, K. (1995). Family preservation services in context: Origins, practices, and current issues. In I. M. Schwartz & P. AuClaire (Eds.), *Home-based services for troubled children* (pp. 1-28). Lincoln: University of Nebraska Press.

Wells, K. B., Benson, M. C., Hoff, P., & Stuber, M. (1987). A home-visit program for first-year medical students as perceived by participating families. *Family Medicine, 19*, 364-367.

Whall, A. L. (1986). The family as the unit of care in nursing: A historical review. *Public Health Nursing, 3*, 240-249.

White, B. L. (1975). *The first three years of life*. Englewood Cliffs, NJ: Prentice Hall.

White, K. R. (1988). Cost analyses in family support programs. In H. B. Weiss & F. H. Jacobs (Eds.), *Evaluating family programs* (pp. 429-444). New York: Aldine de Gruyter.

Wilt, S., & Olson, S. (1996). Prevalence of domestic violence in the United States. *Journal of the American Medical Women's Association, 51*, 77-82.

Winter, M., & McDonald, D. (1997). Parents as teachers: Investing in good beginnings for children. In G. Albee & T. Gullotta (Eds.), *Primary prevention works* (pp.119-145). Thousand Oaks, CA: Sage.

Winter, M., & Rouse, J. M. (1991). Parents as teachers: Nurturing literacy in the very young. *Zero to Three, 12*, 80-83.

Wolery, M., & Bailey, D. B. (1984). Alternatives to impact evaluation: Suggestions for program evaluation in early intervention. *Journal of the Division for Early Childhood, 9*, 27-37.

Wolfe, B., & Herwig, J. (Eds.). (1986). *The Head Start home visitor handbook*. Portage, WI: The Portage Project.

Wolfe, D. A. (1999). *Child abuse: Implications for child development and psychopathology*. Thousand Oaks, CA: Sage.

Wolfe, D. A., & McEachran, A. (1997). Child physical abuse and neglect. In E. J. Mash & L. G. Terdal (Eds.), *Assessment of childhood disorders* (pp. 523-568). New York: Guilford.

Young, M. E. (1998). *Learning the art of helping: Building blocks and techniques*. Old Tappan, NJ: Pearson Education.

Zayas, L. H., Evans, M. E., Mejia, L., & Rodriguez, O. (1997). Cultural-competency training for staff serving Hispanic families with a child in psychiatric crisis. *Families in Society, 78*(4), 405-412.

Zigler, E. F., & Black, K. B. (1989). America's family support movement: Strengths and limitations. *American Journal of Orthopsychiatry, 59*(1), 6-19.

Zigler, E. F., & Freedman, J. (1987). Head Start: A pioneer of family support. In S. L. Kagan, D. R. Powell, B. Weissbourd, & E. F. Zigler (Eds.), *American's family support programs, perspectives, and prospects. New Haven, CT: Yale University Press.*

Zigler, E. F., Kagan, S. L., & Hall, N. W. (Eds.). (1996). *Children, families, and government: Preparing for the twenty-first century.* Cambridge, UK: Cambridge University Press.

Name Index

Subject Index

About the Authors

Barbara Hanna Wasik is a psychologist on the faculty of the University of North Carolina at Chapel Hill. She is a professor in the School of Education, a fellow of the Frank Porter Graham Child Development Center, and the Director of the University of North Carolina at Chapel Hill Center for Home Visiting. She received her Ph.D. in clinical psychology from Florida State University and was a postdoctoral research fellow at Duke University. Throughout her career, she has been concerned with children with social, emotional, and academic difficulties and their social contexts, especially schools and homes, and has conducted both prevention and intervention programs for children in these settings. She helped develop and direct Project CARE, a longitudinal early childhood intervention program, and was codirector for curriculum in the national collaborative study on low birthweight infants, the Infant Health and Development Program. She conducted a longitudinal study of kindergarten children's school success and is currently directing a longitudinal study of family literacy programs. The author of numerous publications, she is a fellow of the American Psychological Association and has served as president of the North Carolina Psychological Association. She currently serves on several national boards and advisory groups.

Donna M. Bryant is a senior scientist at the Frank Porter Graham Child Development Center at the University of North Carolina at Chapel Hill and a research professor in the School of Education. She received her Ph.D. in experimental psychology at the University of North Carolina at Chapel Hill. During the mid-1970s, she was a home visitor in an infant education program for the Developmental Evaluation Center in Durham, North Carolina. This work lead to other research projects with young children and their families, including several studies of early intervention and prevention for children at risk for developmental disabilities: Project CARE, the Infant Health and Development Program, and the Head Start Transition Demonstration Project. Her recent work has focused on Head Start, with current studies including the Head Start Quality Research Consortium and a study of mental health interventions for teachers and parents of children with problems of aggression. Along with colleagues at the Frank Porter Graham Center, she has conducted statewide studies of North Carolina's kindergarten and public preschool programs. She is leading the evaluation of Smart Start, North Carolina's initiative to enhance child care and family services. She has authored many articles and chapters on early intervention and early childhood education, including a book on best practices.

CPSIA information can be obtained
at www.ICGtesting.com
Printed in the USA
FSOW01n1420300118
43973FS